THE CHINESE REVOLUTION

Other Titles in the Greenwood Press Guides
to Historic Events of the Twentieth Century
Randall M. Miller, Series Editor

THE CHINESE REVOLUTION

Edward J. Lazzerini

Greenwood Press Guides to
Historic Events of the Twentieth Century
Randall M. Miller, Series Editor

Greenwood Press
Westport, Connecticut • London

Library of Congress Cataloging-in-Publication Data

Lazzerini, Edward J.
    The Chinese Revolution / Edward J. Lazzerini.
       p.   cm.—(Greenwood Press guides to historic events of the
twentieth century, ISSN 1092–177X)
    Includes bibliographical references and index.
    ISBN 0–313–30110–7 (alk. paper)
    1. China—History—20th century. 2. Revolutions—China—
History—20th century. I. Title. II. Series.
DS774.L39   1999
951.04—dc21   99–10141

British Library Cataloguing in Publication Data is available.

Library of Congress Catalog Card Number: 99–10141
ISBN: 0–313–30110–7
ISSN: 1092–177X

First published in 1999

Greenwood Press, 88 Post Road West, Westport, CT 06881
An imprint of Greenwood Publishing Group, Inc.
www.greenwood.com

Printed in the United States of America

The paper used in this book complies with the
Permanent Paper Standard issued by the National
Information Standards Organization (Z39.48–1984).

10 9 8 7 6 5 4 3 2 1

Front cover photo: Portrait of Mao Zedong overlooking Tiananmen Square faces off with a
statue erected in the square on May 30, 1989. The statue was dubbed "The Goddess of Democracy" by students from Central Academy of Fine Arts, who modeled it after the Statue of
Liberty. Courtesy of AP/Wide World Photos.

For Penny and Repete,
two faces to light up any life.

Contents

A photo essay follows page 68

Series Foreword

As the twenty-first century approaches, it is time to take stock of the political, social, economic, intellectual, and cultural forces and factors that have made the twentieth century the most dramatic period of change in history. To that end, the Greenwood Press Guides to Historic Events of the Twentieth Century presents interpretive histories of the most significant events of the century. Each book in the series combines narrative history and analysis with primary documents and biographical sketches, with an eye to providing both a reference guide to the principal persons, ideas, and experiences defining each historic event, and a reliable, readable overview of that event. Each book further provides analyses and discussions, grounded in both primary and secondary sources, of the causes and consequences, in thought and action, that give meaning to the historic event under review. By assuming a historical perspective, drawing on the latest and best writing on each subject, and offering fresh insights, each book promises to explain how and why a particular event defined the twentieth century. No consensus about the meaning of the twentieth century emerges from the series, but, collectively, the books identify the most salient concerns of the century. In so doing, the series reminds us of the many ways those historic events continue to affect our lives.

Each book follows a similar format designed to encourage readers to consult it both as a reference and a history in its own right. Each volume opens with a chronology of the historic event, followed by a narrative overview, which also serves to introduce and examine briefly the main themes and issues related to that event. The next set of chapters is composed of topi-

cal essays, each analyzing closely an issue or problem of interpretation introduced in the opening chapter. A concluding chapter suggesting the
long-term implications and meanings of the historic event brings the
strands of the preceding chapters together while placing the event in the
larger historical context. Each book also includes a section of short biogra-
phies of the principal persons related to the event, followed by a section introducing and reprinting key historical documents illustrative of and
pertinent to the event. A glossary of selected terms adds to the utility of each
book. An annotated bibliography—of significant books, films, and CD-
ROMs—and an index conclude each volume.

The editors made no attempt to impose any theoretical model or historical perspective on the individual authors. Rather, in developing the series,
an advisory board of noted historians and informed high school history
teachers and public and school librarians identified the topics needful of exploration and the scholars eminently qualified to examine those events with
intelligence and sensitivity. The common commitment throughout the series is to provide accurate, informative, and readable books, free of jargon
and up to date in evidence and analysis.

Each book stands as a complete historical analysis and reference guide to
a particular historic event. Each book also has many uses, from understanding contemporary perspectives on critical historical issues, to providing
biographical treatments of key figures related to each event, to offering ex-
cerpts and complete texts of essential documents about the event, to suggesting and describing books and media materials for further study and
presentation of the event, and more. The combination of historical narrative
and individual topical chapters addressing significant issues and problems
encourages students and teachers to approach each historic event from multiple perspectives and with a critical eye. The arrangement and content of
each book thus invite students and teachers, through classroom discussions
and position papers, to debate the character and significance of great historic events and to discover for themselves how and why history matters.

The series emphasizes the main currents that have shaped the modern
world. Much of that focus necessarily looks at the West, especially Europe
and the United States. The political, commercial, and cultural expansion of
the West wrought largely, though not wholly, the most fundamental changes
of the century. Taken together, however, books in the series reveal the inter-
actions between Western and non-Western peoples and society, and also the
tensions between modern and traditional cultures. They also point to the
ways in which non-Western peoples have adapted Western ideas and technology and, in turn, influenced Western life and thought. Several books examine such increasingly powerful global forces as the rise of Islamic

fundamentalism, the emergence of modern Japan, the Communist revolution in China, and the collapse of communism in eastern Europe and the former Soviet Union. American interests and experiences receive special attention in the series, not only in deference to the primary readership of the books but also in recognition that the United States emerged as the dominant political, economic, social, and cultural force during the twentieth century. By looking at the century through the lens of American events and experiences, it is possible to see why the age has come to be known as "The American Century."

Assessing the history of the twentieth century is a formidable prospect. It has been a period of remarkable transformation. The world broadened and narrowed at the same time. Frontiers shifted from the interiors of Africa and Latin America to the moon and beyond; communication spread from mass circulation newspapers and magazines to radio, television, and now the Internet; skyscrapers reached upward and suburbs stretched outward; energy switched from steam, to electric, to atomic power. Many changes did not lead to a complete abandonment of established patterns and practices so much as a synthesis of old and new, as, for example, the increased use of (even reliance on) the telephone in the age of the computer. The automobile and the truck, the airplane, and telecommunications closed distances, and people in unprecedented numbers migrated from rural to urban, industrial, and ever more ethnically diverse areas. Tractors and chemical fertilizers made it possible for fewer people to grow more, but the environmental and demographic costs of an exploding global population threatened to outstrip natural resources and human innovation. Disparities in wealth increased, with developed nations prospering and underdeveloped nations starving. Amid the crumbling of former European colonial empires, Western technology, goods, and culture increasingly enveloped the globe, seeping into, and undermining, non-Western cultures—a process that contributed to a surge of religious fundamentalism and ethno-nationalism in the Middle East, Asia, and Africa. As people became more alike, they also became more aware of their differences. Ethnic and religious rivalries grew in intensity everywhere as the century closed.

The political changes during the twentieth century have been no less profound than the social, economic, and cultural ones. Many of the books in the series focus on political events, broadly defined, but no books are confined to politics alone. Political ideas and events have social effects, just as they spring from a complex interplay of non-political forces in culture, society, and economy. Thus, for example, the modern civil rights and woman's rights movements were at once social and political events in cause and consequence. Likewise, the Cold War created the geopolitical framework for dealing with competing ideologies and nations abroad and served as the touchstone for political and cultural identities at home. The books treating political events do so within their social, cultural, and economic contexts.

Several books in the series examine particular wars in depth. Wars are defining moments for people and eras. During the twentieth century war became more widespread and terrible than ever before, encouraging new efforts to end war through strategies and organizations of international cooperation and disarmament while also fueling new ideologies and instruments of mass persuasion that fostered distrust and festered old national rivalries. Two world wars during the century redrew the political map, slaughtered or uprooted two generations of people, and introduced and hastened the development of new technologies and weapons of mass destruction. The First World War spelled the end of the old European order and spurred communist revolution in Russia and fascism in Italy, Germany, and elsewhere. The Second World War killed fascism and inspired the final push for freedom from European colonial rule in Asia and Africa. It also led to the Cold War that suffocated much of the world for almost half a century. Large wars begat small ones, and brutal totalitarian regimes cropped up across the globe. After (and in some ways because of) the fall of communism in eastern Europe and the former Soviet Union, wars of competing cultures, national interests, and political systems persisted in the struggle to make a new world order. Continuing, too, has been the belief that military technology can achieve political ends, whether in the superior American firepower that failed to "win" in Vietnam or in the American "smart bombs" and other military wizardry that "won" in the Persian Gulf.

Another theme evident in the series is that throughout the century nationalism has continued to drive events. Whether in the Balkans in 1914 triggering World War I or in the Balkans in the 1990s threatening the post–Cold War peace—or in many other places—nationalist ambitions and forces would not die. The persistence of nationalism is yet another reminder of the many ways that the past becomes prologue.

We thus offer the series as a modern guide to and interpretation of the historic events of the twentieth century and as an invitation to consider how and why those events have defined not only the past and present but also charted the political, social, intellectual, cultural, and economic routes into the next century.

Randall M. Miller
Saint Joseph's University, Philadelphia

Preface

The Chinese Revolution is long in the making. My use of the present tense in the preceding sentence serves as a modest acknowledgment that China's leaders, especially within the Chinese Communist Party, continue to proclaim the revolution an unfinished project. Nearly ninety years have passed since revolutionaries and other anti-Manchu forces in Chinese society toppled the moribund Qing dynasty and monarchical system in roughly four months between October 1911 and early 1912. But that episode was only the beginning. Many other extraordinary events have occurred during the intervening decades. Civil war persisted for years with brief respites, international conflicts caused China's people suffering on a grand scale, leaders and political parties came and went, and mutually hostile ideologies competed with one another for dominance and a chance to shape society.

This book is about China's Revolution, an unfolding process that has spanned most of the twentieth century in search of the country's transformation. Seven essays provide information and analysis of the Chinese Revolution from the first decades of this century through 1998. Following an introduction that offers background about key features of Chinese culture and practice, the first essay emphasizes the significance of Confucian teaching. It also identifies frequently complex developments—national and international—emerging between the mid-eighteenth and early twentieth centuries that contributed to the perceived need for revolution.

Five topical essays focus on selected themes that helped shape the revolution and/or were affected by it. The first examines the thought of Mao Zedong, the most important figure in the history of the Chinese Communist

Party. The second does the same for Deng Xiaoping, a companion of Mao from the beginning but one who turned against The Great Helmsman's (as Mao came to be called) legacy and dramatically moved China in new and profoundly different directions. The third explores the multiethnic character of China, with particular emphasis on Chinese (Han) relations with non-Chinese and the role of the latter in the revolutionary process and its consequences. The fourth takes us into the realm of international relations with treatment of China's mixed and frequently ambiguous relationship with the United States and the former Soviet Union. The fifth focuses on the thorny issue of the People's Republic of China and its interests in two neighboring territories that it claims: Hong Kong and Taiwan.

A concluding essay offers an interpretation of China's Revolution that emphasizes the importance of both Marxism and nationalism in its unfolding and then attempts to assess its consequences. Biographical sketches of seventeen major participants in various phases of the revolution offer ready-reference value. The texts of thirteen primary documents, each of which offers direct access to words that have shaped the revolution, accompanied it, or emerged in response to it will assist the student researcher.

No single portion of this book is meant to stand alone. Rather, each provides a different angle from which to view aspects of China's Revolution and to develop some understanding of one of this century's major forces in the making. Taken together, the components make up a whole that we hope will serve an audience of advanced secondary school and college students needing an introduction and reference guide to a vast subject.

Other than my debt to teachers in graduate school at the University of Washington who introduced me to Chinese history, both traditional and modern, I owe most to my students at the University of New Orleans these past twenty-five years who kept me searching for ways to make China intelligible. I would like to think that this book reflects that challenge and does it honor. I need also to thank my editor, Randall Miller, whose reading of this text on more than one occasion was invaluable in catching errors of expression, in offering challenges to vague or ambiguous arguments, and in suggesting what should be added. For her extreme patience, I owe Barbara Rader of Greenwood Press a commendation. Finally, to my wife Cindy, who sustained me throughout the preparation of this book, I can only say that the plate is getting empty.

A Note on Chinese Transliteration, Pronunciation, and Names

The system for romanizing Chinese that is used in this book is pinyin, introduced from the Soviet Far East into parts of China in the late 1930s, then reintroduced by the Chinese themselves during the 1950s. Since January 1, 1979, it has served as the official romanization system in the People's Republic of China, but not in the Republic of China on Taiwan, which continues to use the older Wade-Giles system. The only exceptions will be for a small number of commonly known personal or place names, such as Chiang Kai-shek and Canton (instead of Jiang Jieshi and Guangzhou), whose Wade-Giles forms have become standard,

The primary benefit of pinyin to English speakers is that it is pronounced largely as it looks, with the following exceptions for initial consonants:

Pinyin	English
c	ts
q	ch
x	hs (close to a soft sh)
z	dz
zh	j (as in jump)

In Chinese, people's names are presented in their opposite order from English. Thus, the surname (family name) comes first, followed by the given (personal) name or names.

Chronology of Events

1839–1842	First Opium War with England; concluded by Treaty of Nanjing, the first of the "unequal treaties"
1894–1895	Sino-Japanese War
1898	China forced to lease territories to Germany, Russia, France, and Britain; "Hundred Days Reform"
1899	"Open Door Doctrine" proposed by United States
1899–1901	Boxer Rebellion: a popular uprising turned against the Western presence in China
1904–1905	Russo-Japanese War
1911 (October)	Revolution breaks out in Wuchang, signaling the end of the monarchy and beginning of the Republic
1912 (February)	Yuan Shikai becomes president of the Republic of China
1912 (August)	Guomindang (GMD) revolutionary party formed
1915 (January)	Twenty-One Demands presented by Japan
1915 (December)	Yuan Shikai attempts to restore monarchy
1916 (June)	Death of Yuan Shikai
1917	Civil war breaks out between Beijing and Guangzhou governments

1917 (September)	Sun Yat-sen establishes Republic of China Military Government in Guangzhou (Canton)
1918	Warlords begin claiming territory across China
1919	May Fourth Movement
1921	Chinese Communist Party (CCP) founded
1924	China recognizes the Soviet Union; first Guomindang-CCP united front
1925 (March 12)	Sun Yat-sen dies
1926	Chiang Kai-shek begins "Northern Expedition" to reunify the country
1927 (April 12)	Chiang Kai-shek turns against communists
1931	Japanese army takes over northeast China; communists set up Chinese Soviet Government in Jiangxi Province
1932	Japan creates puppet state of "Manchukuo" in China's northeast
1934	Communists start "Long March" to escape GMD encirclement
1937	Second GMD-CCP united front; Japan begins full invasion of China
1943	Mao Zedong elected chairman of the CCP's Politburo
1945	Japan surrenders; U.S. General George C. Marshall arrives in China
1946	Chinese Civil War recommences; Marshall mission fails
1949 (October 1)	Founding of People's Republic of China; Chiang Kai-shek and GMD government retreat to Taiwan
1950	Sino-Soviet Treaty of Friendship, Alliance, and Mutual Assistance is signed in Moscow; Chinese "volunteers" sent to Korea where war had broken out
1950–1952	Land Reform campaign
1953	Beginning of First Five-Year Plan
1954	First National People's Congress adopts PRC constitution
1955	Agricultural cooperatives launched as a step toward communization of the countryside

1956 (January–February)	Soviet Premier Nikita Khrushchev criticizes Stalin's "cult of personality," and, by implication, Mao Zedong
1957	"Hundred Flowers" campaign
1958–1961	The "Great Leap Forward" campaign
1959	Border clashes between China and India; abortive rebellion in Tibet
1960 (April)	Exchange of polemics between China and the USSR signals a deterioration of their relationship
1962	Border war between China and India
1964 (October)	China explodes its first atomic bomb
1966	Outbreak of "Great Proletarian Cultural Revolution"
1967	China explodes its first hydrogen bomb
1968	Liu Shaoqi expelled from CCP "forever"
1969	Soviet and Chinese troops clash along the border
1969 (April)	Ninth Congress of the CCP adopts a new constitution that reaffirms Marxism-Leninism-Mao Zedong Thought as the theoretical basis of the party
1971	The PRC is admitted to the United Nations
1972 (February)	U.S. President Richard Nixon visits China
1975	Zhou Enlai proposes policy of "four modernizations"
1975 (April)	Chiang Kai-shek dies on Taiwan
1976 (January 8)	Death of Premier Zhou Enlai
1976 (July 6)	Death of Zhu De, Commander-in-chief of PLA
1976 (September 9)	Death of Mao Zedong
1976 (October 6)	"Gang of Four" arrested
1977	Hua Guofeng named chairman of the Central Committee of the CCP and its Military Affairs Committee
1979	Full diplomatic relations established between China and the United States
1980	Hu Yaobang becomes General Secretary of the CCP; Liu Shaoqi posthumously rehabilitated
1981 (January)	"Gang of Four" sentenced by special tribunal

1984	Sino-British Joint Declaration on Hong Kong signed; the PRC will resume sovereignty over Hong Kong on July 1, 1997
1987 (January)	Hu Yaobang "resigns" as general secretary of the CCP and is replaced on acting basis by Zhao Ziyang
1988 (January)	Taiwan's president, Chiang Ching-kuo, dies and is succeeded by Lee Teng-hui
1989 (April 15)	Hu Yaobang dies
1989 (May–early June)	Start of events leading to the occupation of Tiananmen Square by student-led demonstrators
1989 (June 24)	Zhao Ziyang, who had been sympathetic to the student demonstrators, is stripped of all his posts
1989 (November)	Jiang Zemin is elected general secretary and member of the Standing Committee of the Politburo; Deng Xiaoping resigns as chairman of the Central Military Commission, his last formal post in the CCP; Jiang Zemin is appointed to succeed him
1990 (January)	Martial law lifted
1992 (January)	Deng Xiaoping tours the southern "Special Economic Zone" at Shenzhen and calls for further economic reforms
1994	Creation of a market-based foreign exchange rate, thereby ending the dual-rate foreign exchange system in place since 1949
1996 (March)	Taiwan holds its first free election for president
1996 (August 7)	China agrees to support the global ban on nuclear explosions
1996	Pro-Beijing businessman, Tung Chee-hwa, is chosen as the chief executive of Hong Kong after July 1, 1997
1997 (February 19)	Deng Xiaoping dies
1997 (May)	A Sino-Soviet summit during Mikhail Gorbachev's four-day visit to Beijing announces normalization of relations between the two nations
1997 (July 1)	Hong Kong reverts to Chinese control as a special administrative zone
1998 (June 25–July 3)	U.S. President William J. Clinton visits China

THE CHINESE REVOLUTION EXPLAINED

1

The Chinese Revolution: An Overview

Any effort to understand the Chinese Revolution, which has run virtually the length of the twentieth century, must start well before 1900. Scholars of modern China have long disagreed over how far back one needs to look to find the forces, trends, personalities, and events that together established the backdrop for such an enormously significant process. Nevertheless, a consensus has emerged during the last few decades around several basic arguments. First, the technological and cultural influence of Europe, while undeniably challenging to Chinese self-perceptions and practice, was not as overwhelming as once thought. The intrusion of the West cannot be ignored, but it also cannot be treated as an irresistible force against which the Chinese were constantly responding as if helpless victims. Second, regardless of the extent of European influence, China had to confront powerful demographic, social, and economic circumstances so unusual in Chinese experience that they would have reshaped the empire in any event. Third, the signs of distress afflicting Chinese society by the late nineteenth century were the consequence of forces at work since at least the mid-eighteenth century and in some cases much longer.

Although subject to reform many times over in response to changing circumstances, the Chinese imperial order had survived for roughly two millennia by the beginning of the nineteenth century. It did so by creating a powerful symbiosis between state and culture that was legitimized during the Han dynasty (202 B.C.–A.D. 220) by the official adoption of the teachings of Confucius (Kongzi), the sixth-to-fifth-century B.C. sage.

Like many philosophies, Confucianism was subject to reinterpretation time and again by succeeding generations of teachers and scholars. Attempts to render it easily understood run the risk of distortion. Nevertheless, several features of this body of wisdom stand out for their overriding significance in explaining the character of the state, the relationship between it and society, the nature of elite culture, and the accepted values affecting daily life and social aspirations.

At its most basic level, Confucian thought is concerned with the creation and maintenance of the good society as defined principally by the harmony and balance in and among all things. In pursuit of this goal, the behavior of humans as social animals commands attention. Drawing upon older Chinese traditions, Confucianism assumes a cosmic order without a creator-god, thereby freeing humans to be responsible for their individual and collective fates. What one does or does not do is believed to affect not merely the self and the larger human community but the cosmic order as well, since the three are understood to be fully integrated. Hence the success of human society—always linked to human actions—can be determined at any given moment from the "opinion" of nature as expressed through astronomical events, earthquakes, floods, blights, infestations, and other "natural" signs.

To ensure that individuals act according to principle and the social good, Confucius and his later commentators stressed the necessity of conscious and focused attention to personal development whatever one's calling in life. For some who would serve society as its leaders, this might mean intense and relentless study, lasting a lifetime, of particular forms of wisdom, but no one was exempt from trying to be the best he or she could be within the context of even the simplest life's experiences. Two short passages, a millennium and a half apart in their composition, one attributed to Confucius and the other from a text by the twelfth-century neo-Confucian scholar Zhu Xi (1130–1200), reveal the continuity and timelessness of the admonition that "knowledge is painfully acquired"[1]:

Confucius said, "At fifteen my heart-and-mind were set upon learning; at thirty I took my stance; at forty I was no longer of two minds; at fifty I realized the possibilities of life; at sixty my ear was attuned; and at seventy I could give my heart-and-mind free rein without overstepping the mark."[2]

[Zhu Xi writes:] "So let us now set our minds on honoring our virtuous natures and pursuing our studies. Let us every day seek in ourselves whether or not we have been remiss about anything in our studies and whether or not we have been lax about anything in our virtuous natures. . . . If we urge ourselves on in this way for a year, how can we not develop? Every day we must seek some amount of improvement, learning what we do not yet know and changing for the better whatever is not good; thus we shall improve our virtuous natures. . . . We must never relax for a moment. If we pass our days in this fashion, then in three years we might have made a bit of progress."[3]

Few people practice dedication of the kind suggested by Zhu Xi, a fact that Confucius and his disciple understood well. All of us need assistance in identifying and keeping to the proper path, and it is one of society's clear and primary obligations to provide such assistance in as many ways as possible. For Confucius, the key was found in the training and subsequent behavior of those responsible for leading society. They must be the best of the best, understand yet accept the terrible burden and personal cost of leadership, seek their pleasure in serving society, and be models for ordinary people to emulate. If they fail, those below them can be expected to do no better.

The state, then, was not just the arbiter of morality and justice, but the bearer of their spirit, the responsible agent for their preservation across generations, the well from which the public conscience drank. Over the many centuries an unusual class of men, trained as Confucian scholars and generally subject to written examination in order to ensure their credentials, provided China not just with its intellectual elite but with its artistic and literary practitioners, and its bureaucrats. These men controlled China in the name of the emperors and their dynasties. Dynasties rose and fell, but the scholar-official class always remained to serve China and help it endure. Their values came to define China, not just at the top in its high culture, but even lower down, among the peasants and other subjects. This was possible for many reasons, not least that the elite usually sought to maintain a rural base close to nature and that it shared with the villagers a common cosmology, a common set of religious attitudes, property concepts, views of authority, and other cultural traits and practices, such as sexual inequality, equal inheritance among brothers, and even footbinding.[4]

The stability, order, and harmony to which Confucian China aspired ebbed and flowed with time, but that dynamic seemed normal to the Chinese. In their view, all living things have their cycles of development and their life spans, and societies are no different. Famine comes with prosperity, disease with health, chaos with order, and pain with joy. Everything is appropriate within the cosmos, and everything is to be expected. What explained the dynamic, epitomized by the concept of yin and yang (complementariness), was human nature, potentially strong but too often weak, able to be focused but too easily distracted from the proper way.[5] Fixing life and society meant fixing character.

By the end of the eighteenth century, and for several decades thereafter, more and more Chinese experienced such disruption in their lives that they were encouraged to look for and find evidence of unusual and large-scale corruption in public affairs, mismanagement of resources, dereliction of official duty, and a general decline in standards of behavior. They were supported in their observations and impressions by the expected signs of nature's displeasure with human endeavor, as famine, malnutrition, disease, and death swept a broad swath across the empire. Amid such tribulations, Chinese responded in traditional fashion by focusing on the responsibilities of leadership and the fulfillment of the state's moral obligations to protect the people's well-being. What was wrong could be rectified by adjusting human behavior or, if that was impossible, by replacing those in power.

But what China faced in the century before 1900 was radically different in two fundamental ways from anything experienced before. First, its leaders had to devise effective responses to uncommon domestic challenges that looked at first as if they could be handled by time-honored means; second, they had to accept the task of finding their way in a larger world that was in the process of being reordered decisively under European military, technological, and economic power. In both cases, the rules of behavior and their justification came under relentless assault, and reliance on Confucian "character" fixes seemed increasingly ineffectual.

Because of a remarkable demographic explosion that saw the empire's population nearly double from 200–250 million in 1750 to 410–430 million by 1850[6] without any corresponding breakthrough in agricultural technology or organization, per capita productivity declined for many peasants and opened the door to famine, disease, higher levels of human misery, and the inevitable rebellions. But overpopulation caused or abetted unusual and more-subtle changes in many aspects of Chinese life that were unanticipated and could not be reversed, and that collectively helped to shape the emergence of a different China. It encouraged increasing privatization of formerly public activity, commercialization of agriculture, increased reliance on and growth of a money-based economy, the development of new social classes, the blurring of class lines and identities, and the emergence of more-intense competition between bureaucratic leaders of the central government and a variety of social elites in the provinces. It also stimulated urbanization and affected the opportunities of ambitious young men who continued to train themselves in the classical manner for access to elite status and possibly government service, only to find that the authorities refused to raise the quotas for success on the examinations to match the new demographic realities.[7]

These slowly progressing internal changes were novel and disturbing enough, but they were accompanied by much higher levels of official corruption than usual,[8] a growing incidence of opium addiction,[9] and short-term instabilities that propelled China along a trajectory of increasing popular dissatisfaction and disorder, and, among its leaders, consideration of reform. By the close of the nineteenth century, even when rejected as unnecessary, reform was typically discussed in relationship to the power and influence of Europe, whose intrusion into the Chinese world could no longer be ignored or belittled by the empire's ruling class and policymakers. Historians and others continue to argue over the impact of the West, with strong cases made for both positive and negative consequences, and at the time Chinese opinion was certainly mixed. The trend in China from the mid-nineteenth century to the present, however, has been along a path that has led to the increasing abandonment of traditional Chinese attitudes and practices, habits of thought and perspectives, institutions and structures that demand our attention to international matters as well as domestic ones.

During imperial China's long history, relations with the outside world, principally with neighbors on all sides, had been a constant and deep concern, more so than historians (Chinese and non-Chinese alike) have acknowledged adequately until recently. Relations with such cultures as the Korean, Japanese, and Vietnamese have figured into this mix, but clearly the most important have been those resulting from engagement with various nomadic and seminomadic peoples to the north and west. The importance of such engagements can be seen in a startling fact: Of the sixty or so dynasties that had governed China until the end of the monarchical system in February 1912, nearly one-third had been created by northern "barbarians," as traditionally characterized by the Chinese. Unusually conscious of history generally, the Chinese elite learned to appreciate profoundly the potential power of confederated tribes under charismatic leaders because of the very successes that such forces had had again and again.

Following a lifestyle rooted in pastoralism—livestock raising and nomadic—rather than agriculture, the tribal peoples beyond China's northern and western borders held certain advantages over the Chinese, despite the huge disparity in respective populations. Theirs was a life inherently more mobile and, therefore, less vulnerable to attack. Unlike the Chinese, who were fully sedentary, they had few meaningful urban centers whose loss might prove disastrous. Moreover, they possessed greater access to and developed greater skills in the use of the premier weapon available to humans before the so-called gunpowder revolution: the horse. So valuable was the horse, particularly those bred by the pastoralists themselves, that annually the Chinese purchased large numbers of them from their erstwhile enemies.

These strengths were balanced by a weakness that stemmed mainly from the pastoralists' desire for access to Chinese goods, to Chinese prestige and authority, and to Chinese patronage. Of primary concern, these typically took precedence over ambitions to attack and attempt conquest of their giant neighbor. The dynamics of pastoral-Chinese relations that emerged took form under these conditions, leading both sides to strive for mutual ac-commodation—despite their profound cultural differences—based upon self-interests that reinforced those of the other. For the Chinese, peace with the pastoralists was, with occasional exceptions, prompted by a breakdown of the *modus vivendi*, and was the preferable course to pursue, both because it was less expensive (minimizing military costs and wall building or strengthening) and justified Chinese self-representation as culturally supe-rior, beneficent, and munificent.

Centuries of exercising a range of approaches in dealing with its neigh-bors, the basic principles of which seemed to create a system of foreign management (the so-called "tributary system") that could be applied to all and sundry, at times worked and at others did not for China. By the time that Europeans—first the Portuguese and Dutch, then the English—appeared along the Celestial Empire's southern shores beginning in the sixteenth cen-tury, the Chinese were quite comfortable with their traditional international practices and insisted upon forcing the most recently arrived "barbarians" to fit into a predetermined mold. As a result, by 1760, Chinese regulations limited the European presence to the period between October and March annually at one point of entry, the city of Canton (now Guangzhou), where these foreigners had to reside in a special, confined quarter, and had to con-duct their business through local Chinese merchants headed by a monopo-listic guild known as the Cohong. Catholic missionaries, from Jesuit, Dominican, and Franciscan orders, had been prohibited from Chinese soil since the 1730s.[10]

The "Canton system," as it became known, reflected a practical desire to control the foreign intruders and limit their influence on Chinese society. It also reaffirmed long-held views regarding commerce. Rooted in Confu-cianism, these held that commerce was incidental to the goal of creating and maintaining the properly functioning society. Worse, because business dealings involved little more than the transferral of goods for the sake of profit, they were *ipso facto* suspect and socially dangerous. Therefore, al-lowing the Europeans to trade in Canton was treated by the Chinese as a ma-jor concession, virtually a privilege. Trade's sole purpose was to appeal to the baser instincts—such as greed—typical of "barbarians," so that the Chinese concern was ensuring that those instincts would not penetrate China proper.

As the eighteenth century drew to a close, however, the English pressed their Chinese hosts unsuccessfully to expand commercial opportunities by opening additional ports, reducing the control of the Cohong, and permit-ting penetration of the Chinese interior. Three other issues added to accu-mulating tensions: the trade deficits that befell British merchants annually because of an imbalanced exchange, forcing them to pay with silver bullion for the silks, porcelains, and ever-growing amounts of tea that they purchased in China; the failure to persuade the Qing dynasty (1644–1912) to grant the right of diplomatic residence in Beijing, a concession that would acknowledge a level of international equality unknown to Chinese theory or practice but institutionalized within Europe; and the differences between the Chinese and English theories of jurisprudence, organization and purposes of judicial process, and the character of punishments.[11] Important separately, these matters together produced among the English the impression that China was not as enlightened as European eighteenth-century thinkers—such as Voltaire—believed, nor was its culture a haven for "modern" values rooted in ideals proclaiming all men free and deserving of equal justice. By the early nineteenth century, the English and other Europeans were convinced that China in fact represented a stage of human development—Asiatic, as it came to be categorized—inadequate to the demands of the "modern" age and incapable of engaging the contemporary world because of its unrelenting commitment to history.

The response of the Chinese elite to the resurgence of domestic instability and the challenges of European culture was consistent with habits of observation and analysis embedded in long-cherished Confucian perspectives. Political and cultural leaders were encouraged to view what they saw occurring to their empire as recurrences of what generations of predecessors had witnessed time and again. At the beginning of the nineteenth century there was little chance of innovative ideas being tested, even among those recognizing that something had to be done. A combination of increasingly dramatic and wrenching events, from domestic rebellion—the most famous being two Muslim rebellions (1855–1873), the Nian rebellion (1851–1868), and the Taiping rebellion (1850–1864)—to international wars and their costly settlements, particularly with England from 1839 to 1842 (the Opium War) and from 1856 to 1860, would have to occur before some among China's elite began entertaining reform.

Despite growing support for borrowing the results of military and civil technology as well as institutional approaches from Europe, Chinese thinking about reform remained limited until the end of the nineteenth century by an understandable desire to hold on to as much of China's character as possible. How to keep China Chinese despite growing European influence was a constant concern, giving rise to elaborate arguments that sought to justify acceptance of that influence while allaying fears of its consequences. Yet for a culture like China's, with its exaggerated Confucian concern for appropriate behavior as defined by a political class that was also the empire's intellectual, social, and cultural elite, the domestic and international challenges that emerged from the eighteenth century were particularly unnerving and subversive. What Chinese leaders, would-be leaders, and ordinary people did or did not do in the face of these challenges by the beginning of the twentieth century contributed extensively to what has been called "the titanic drama of the Chinese revolution,"[12] a much more radical solution to China's problems than reform.

But what kind of revolution? Several, in fact: a Republican, a Nationalist, and a Communist. The first occurred in 1911. It brought an end to the monarchy that had been at the center of Chinese political life for more than two thousand years, and inaugurated an experiment in republicanism lasting in principle until the late 1920s. The second, beginning in the early 1920s and lasting in theory until 1949, placed the Guomindang party (GMD)[13] into power under the banner of Sun Yat-sen's "Three People's Principles"—anti-imperialist nationalism, democracy, and socialism—and the leadership of Chiang Kai-shek (1888–1975). The third, propelled by the egalitarian premises and promises of socialism and a renewed and invigorated popular Chinese nationalism, established the People's Republic of China in 1949. Owing to certain features of the thought of Mao Zedong (Mao Tse-tung), the preeminent figure in the history of Chinese communism, an argument can be made that the third revolution produced a subset of others, including the Great Leap Forward (1958–1960) and the Great Proletarian Cultural Revolution (1966–1976).

THE REPUBLICAN REVOLUTION
(1890s–LATE 1920s)

This first phase of the Chinese Revolution resulted from popular frustration over the accumulated burdens of China's wrestling with decades of socioeconomic changes; failed imperial leadership; the threatening, disruptive, and humiliating presence of Western and Japanese power on Chinese soil; and disenchantment with reform. It was largely the product of new social forces, including the first generation of modern students, many of whom were educated in Japan, Europe, or the United States; intellectuals with severed or no ties to the traditional order; members of a budding middle class of entrepreneurs and urbanites most involved with the modernizing sectors of the country's economy; and even peasants receiving some modicum of modern-style education.

In the 1890s a revolutionary movement was born whose most visible leader became Sun Yat-sen (1866–1925). Sun was a young man from south China who lived for some years with a brother in Hawaii, where he attended a local missionary school and graduated from Oahu College in 1883. He subsequently studied medicine in Canton and then Hong Kong before taking up practice in Macao in the early 1890s. In those years he also began to ponder China's plight, increasingly believing that only the ouster of the dynasty with its Manchu roots could save the country. He commenced serious, although long, unsuccessful, revolutionary activity in 1895.

Sun's political ideas were never well articulated, although he remained fundamentally a constitutionalist throughout his life, admiring the French Third Republic but seeing his country's most logical model in Japan—Asian and successfully modernizing by the turn of the twentieth century. Owing to China's lack of experience with anything but monarchy, Sun argued that before arriving at a constitutional order, its people would need guidance and would have to pass through phases of military control and political tutelage. This part of his legacy to the revolutionary movement proved costly to the Chinese people in that it encouraged political leaders in their all-too-frequent tendency toward dictatorial politics.

Although one of China's earliest revolutionaries, Sun missed the Republican Revolution when it erupted in late 1911, being on one of his many fund-raising trips abroad. The specific events that led to the abdication on February 12, 1912, of the last Qing emperor, Puyi, and the end of the monarchical form of government, began on October 9, 1911. An accidental bomb explosion occurred in Hankou, one of several cities in the Wuhan area that had become a haven for radical young Chinese. With strong branches of secret societies, a large number of industrial and other workers, modern schools, and units of the New Army (the main state military force, created as part of governmental reforms in 1901), the area was ripe for revolutionary infiltration and agitation.

A group of the revolutionaries was making bombs in the Russian Concession area of the city when the accident occurred. A police raid during the confusion provided authorities with membership registers for the network of revolutionary societies that had been forming since 1904. Now vulnerable to wide-scale and potentially disastrous repression, the revolutionaries had little choice but to unleash an uprising immediately. It began early the next morning with the mutiny of the Wuchang Eighth Engineer Battalion. On October 11, the uprising spread to Hanyang, and on the twelfth to Hankou. By October 22, it extended to Hunan and Shaanxi provinces, and by the end of the month three more provinces had succumbed: Shanxi, Jiangxi, and Yunnan. At the same time a group of field commanders sent a list of demands to the Qing court. The document called for establishing a parliament before the year was out, promulgating a constitution, electing a premier, and reducing the power of the emperor.

Once the monarchy had passed into history, Sun Yat-sen's popularity among progressives made him the logical choice for the new republic's first president, but the presence of a formidable rival in Yuan Shikai (1859–1916), a military leader who commanded China's most powerful and disciplined army and controlled Beijing, as well as the fear of forcing a civil war, prompted Sun to step aside in Yuan's favor.

Despite committing to a constitutional order in China, Yuan was more interested in ensuring his own power. Remaining in Beijing and refusing to cooperate with the fledgling national assembly meeting in Nanjing, he turned his troops against the assembly and dispersed its delegates, scrapped the constitution, and proclaimed himself president for life. The storm of opposition that erupted after he announced plans for the restoration of the monarchy and the commencement of his "reign" in 1916 drove him from power. Yet, far from improving China's political situation, Yuan's ouster left a vacuum in national politics that no successor could fill adequately. In the absence of strong central government in Beijing (where the fiction of republicanism was preserved), local military leaders (warlords), with private armies, emerged across the country. Their separatist ambitions as well as lack of commitment to republicanism and nationalism kept China politically fragmented and internationally weak for nearly two decades. For his part, Sun Yat-sen would struggle in vain over the next few years to establish a workable government in Canton as a base from which to lead the struggle for national unification.

Meanwhile, a new generation of Western-educated or at least Western-influenced intellectuals emerged to challenge not merely the old politics but also the philosophical basis of traditional China. As yet politically impotent, these progressives nevertheless wielded enormous influence over a growing reading public increasingly willing to entertain radical solutions to China's problems. Western standards became the yardstick by which the "new" men and women judged China, and Western political institutions, culture, scientific knowledge, and technology promised the means by which they sought to forge a modern nation.

To achieve the complete transformation of national life, men like Chen Duxiu (1879–1942), Cai Yuanpei (1868–1948), and Hu Shi (1891–1962), all products of foreign education, called upon their countrymen to eliminate the last vestiges of the past. Unlike previous reformers, they had no desire to purify or revitalize Confucianism. Rather, they strove to discredit the teachings of Kongzi as a reactionary, obscurant philosophy whose continued domination of Chinese society would impede progress only further. To replace Confucian ideas, men like Chen, Cai, and Hu published magazines (*New Youth*, *New Tide*, and *Weekly Critic*) in which they offered a tantalizing array of Western substitutes, including the philosophies of Kant, Nietzsche, Dewey, Bergson, and Marx. Within a few years, Chinese intellectuals and other elites were introduced to ideas and systems of thought that had taken Europeans more than a century to develop and digest. For the time being, few people made a personal commitment to any particular philosophy. Most merely dabbled in the vast reservoir of Western wisdom available for the first time. Glorification of science may have been excessive, but the debates and controversies that flourished in those years had two major consequences: They enormously stimulated the thinking public in China and strengthened nationalist sentiment, and they popularized such notions as progress, democracy, freedom, and individualism, particularly through the new magazines whose editors and writers abandoned classical Chinese in favor of the vernacular (*bai hua*).

Together with the intellectual revolution sweeping China, Great Power conflicts in Europe and Asia that produced the Russo-Japanese War (1904–1905) and led to World War I (1914–1918) also had the effect of altering the geopolitical framework of foreign influence in China. Some Western powers diminished their presence, while others, particularly Germany and Japan, moved toward greater prominence. This trend, as well as developments at the Paris Peace Conference (1919) that settled World War I and betrayed Chinese interests, contributed to the growing activism of many Chinese in the early 1920s. For their participation in the war on the side of the victorious allies, they hoped to see an end to the "unequal treaties."[14] If the pronouncements of world statesmen about "territorial integrity" and "national self-determination" had any meaning, Chinese progressives felt certain that Germany's concessions would be returned to China. However, because of a secret agreement signed in early 1917 by England, France, and the warlord government in Beijing, Chinese hopes were frustrated. The revelation of allied duplicity, and the transferral of Germany's Shandong holdings to Japan, released a torrent of protest among incredulous Chinese of all classes that culminated in a major eruption on May 4, 1919. On that day, over 3,000 university students assembled at Tiananmen to condemn allied decisions. Organizing a union, the students were able to prolong the protest, thereby attracting support from around the country that, joined by many patriotic Chinese merchants, culminated in a large-scale and effective boycott of Japanese goods. Although this public outcry had little effect on China's relations with the outside world, it represented a significant advance in the growth of Chinese nationalism. Many people received their initial taste of political activity by participating in the strikes, demonstrations, and boycotts that swept the country—particularly its urban centers where the earliest signs of popular nationalist sentiment appeared—as part of what became known as the "May Fourth Movement."

Perhaps more than anything else, party politics in China benefited from the spirit of activism that now pervaded society. Hundreds flocked to Sun Yat-sen and his Guomindang, revitalizing it after years of precarious existence, while a smaller number joined the Chinese Communist Party (CCP), founded in 1921. Increased membership provided the GMD with the broad popular support it sorely needed, but the infusion of new blood only exacerbated the longstanding problem of discipline and organization.

To overcome these weaknesses, Sun turned to the Soviet Union and its Bolshevik leadership. Inspired by Vladimir Ilich Lenin's success in forging a new state system in Russia (a feat that owed much to the kind of party that he had created), grateful for the Soviet offer of assistance, and concerned with the growing influence of the Chinese Communist party (CCP), Sun opened contacts with China's northern neighbor. In early 1923, after months of negotiations, he agreed to the establishment of a united front with the CCP in return for guidance from Soviet political and military advisers and financial backing.

Soviet advisers, money, and weapons induced Sun to modify his "Three People's Principles," thereby stressing the anti-imperialism, authoritarian leadership, and anti-capitalism central to Soviet theory and practice. Doing so created dissension within the ranks of the GMD because some of his followers refused to accept the party's reorientation. Despite Sun's best efforts, many conservatives persisted in their disapproval of the united front. When they came to dominate the party in 1927, they moved quickly to destroy the alliance.

Political reorganization along Bolshevik lines, nevertheless, invigorated the GMD. Under the direction of Comintern agent Michael Borodin, Soviet advisers helped to centralize the party's administration, regularize its finances, and coordinate its propaganda. With Sun and his associates assuming effective leadership, Canton became the center of a small but workable government by 1925, a microcosm of Nationalist aspirations. Although recognized by neither warlords nor foreign powers, the Canton government rapidly consolidated itself and created its own "new model" army, which would provide the main force for the anticipated military effort to reunify China.

THE NATIONALIST REVOLUTION
(EARLY 1920s–1949)

Following Sun Yat-sen's death in March 1925, a struggle for control of the GMD ensued. One of the claimants was Chiang Kai-shek, a young military officer and director of the Whampoa Military Academy near Canton. Chiang had met Sun in Japan and later participated in the revolutionary events of 1911–1912. For the next ten years, however, he remained relatively aloof from politics. Not until 1923 did he emerge as a devoted follower of Sun's cause. Within four years, he would become the leader of the GMD.

By 1926 the Canton government was capable of launching the long-awaited campaign against the northern warlords. Under Chiang's command, Nationalist forces swept into the Yangzi valley, overran half of China's provinces, and "liberated" scores of important cities, often with the assistance of local communist party cells. In the midst of the campaign, however, an open break occurred between conservative and radical wings of the GMD, fomented by communist-inspired riots among the peasant and working classes and the killing of numerous foreigners. Both actions frightened the wealthier and more-conservative members of the Guomindang, the very people who were Chiang's principal supporters.

In a surprise move following the capture of Shanghai, he attacked communist strongholds. By late March 1927, the GMD conservatives triumphed and severed the party's alliance with the CCP. By mid-April, leftists within and outside of the party were assaulted, and Soviet advisers to the GMD were sent packing. Mao Zedong and Zhu De, youthful leaders of the CCP, led two shattered contingents to the frontiers of Jiangxi, a southeastern province. Protected by its mountains and forests, they kept alive the communist movement, regrouped its forces, and turned to guerrilla action against Chiang and his party.

Meanwhile, his opposition temporarily crushed, Chiang resumed the Northern Campaign. By the end of 1928 his armies had occupied Beijing and achieved at least nominal control over most of China. While many warlords continued to ignore his authority, the foreign powers recognized the new government that he established at Nanjing. Financial assistance from abroad bolstered Chiang's regime, and tentative steps were taken toward a revision of the unequal treaties left over from the nineteenth century. Following the lead of the United States, the great powers agreed to relinquish control of the country's customs and tariffs, and over the next couple of years they abolished a number of foreign-held concessions. In such circumstances, there was every reason to expect that the victorious Guomindang could now undertake the reconstruction of the country. Japanese aggression and the persistent opposition of the communists, however, distracted Chiang's attention from this critical task.

For Japan, the 1920s were a decade of growing crisis and disillusionment. The dislocations accompanying modernization, coupled with population pressure and a weakening economy, created domestic tensions that increasingly found release in foreign adventurism. Alarmed by the worsening circumstances of Japanese rural life and resentful of their own lack of influence in determining their country's policies, military leaders maneuvered for political power and advocated a program of expansionism (beginning against China) as a cure for Japan's problems. They especially coveted the rich province of Manchuria. Convinced that Japan must control directly the region's raw materials vital to its industrial needs and great-power status, local officers in charge of the Japanese Guangdong Army demanded immediate action. On September 18, 1931, an explosion on the South Manchurian Railway near Mukden, set off by the Japanese but blamed on the Chinese, provided the pretext for a full-scale invasion of Manchuria. Meeting little resistance, the Japanese overran the entire region within five months.

For the moment, Chiang Kai-shek chose not to fight. In the southeast his armies were struggling against the communists, whom he regarded as the more significant enemy ("internal pacification before resistance to external aggression"). It was for that struggle that he hoped to save his resources. At the same time, he recognized that his military capability was no match for the Japanese and that a major armed clash would lead to certain defeat and the collapse of his own power. By May 1933 the Japanese had occupied China's four northeastern provinces. A truce signed shortly thereafter temporarily halted Japanese expansion in China and acknowledged their conquests. Chiang's strategy seemed successful, but its adoption proved a miscalculation for the long run. Refusal to resist the Japanese eroded patriotic support for him and his party.

When many of the communists fled to Jiangxi following Chiang Kai-shek's attempt to liquidate their movement in 1927, their future looked bleak. Yet, by taking advantage of popular discontent to broaden its base of support, the party created a professional military force (the Red Army) that shaped the technique of guerrilla warfare into an effective strategy. Thus, the communists were able to resist Chiang's armies successfully. While organizing a network of local cells, they established a Chinese Soviet Republic in the southeast.

Late in 1930 Chiang Kai-Shek launched the first two "bandit annihilation offensives" designed to encircle the communist stronghold. Rather than encountering a disorganized rabble, Chiang's troops confronted well-trained, aggressive, and highly mobile Red Army units that fought skillfully against a more numerous foe. The GMD suffered serious setbacks. In 1931 Chiang led a new attack himself. Success seemed imminent, but news of renewed Japanese aggression in Manchuria forced a Nationalist withdrawal.

When the situation in North China stabilized, he conducted a fourth campaign against the communists in late 1932 and 1933, but this ended in a stalemate. Advised by volunteer German officers, the Nationalists constructed a series of blockhouses along the perimeter of the communist-held territory. By early 1934 Chiang was ready to strike the final blow.

With the Nationalists closing in, the communist leaders decided to abandon their base. In October 1934 the main force of some 100,000 men, women, and children slipped through the battlelines, headed west as far as the border of Tibet, and then turned northward. Over the next year they traversed more than 5,000 miles to complete what became known as the "Long March." Only 20,000 arrived at the final destination. Mao, who during the withdrawal had succeeded in wresting leadership of the party, settled his force around Yan'an in Shaanxi province. The communists' headquarters would remain there until 1947.

The Long March had decimated the communist ranks and thoroughly exhausted the survivors. Under the circumstances, their chances of withstanding the expected GMD attack on their new base seemed slim. Chiang counted on Manchurian troops under the command of Zhang Xueliang in his "final" battle with the communists, but their commitment to an anticommunist offensive was secondary to liberating their home region from Japanese occupation. When Zhang failed to move against Mao's forces as ordered, Chiang Kai-shek flew to Zhang's headquarters at Xi'an in December 1936. There he was confronted by rebellious officers who, encouraged by the communists, demanded an end to the civil war and the formation of a united front against the Japanese. Arrested and detained for two weeks, Chiang finally agreed. As a result of the new alliance, the Red Army was nominally placed under GMD command. In view of the failure of the first GMD-CCP cooperation in 1927, neither Mao nor Chiang had any illusions about the long-term success of this second effort. Nevertheless, for a short time most of China rallied behind Chiang in an outpouring of patriotic sentiment that reflected a desire for all-out resistance to the Japanese.

Within a year full-scale war broke out between China and Japan, fighting that would merge with World War II. Even though the Japanese eventually overran the great coastal cities and almost all of eastern China, thereby forcing the Nationalist government to transfer its capital far inland to Chongqing, they never planned to absorb the entire country. Safe behind the protective barriers of the upper Yangzi and the mountains of Sichuan, Chiang refused all peace offers while pressing for American entry into the conflict and tying down sizable Japanese forces. But his prolonged refuge in this inland capital separated him from important segments of his supporters. Settled in Chongqing, cut off from the industrial and banking resources of the coastal urban industrial centers, Chiang had to rely more and more on the conservative landlord class whose main goal was to preserve the old agrarian social system. In time, the interests of this group prevailed over the more progressive urban intellectual and business elements who had fled with the Nationalist government and who were more inclined to support needed social and agrarian reforms. In addition, evacuation of the eastern areas abandoned millions of peasants to brutal Japanese occupation, forcing many to turn away from the Nationalists and toward communist guerrilla units for protection.

Meanwhile, in Shaanxi province the communists slowly rebuilt their shattered movement. By 1941 the failure of the united front and severe losses to the Japanese had revealed shortcomings in prevailing CCP policies and tactics. As a consequence, the party leadership devised a new strategy to sustain the movement, prevent further erosion of support, and ultimately strengthen the communist cause and prepare it for renewed action. The "rectification" campaign of 1942–1944, through intense criticism and self-criticism and the study of selected documents reflecting Mao's views, was an essential step in that direction. It sought an end to party heterodoxy by instilling in cadres a common ideology and set of goals.

Rectification was accompanied by other campaigns, moderate in spirit, yet designed to indoctrinate the people, exclude as few as possible from the revolutionary process, unleash the energies of the masses, and direct them toward the task of solving social problems in the communist-held base areas. Among these programs were the "to the village" campaign (1941–1942), which broke down the isolation of many communities by sending cadres into their midst and shifting the focus of government work to the lower levels of society; the campaign for the reduction of rents and interest (1942–1944), which served to awaken apathetic peasants by rallying them around an issue that had great appeal; the cooperative movement (1942–1944), which, by stressing the concept of mutual aid, increased production and developed new relationships among peasants; and the education movement of 1944, which spread literacy and indoctrinated the masses in communist ideology. The party's emphasis on adult education rather than that of children reveals how literacy could be placed in the immediate service of the revolution.

Through programs such as these, the party sought to mobilize the masses, involve them actively in resolving their many problems, and gain their commitment to the communist cause by seemingly equating its goals with theirs. The success of the campaigns, however, depended on the effectiveness of mobilization. To encourage and increase popular involvement, the party developed a propaganda technique known as the "mass line." The technique comprised a three-stage process. First, cadres would go to the people to determine what kind of program appealed to them. Once the determination was made, the second step was to square popular desires with party ideology and goals. This was often the most difficult task because in the third stage the cadres had to persuade the masses that to support the program was in their best interests. Even more than that, the key to the success of the mass line technique was in arousing the people to believe in the program and to act upon it with genuine commitment. The technique's application resulted, for example, in the party's decision to replace its radical land reform policy with a more moderate one focusing less on social issues (class struggle, for example) than on economic ones. As a technique, the mass line became a permanent feature of Chinese communist practice.

The campaigns of the early 1940s and use of the mass line technique achieved major results by the end of the Sino-Japanese War in 1945. Communist propaganda reached millions of people, party membership rose to 1.2 million (compared with 40,000 in 1937), and the Red Army numbered about 1 million men. What had been a movement on the verge of extinction only ten years before was now capable of challenging the GMD for the leadership of China. It not only had developed the material resources, the organizational ability, and the military tactics to succeed but had the support of millions believing communist ideals and feeling confident in the struggle's outcome.

World War II in the Pacific ended in August 1945, but peace did not come to China. No sooner had the Japanese capitulation been announced than both communist and Nationalist forces rushed to fill the vacuum created by their departing enemy and secure control of as much of China as possible. In the scramble for territory, the advantage seemed to lie with the Nationalists. For one thing, the Japanese had been ordered to surrender only to Chiang Kai-shek's forces; for another, American ships and planes facilitated the movement of Nationalist troops from their inland positions to the coastal areas and northern China. Chiang, however, made two major tactical errors that significantly affected the outcome of the civil war. The first was to concentrate on the occupation of China's principal cities. Though not a surprising move on his part, in view of the GMD's long-standing reliance on China's urban economy and population, it was militarily disastrous because it allowed the communists to gain firm control of the countryside. The second was to commit some of his best divisions to Manchuria in an effort to prevent splitting the country between north and south. He hoped to seize this industrial region and strike a crippling blow against the communists; instead, he found out quickly that his lines of communications and supply were stretched dangerously thin, making them extremely vulnerable to the guerrilla tactics used so effectively by the Red Army. Also, the Russians had thoroughly looted the province and then presented stored Japanese arms to the Chinese communists as they entered Manchuria.

Meanwhile, American efforts to mediate GMD-CCP differences in the hopes of avoiding a full-scale civil war continued through the mediation of General George Marshall, though the spirit of compromise was weak and almost immediately violated. Communist complaints were directed not only at the refusal of some Nationalist commanders to honor the truce but also at the GMD government for its clear lack of commitment to the proposed establishment of a constitutional order in China. Moreover, as mediator, Marshall found his neutral position compromised because the United States openly supported one of the belligerents. By the beginning of 1947, his last effort to reconcile the country's contending forces proved a failure, and both GMD and CCP leaders prepared their supporters for all-out civil war to determine the future leadership of China.

Through 1947 the outcome of the struggle remained in doubt, but by the spring of 1948, Red Army tactics of avoiding major clashes with GMD troops in favor of harassing supply lines and encircling Nationalist-held cities had begun to tip the balance in its favor. The communists achieved a major success in Manchuria, where Chiang's forces had isolated themselves and had taken up defensive positions in and around the major urban centers. Denied the opportunity to either attack or withdraw, GMD troops found themselves caught in numerous traps, surrounded, and cut off. By the summer of 1948, Red Army units had succeeded in completely severing overland supply lines to Manchuria, leaving Nationalist troops to be provisioned by air.

From summer through late autumn, the GMD military situation deteriorated rapidly. Heavy troop losses following the evacuation of several Manchurian cities and the surrender of the army at Mukden were accompanied by the abandonment of huge amounts of American supplies and armaments that then fell into the eager hands of the communists. By December, China north of the Yangzi was under Red Army control, and Nationalist resistance had been all but shattered.

Defeated on the field of battle, hamstrung by economic collapse, panicked by runaway inflation (the yuan-to-dollar exchange rate had risen from 1,000 to 1 in 1945 to 45,000 to 1 in mid-1947) and cancerous fiscal corruption, unable to maintain the morale of its supporters, and abandoned by millions who felt that their interests had been too long ignored, the Nationalist government faced a situation that few would have thought possible even five years before. In one last desperate ploy to salvage at least something of GMD influence in Chinese affairs, Chiang resigned the presidency and sought a negotiated settlement with his adversary. The time for such maneuvers, however, was long past. Flushed with their victories in the north, the communists used the negotiations to consolidate their hold over territory already acquired and prepare for the anticipated campaign to "liberate" China south of the Yangzi. In 1949 the final push commenced, meeting only token resistance as one after another of the great cities—Nanjing, Shanghai, and Canton—fell. Meanwhile, with most of his government, some 50,000 troops, and two and a half million civilians, Chiang Kai-shek withdrew to the island of Taiwan (Formosa). The civil war was over.

THE COMMUNIST REVOLUTION (1949–PRESENT)

On October 1, 1949, before cheering throngs in Beijing's famous Tiananmen Square, Mao Zedong proclaimed the People's Republic of China (PRC). This great turning point in recent world history inaugurated an attempt to transform China and its people that has continued ever since. If the goal of constructing a new China has gone virtually unchallenged since 1949, the means for its achievement have not been so easily agreed upon. Much of the history of the People's Republic over the past half century has been determined by shifts in policy reflecting an on-going dispute over related questions about the revolution. What are the goals of that revolution and have they been achieved? Is it necessary to continue the effort to transform the character of the Chinese people, or can the elite and society focus on developing the material base of the country? What role should ideology play in China's development? What should be the nature and goals of policy? By what means should policy be implemented? These questions have not been posed in isolation of politics but have defined the main parameters of factionalism at the highest levels. Above them all has hovered the personality, thought, and vision of Mao Zedong.[15]

Like all revolutionaries who spend years in the struggle to win power, the Chinese communists before 1949 devoted little attention to specific policies that they would pursue after attaining victory. Concerned more with the survival and expansion of the revolutionary movement, Mao and his colleagues gave little consideration to the future. As a result, when the "future" arrived at mid-century, the CCP was suddenly faced with all the responsibilities that come with wielding power as well as the pressing need to undertake two major tasks immediately: the reintegration of political authority after nearly four decades of ineffective central control over all of China; and the reconstruction of an economy shattered by years of civil and international strife.

In spite of the mood of optimism that permeated the ranks of the CCP in 1949, the wide popular support that the party enjoyed, and the dedication and discipline that the rank-and-file would bring to the tasks at hand, the new regime had to proceed slowly and with moderation over the next several years. As Mao pointed out repeatedly, China was not yet prepared for the "second revolution" intended to transform it thoroughly. Socialist construction, the first stage in this process, would have to await the political and economic stabilization of the country.

Given the limited numbers and inadequate training of party cadres, success in achieving the goals of rehabilitating the country and consolidating the new regime depended in part on the party's ability to approach China's problems with ideological flexibility and moderation. The conscious decision to deemphasize theoretical considerations for more-pragmatic goals enabled the party to mobilize all available human resources, accept temporary solutions, and retain many of the former Nationalist administrators. Along with ideological temporizing (compromise), the party worked to organize the population, much as it had done on a lesser scale during the Yan'an period, in order to achieve major political and/or social change with full mass participation.

Between 1950 and 1953 several movements were launched that left hardly any of China's millions untouched:

1. The land reform movement (1950–1952), conducted to involve the rural masses in peasant associations and "people's courts" for the purposes of completing the process of breaking up large landholdings, equalizing the distribution of land among farm owners and laborers, and undercutting the traditional power of the landlord class

2. The campaign for "implementation of the marriage law" (beginning in 1950), designed to end the inequality of Chinese women (epitomized and maintained by the traditional marriage system) and involve them in public activity of all kinds

3. The "Resist America-Aid Korea" campaign (1950–1953), begun to intensify patriotic sentiment and recruit volunteers for the army in support of Chinese participation in the Korean War

4. The "thought reform" campaigns (1950 and after), organized to attack traditional and "bourgeois" ideas and values through programs of self-evaluation, mutual criticism, and indoctrination

5. The "bandit suppression" campaigns (1951), launched to root out remnants of active Nationalist resistance and persons suspected of inadequate loyalty to the new regime

6. The "three anti" campaign (1951–1952), initiated to rectify the behavior of party cadres and government officials who were accused of corruption, waste, and bureaucratism

7. The "five anti" campaign (1951–1952), directed largely at urban middle-class businessmen for their alleged "bribery, tax evasion, theft of state assets, cheating on government contracts, and stealing of state economic secrets"

By 1953 not only was the economy revived, state control over it increased, and the political system strengthened, but society was also organized to a degree that seemed to prove China's readiness for the transition to socialism.

In late 1952 the leadership announced the First Five Year Plan (FFYP). Designed to move the country rapidly forward economically, it had all the earmarks of Soviet Russian influence: emphasis on industry rather than agriculture, heavy industry rather than light, large enterprises rather than small, centralized planning, and full exploitation of the peasantry through collectivization in order to finance economic development. To accompany the plan and assist its fulfillment, technical and monetary aid flowed from the USSR, the population was mobilized to increase production, moderation prevailed in political life, and a policy of "peaceful coexistence" and renewed contact with the outside world characterized China's foreign relations. In sum, at least until 1956, the general thrust of party policies was in the direction of minimizing social and political tensions so as to avoid disrupting production and proceed with the task of nation-building.

The successes of the First Five Year Plan quickly seemed patent. Agriculture, although underfunded, appeared to be thriving—the summer of 1955 provided the best crop since 1949—and practically all peasant households had been collectivized (although not without growing peasant objection). As for industrial development, gains were even more impressive.

An intense debate within the party, however, ensued in 1956–1957 over the implications of FFYP results and trends. The antagonists—on the one hand called pragmatists, conservatives, and rightists, and on the other hand radicals and leftists—found themselves at odds over issues of policy and ideology. First, should priority continue to be given to industrial development? That is, should economic growth be "uneven" between industry and agriculture? Second, should the socialization, even communization, of the countryside continue regardless of its potentially disruptive effect on the economy? In other words, should economic development continue to receive higher priority than social revolution? Third, should the bureaucratization of Chinese administrative practice and planning proceed unchecked because it was "necessary" for the kind of rapid economic development implied by the FFYP? Fourth, should the revolution be institutionalized instead of perpetuated (that is, should greater emphasis be placed on establishment of regular procedures and institutions so as to provide the needed social stability for orderly national growth, or on the notions of social struggle and "contradictions among peoples" and the practice of mass mobilization)? Fifth, should the party continue to rule unopposed? Regardless of one's position on these issues, the FFYP offered ammunition that could be used against one's opponents. The pragmatists could point to solid evidence of growth and the potential for continued growth if only realism would prevail among China's decision-makers; as for the idealists, they could point to the threat that bureaucratization, institutionalization, centralization, and excessive pragmatism posed to the revolution.

As the chief spokesman for the leftists, Mao felt compelled to intervene directly and use his enormous prestige to challenge the thinking of the pragmatists, modify the FFYP, and "correct" some of the worst tendencies emerging from it. He was driven to this course of action not only by domestic Chinese concerns but by events within the Soviet Union and eastern Europe—specifically, Soviet Premier Nikita S. Khrushchev's denunciation in February 1956 of Stalinism and the uprising in Hungary from late October to early November of the same year.

At first, Mao was unsuccessful. We now know that his opponents, led by Liu Shaoqi, a revolutionary comrade since 1921, had enough support within the party and government to temper and control the radicals and their policies. This was certainly the case with regard to the countryside. There the collectivization process continued but was slowed, steps were taken to make it less disruptive of traditional rural village organization, and the peasants were restored the right to maintain private plots and livestock. Pragmatist domination of the ruling organs was revealed in efforts to slow down collectivization and in the public assertion of collective leadership within the party, a concept which, inspired by Khrushchev's critique of Stalin's "cult of personality," directly challenged Mao's authority. Mao continued to defend his positions in private and public, with articles in the press and speeches (notably his "On the Correct Handling of Contradictions Among the People," delivered in February 1957), and by means of the "Hundred Flowers" campaign (May–June 1957), which invited people in and out of the party to speak their minds about the state of the country and the CCP leadership. The volume and range of criticism, however, surprised all of China's leaders, including Mao. The party's response was to close the door immediately and launch "anti-rightist" and rectification campaigns to root out erroneous and counterrevolutionary tendencies among elite groups and expand socialist education (ideological training) among the masses. In addition, party leaders, only recently opposing one another, agreed to seek accommodation, gloss over their differences, and present a united front against a society that was obviously not yet imbued with the revolutionary spirit needed to build communism in China. Maintaining the party's political hegemony was unquestioned, not only in light of the "weeds" that had sprouted during the "Hundred Flowers" campaign but also the "counter-revolutionary" character of the Hungarian uprising some months earlier.

The temporary healing of party wounds seems to have benefited Mao the most. He could now impress his views on the economic and political decisions that would affect China for the next several years. The set of policies that emerged during the Third Plenum of the Central Committee in September–October 1957 acquired the designation of the "Great Leap Forward."

The Great Leap Forward

The Great Leap Forward (GLF) was less a program of specific measures than a set of ideological assumptions whose purpose was to harness the total energies of the Chinese people for the task of propelling the country into the future. The assumptions, not necessarily novel but certainly expressed with extraordinary vigor and zealotry, were three in number. One was that human will can accomplish the impossible and be a decisive factor in history—an idea with seeming Confucian underpinnings but more a product of modern Leninist belief in human agency. Another was contained in the slogan "politics takes command," which implied that China's problems and its very backwardness were less matters of economics than politics. Ultimately, "correct" politics and "proper" thinking would be more important than investment capital, fertilizer, or technical expertise, and one's political reliability ("redness") would count for more than one's specialized skills. The third cornerstone of the GLF was the belief in the possibility and necessity of simultaneously developing all areas of Chinese life. To give priority to some spheres would only delay the arrival of full communism as other aspects lagged behind.

During the First Five Year Plan, investment in heavy industry consumed roughly one-half of Chinese capital, with perhaps another 10 percent going to light industry. Total industrial production grew by about 140 percent as a result, thereby justifying the large investment. Agriculture, however, which was to help finance further industrial growth through surplus production, was able to increase output during the same period only enough to provide for China's expanding population. Failure to raise agricultural production in 1956 and 1957 only added to the problem, as did declining peasant willingness to continue making the sacrifices demanded of them. As a result, the party found itself faced with a major dilemma: how to win over the masses to the effort of increasing agricultural production while at the same time continuing the rapid industrialization of China without adequate investment resources.

For Mao and his supporters, the solution was to exploit to the fullest China's massive population, to do with people what was otherwise impossible. By emphasizing the mass line and mass mobilization, socialist education, economic decentralization (epitomized by the backyard furnaces that sprang up by the thousands to produce steel), competition and quotas rising to extraordinary heights, a foreign policy that encouraged belief in China as a beleaguered nation, and the reorganization of rural life into communes, Mao sought to turn liabilities into assets and weaknesses into strengths. Above all, the radicals thought that the GLF would lead not only to economic progress but also to the creation of a new society by breaking down traditional barriers between city and countryside, industry and agriculture, intellectual and physical labor. The results would ensure progress toward full communism at a more rapid pace.

Launched in late 1957, the GLF was in trouble well before the end of 1958. Production of many commodities probably did increase as a consequence of mobilizing the country's human resources as never before and encouraging the kind of feverish labor reminiscent of Stalin's Five Year Plans in Soviet Russia during the 1930s. The positive results, however, were easily overshadowed by the failures and the damage done to agriculture and industry. The GLF simply did not work, whether owing to adverse weather conditions and party cadre failings, as claimed by Mao, or the economic irrationality of the Great Leap concept itself and the resistance of the peasantry to communization and regimentation, as argued by many Western specialists (and since Mao's death, by many Chinese themselves). Rather than advance the economy, the GLF nearly wrecked it; and rather than lead China to some happier circumstances, it only stirred crisis. Moreover, the unity that had characterized the party leadership in the autumn of 1957 was now dissipated, and differences of opinion over policy reemerged to coalesce into several factions that would engage in a power struggle for most of the next decade.

As criticism of the GLF grew, numerous conferences were held in 1958 and early 1959, during which Great Leap policies came under increased attack. Toward the summer of 1959, Mao attempted to counter his opponents and salvage the GLF. He succeeded temporarily when the Eighth Plenum of the Central Committee (July–August) called for a campaign against rightists, reasserted the correctness of GLF policies, and forced the dismissal of Defense Minister Peng Dehuai, the pragmatists' leading spokesman. Mao's victory, however, was short-lived. By the end of 1960, his influence had once again declined as more discouraging and negative news concerning the economy poured in. By the time the Ninth Plenum of the Central Committee met in January 1961, the pragmatists had succeeded in wresting control of the party and rejecting the Great Leap approach.

Accompanying the drama and disruption of the GLF, China's relationship with the Soviet Union experienced increased tensions. Much had to do with the GLF itself, which from the Soviet perspective represented a rejection of its own developmental model. Under Khrushchev, the path to socialism and communism was to be cautious and less dependent upon full-scale mass mobilization. The process required an international environment that was nonconfrontational and based on the notion of the "peaceful coexistence" of different socioeconomic systems.[16] The unfolding Soviet critique of Joseph Stalin and his decades of preeminence conversely disturbed Mao and his supporters for its implications about Mao's own leadership. These current events served to release decades of mutual distrust and resentment rooted in differing histories and national experiences as well as ideological and practical competitiveness.

Throughout 1960 and 1961 the socialist bloc was rent with increasingly bitter polemics, sometimes focusing on surrogates for the USSR (Yugoslavia) and the PRC (Albania), but always understood to be part of the acrimonious jousting between the bloc's two leaders. The Soviet Union removed all its experts and advisers stationed in China by September 1960, thereby undercutting major contracts and projects between the two countries. For its part, the Chinese continued to attack Khrushchev as a "revisionist." The October 1961 meeting of the Congress of the Communist Party of the Soviet Union (CPSU) in Moscow proved something of a watershed. Invited to attend, Mao sent his confidant Zhou Enlai, possibly as a conciliatory gesture. But when Khrushchev delivered a sharp attack on Albania (read China) and Stalin, Zhou walked out and returned to Beijing. Although the Cultural Revolution (1966–1969) and domestic events leading up to it distracted the Chinese from foreign affairs, tensions remained, erupting in 1969 in military clashes along the Xinjiang and Manchurian borders.

The Cultural Revolution

As for domestic matters, the years from 1961 to 1965 witnessed two concurrent developments. On the one hand, with the reins of party and government firmly in their grasp, the pragmatists under Liu Shaoqi devoted their attention to economic restoration and political retrenchment. In order to revive the economy, measures were taken to centralize planning once again, increase the production of consumer goods, establish incentives for the peasants (including permission to use private plots and organize free markets), emphasize expertise rather than "redness," and deradicalize the communes by reorganizing them and limiting their size. In the political sphere, along with efforts to play down mass mobilization and socialist education, the Liuists purged the middle and lower-level party organs and replaced leftist cadres with their own supporters and "experts." Veiled attacks against the Great Leap and Mao's leadership multiplied.

Meanwhile, those same years witnessed a persistent, initially low-keyed effort by Mao to win back his former influence over the CCP. Unhappy with his own political demise and the current "line" of the pragmatists, and convinced that the Great Leap was a sound approach to solving China's problems, he campaigned to win new supporters and lay the foundation of yet another attempt both to rectify the party and change the thought and behavior of the Chinese people. Finding himself without a sufficient audience in the central organizations of the party and government, Mao turned to local and provincial cadres (notably in Shanghai) for allies. He also engaged the services of the army through his protégé Lin Biao, named Defense Minister after Peng Dehuai's dismissal in 1958. Finally, as the struggle for power came increasingly into the open, Mao appealed to China's youth to rally to his cause. With these allies, he launched a nationwide campaign known as the Great Proletarian Cultural Revolution (GPCR) in 1966. The battle was joined—"Red vs. Expert."

One of the most surprising features of the GPCR, a phenomenon filled with startling and bizarre events, was Mao's apparent willingness to risk the destruction of the very party that he had spent so many years nurturing and shaping. In his view, the CCP had become a haven for rightists and "capitalist-roaders," and having lost touch with the masses, had betrayed the revolution. Because the party was dominated by those who would not accept Mao's views, he had no choice but to strike out at the country's leading institution. His weapons were propaganda, hence the enormous emphasis on the "Little Red Book" and the "thoughts of Mao," and a politicized army and youth. The army, in fact, was increasingly portrayed as a model for society, and students and other young people were formed into units of Red Guards. As the GPCR unfolded, demands for rectification of the party were accompanied by an extraordinary effort to change the content of literature, art, and the theater (in this work Mao's wife, Jiang Qing, was prominent), reform the educational system, and reject the values and attitudes of traditional China, all in the name of vague "proletarian" virtues and orientation. Mao's goal was to preserve for and transmit to the rising generation the revolutionary spirit that it had never experienced.

The course of the Cultural Revolution is too complex to be dealt with here in any detail. It should be noted, however, that one of Mao's chief tactics was to isolate his major enemies and tarnish their names by turning on their subordinates and/or persons known to be associated with them. This he did successfully early on with Peng Zhen, Beijing's mayor, later with Deng Xiaoping, the party secretary-general, and ultimately with Liu Shaoqi himself. At the Eleventh Plenum of the Central Committee (August 1–12, 1966), Mao's forces succeeded in winning control of that body and issuing in its name a "Sixteen-Point Decision" that officially sanctioned the Cultural Revolution. Thereafter, the GPCR escalated and spread throughout the country, bringing with it a tidal wave of unrest, economic and political disruption, and near civil war. By the time that revolutionary committees had been set up nationwide in September 1968, Mao, probably under the calming influence of Premier Zhou Enlai, had begun the process of restoring order, phasing out the activities of the Red Guards, and consolidating the changes that had occurred in Chinese life. His victory seemingly won, his enemies purged from positions of authority, and his vision of the new China in everyone's mind, Mao now could pause in his race to the future to rebuild the party and the economy that lay in rubble about him.

The meeting of the Ninth Congress of the CCP in April 1969 marked the conclusion of the Cultural Revolution and the seeming culmination of Mao's struggle with his opponents. But the coalition of factions that controlled the ruling organs of party, state, and army were hardly of one mind. As reconstruction and consolidation became primary goals in the immediate aftermath of the GPCR, Zhou Enlai began to play an increasingly prominent role in managing affairs of state, all the more so as Mao once again withdrew from public life and Lin Biao (his heir apparent) was killed in a plane crash (September 1971) while reportedly trying to flee China following a failed coup against Mao. Factional relationships in the early 1970s are especially intricate and resistant to easy analysis. Despite this, it has become clear that already in this period moderate and pragmatic leaders were beginning to return to positions of influence, and that Deng Xiaoping, with support from Zhou, was being groomed to succeed his benefactor as premier. The visit to China by United States President Richard M. Nixon in 1972, while certainly an outgrowth of American initiative and rethinking, was likely also a reflection of Chinese pragmatism and a counter to Soviet power.

During this latest phase of a seemingly perennial problem (the waning of revolutionary fervor, bureaucratism, capitalist backsliding, careerism, and other "evils"), Mao gave his blessing to two major campaigns: the "anti-Lin Biao, anti-Confucius" campaign of 1973–1974 (aimed, through allusion, at Zhou Enlai), and the "beat back the right deviationist wind" campaign of late 1975 (targeted at Deng). Leading the way were Mao's wife, Jiang Qing, and three of her associates—Wang Hongwen, Zhang Chunqiao, and Yao

Wenyuan—who had all been promoted to leadership positions during the Tenth Party Congress in 1973 and were clearly favored, and protected, by Mao. Aided by the secret police and taking advantage of Mao's increasing debility, this "Gang of Four" tyrannized the country for the next several years and plotted its own seizure of Mao's legacy.

Within the space of nine months in 1976, three of the country's preeminent revolutionary leaders passed away: Zhou Enlai in January, Marshal Zhu De in July, and Mao himself in September. In the midst of these events, political maneuvering intensified. Deng Xiaoping offered a stirring eulogy to Zhou Enlai at a memorial service on January 15 but then disappeared from public view without explanation. Mao made known his choice for premier: Hua Guofeng, the sixth-ranking vice-premier. Under the circumstances, Hua was a clear compromise between radicals and pragmatists, but his nomination as acting premier had the added purposes of giving the Gang of Four time to expand its base of support while preventing Deng from moving into the position himself. While Mao remained alive, Hua proceeded cautiously, making allies among senior cadres and military leaders but angering Jiang Qing and her friends. As the Gang of Four proceeded confidently and brashly toward what it thought would be a successful seizure of power, Hua completed his own plans for a preemptive strike. Under the guise of an emergency meeting of the Politburo in the early hours of October 6, the Gang of Four and its chief allies were arrested and placed in solitary confinement by sunrise. The following day, the Politburo heard three reports, two from Hua Guofeng, outlining charges against Jiang Qing and company. Hua was rewarded with additional chairmanships: those of the Central Committee and the Military Commission. On October 24 an enormous rally filled Tiananmen Square to celebrate the Gang's smashing and recognize the triumph of Hua as Mao's successor.

Meanwhile Deng Xiaoping, hiding in the south since February, was plotting his own political comeback. With the invaluable protection and support of General Xu Shiyou, the military governor of Guangdong and former military chief of the Nanjing region (comprising the wealthy provinces of Jiangsu, Anhui, and Zhejiang), as well as the backing of the first party secretary of Guangdong, Deng's case for rehabilitation was pushed in the CCP's Central Committee. The pressure worked: Deng was reappointed to a vice-premiership, to the Politburo, and to the Military Affairs Commission (MAC) in July 1977, albeit over the objections of Hua Guofeng and other party and PLA officials. Throughout the remainder of that year and most of 1978, the unfolding of China's domestic and foreign policies reflected the ambiguous relationship between Hua and Deng. Supposedly, Hua was still in control; in reality, however, by the Third Plenum of the Eleventh Central

Committee in December 1978, Deng and his allies had succeeded in neutralizing Hua's influence and capturing control over main party organs. For a time, Hua retained his official titles, but these too he gradually was forced to relinquish to Deng and two protégés: in September 1980, the post of premier was passed to Zhao Ziyang; and in June 1981, the chairmanship of the party went to Hu Yaobang and of the Military Affairs Committee to Deng himself.

With protégés in key positions and the powers of party vice-chairman, vice-premier, and PLA chief-of-staff in his own hands, Deng completed his comeback, and through the time of his death in 1997, he remained China's paramount leader, the arbiter of unresolved political rivalries, and the architect of the country's domestic and foreign policies. Those policies have been intertwined in an overriding effort to ensure China's entrance into the world of economically advanced countries by the early twenty-first century, to achieve what have become known as the "four modernizations" in agriculture, industry, national defense, and the linked areas of science and technology. First proposed by Zhou Enlai and subscribed to by virtually all of China's leaders since the mid-1970s, pursuit of the "four modernizations" has nevertheless produced unending and often vitriolic debate over questions of scope, timetable, and implementation. Deng's position derives from his understanding of the consequences of the Cultural Revolution and the underlying "leftist" (Maoist) assumptions that produced the phenomenon. To him, the Cultural Revolution nearly ruined the country, setting it back economically in ways that are incalculable and simultaneously undermining the legitimacy of the CCP in many minds. In fact, unless a way could be found to correct China's economic weaknesses and deficiencies rapidly, the very survival of the party, he believed, would be in doubt.

The problem was ideology: not its central role in Chinese experience, but its emphases. If Mao insisted on the priority of class struggle over economic productivity, Deng argued for the availability of more and more consumer goods; if Mao preferred ideological rectitude to technical expertise, Deng valued the technicians; if Mao looked askance at and punished individual enterprise, Deng wanted to stimulate the search for profit; and if Mao proclaimed the virtues of self-sufficiency, Deng advocated looking to workable models wherever they might be found. In a classic example of the Chinese penchant to reduce policy to number-based slogans, Deng's approach has been aptly proclaimed as comprising "one central task, and two fundamental points." The central task is economic development, the achievement of which will, Deng believed, not only move the country forward into the ranks of the most highly productive in the world but also make possible the achievement of a socialist society with a high standard of living for all.

Of the two fundamental points, one focuses on persevering in the policy of economic reform and openness to the outside world, meaning, among other things, maintaining the system of privatized agriculture that replaced collective farms, closing or eventually privatizing much unprofitable state industry, dismantling central planning generally in favor of private entrepreneurship and the market, and fully integrating China into the global economy. The second fundamental point concerns domestic politics and the need to ensure political stability by fostering the "four cardinal principles" (first enunciated in 1979): socialism, the dictatorship of the proletariat, communist party leadership, and Marxism-Leninism Mao Zedong Thought. These principles are not to be challenged publicly, a fact requiring the removal from the Chinese constitution of the "four great freedoms" (speaking out freely, airing views freely, holding great debates, and writing big-character posters).

The work of redirecting China was launched officially at the Third Plenary Session of the Eleventh Central Committee of the CCP in December 1978. From the late 1970s through the early 1980s the main goal was to create a market economy in food that meant freeing most prices (grain being the notable exception). Once the mechanism of supply and demand was reintroduced, the next step was to abolish the communes as units of production and replace them with family farms. In this, Deng not only reversed a major feature of Maoism but rejected the experience of the Soviet Union under Stalin; and in the process, he significantly eased the policy of "milking the peasants" to help pay for development. At the same time, the government's monopoly of foreign trade was eliminated, opening up opportunities not only for domestic entrepreneurial activity but for foreign capital and expertise as well. To affirm the government's commitment to an emergent private business sector, four experimental "special economic zones" were set up in 1979 (three in Guangdong and one in Fujian), all close to Hong Kong and Taiwan with their large ethnic Chinese populations. From 1984 to 1987, attention turned to industry, where, as in agriculture, prices were allowed to reflect relative scarcities rather than the dictates of a plan, competition was encouraged, and efficiency declared a major goal. Between the beginning and end of the 1980s, the number of people in private business rose from 2.3 million to 23 million and the volume of retail trade in free markets increased by a factor of 14.

Despite the unmistakable progress from an economic standpoint, some within the CCP grew concerned over the negative consequences of the reforms. These included urban inflation that seemed to be careening out of control; official corruption that took advantage of the tiered marketing system, the partial nature of deregulation, and the economy's growing decentralization; profiteering and tax evasion; the tensions resulting from uneven economic development, rising economic inequality, and confusion over the rules of upward social mobility; and fear about the subtle impact of foreign influences. Deng Xiaoping's argument that "Time is money, efficiency is life" seemed increasingly to miss the most important point: the preservation of CCP control over China under conditions of fundamental change that were breeding public restiveness, widespread concern for narrow self-interest at the expense of social goals, and rampant cynicism about politics (and political leaders) generally. When public-opinion research revealed what many had suspected, those leaders more interested in social welfare and equity were able, in late summer and early fall 1988, to force a retreat from economic reform so as to cool the overheated economy and rein in the private sector.

These measures were accompanied by a resurgence of political tensions in the second half of the 1980s and complaints from intellectuals and students about limits to democratic practices. Demonstrations in late 1985 in Tiananmen Square spread to other urban centers, as did such actions a year later that began in Hefei but quickly involved students in Shanghai and sixteen other cities. Though these events were easily suppressed by the authorities, they managed to confuse further the political situation at the top of party and government. Hard-liners railed against the protests, complaining about the spreading tide of "bourgeois liberalization" and excessive "rightism"; more-moderate leaders, such as Hu Yaobang, advocated conciliation. When Deng Xiaoping sided with the hard-liners, Hu's fate was sealed: He resigned as general secretary on January 16, 1987, and with his departure, reprisals against students, intellectuals, and academic officials ensued.

But the campaign against "bourgeois liberalization" and the effort to bring more-conservative party cadres into leadership positions did not succeed in turning the tide of reform. Dissatisfaction persisted and critics of the regime found daring and imaginative ways to express themselves. Students continued to request permission to demonstrate but typically had their petitions denied; some newspapers risked retaliation for their bolder reporting; Chinese Central Television broadcast a startling series, entitled "River Elegy," that, using the metaphor of the Yellow River, pointedly lamented the albatross of oppressive "old" ways that stood in the path of progress; and early in 1989 prominent intellectuals urged the party to release political prisoners, including Wei Jingsheng, who had a decade before called for a "fifth modernization" (political democracy).

Tiananmen Square

In the midst of inflation and an overheated economy, faced with a growing list of popular grievances, and confronted by increasingly bolder intellectual challenges to fundamental features of the communist system, the party seemed less able to lead the country and command society's respect. Rent by its own ongoing political infighting and further weakened by the emergence of multiple centers of power in the provinces, it seemed locked into a cycle of unimaginative responses that reflected above all the unresolved tension between conflicting desires: economic development and maintenance of authoritarian rule. Commencing on the night of April 17–18, 1989, the world began to witness seven extraordinary weeks of unprecedented behavior on the part of students, many ordinary citizens, and the authorities themselves. What started as a heartfelt response by students to the sudden death of the popular Hu Yaobang mushroomed into a mesmerizing drama that played itself out principally on the stage of Tiananmen Square. Marches, demonstrations, class boycotts, sit-downs, encampment, and a hunger strike, much in full view of the world thanks to television, propelled students into a confrontation with the CCP. Young leaders appeared, such as Wu'er Kaishi, Wang Dan, and Chai Ling, to upstage the country's leaders and force them through one humiliation after another.

The CCP waited until May 18 to impose martial law. Troops began to filter into Beijing, although they were frequently stymied by the outpouring of support for the protesters from ordinary citizens who put up makeshift roadblocks and swarmed around soldiers to remind them that they were part of the people's army. Patience grew increasingly thin as the regime pursued what amounted to a war of attrition against the students. As incidents of violence multiplied on June 2 and 3, the stage was being set for a final showdown. It began to unfold toward midnight on the third, quickly turning the capital into a battle zone. The number of casualties remains unknown, though it was probably higher than the official figure of around 300 dead. Once launched, repression was swift. The CCP reasserted its traditional preeminence, and the elder leaders—principally Deng Xiaoping, Chen Yun, Peng Zhen, and Yang Shangkun—once more were in complete control. Some subordinates had to be replaced, as was the case with Zhao Ziyang who had served as General Secretary of the Central Committee but was ousted for being too conciliatory toward the demonstrators. His successor would be Jiang Zemin, a one-time mayor and party secretary of Shanghai. Jiang's appointment as well as the formation of a new Standing Committee reflected a compromise between the competing factions in the party. That spirit may also have ensured Jiang's selection to replace Deng as CCP head following the latter's death, though Deng's anointment of Jiang was surely a major consideration.

Quelling what was officially described as a "counter-revolutionary rebellion" launched by hooligans was only the first step in getting the country back to normalcy and orthodoxy as defined by the regime. Pursuit of appropriate reform and openness to the outside world were restated as basic policies, but they were now accompanied by renewed ideological work, a push to instill patriotism, especially in the schools, and by a variety of measures to improve the party's standing in the public's eyes. Largely because the economy perked up toward the end of 1989 and through 1990, the conservatives, with Li Peng in the forefront, were able to sustain their political viewpoint. But a downturn in 1991 and the global demise of communism seem to have prompted Deng Xiaoping to push more aggressively for economic development and allow more liberated thinking. In a major speech delivered in January 1992 during a tour of Shenzhen and Zhuhai, the two special economic zones near Hong Kong, Deng set the CCP once more in the direction of reform.

The balancing act between encouraging the rapid development of a market economy and retaining unchallenged CCP control of politics and national decision-making continued during Deng's last and Jiang Zemin's first years as preeminent leader. Creation in 1994 of a market-based foreign exchange that did away with the dual exchange system long in place was an important step toward enhancing the flow of cash from abroad that could be used for economic development. So too was the 1996 decision to allow foreign companies to buy and sell foreign currency freely at designated banks, thereby removing a major obstacle to taking profits out of the country. At the Fifteenth Congress of the CCP that met in September 1997, just six months after Deng Xiaoping's death, Jiang announced a major plan to sell most state-owned industries to a shareholding system. Though the leadership was careful to declare that this step was not a move toward privatization of such enterprises, the long-term reality is likely to be exactly what was disavowed. Concern for development is revealed as well in the 1998 attacks on two serious economic inhibitors. The first is China's "hidden" crime: smuggling, often with the connivance of local authorities, the military, and border guard units. The second is the charge to unravel the vast network of military involvement in legal economic enterprise.

In China's political life, despite the cautious introduction of local elections, the reins continue to be held by a hierarchy of trusted communist cadres. This has meant that dissidents are still imprisoned, exiled, or simply harassed and that the flow of information is still limited (as much as is possible these days) by party determination. The efforts to control access to the Internet is a case in point. In February 1996, new rules to regulate Internet use required that any network offering Internet services would be subject to close supervision by the Ministry of Posts and Telecommunications. Eight months later, censorship of the Internet began when the government blocked access to more than 100 Web sites of the U.S. news media, the Taiwan government, and human rights groups.

We cannot tell how successful Deng's policies in the hands of his successor, Jiang Zemin will prove to be over the longer haul. China has been more successful since the late 1970s in transforming its political economy than has any of the other communist regimes, especially the Soviet Union, which ceased to exist in late 1991. For the most part, China's leaders have managed to avoid rampant inflation and maintain financial stability, even as they have pursued flexible and incremental institutional reform; moreover, their policies have been rewarded with significant economic growth and higher rates of accumulation, and the dismal prospects that have overtaken post–Soviet Russia and some ex-communist regimes of eastern Europe are not visible in China.

Still, the People's Republic faces enormous problems as it approaches the twenty-first century. Many derive from the presence of a huge and ever-growing population (despite implementation of the one-child policy in 1979), but others result from the fact of China's prolonged transition from a centralized economic, social, and political system to one more open, variegated, and free. The legacy of Marxism in its Maoist variant has cost the country dearly and will continue to weigh heavily on any efforts to escape the past and build a different and better society. Defining that better society will itself consume Chinese attention, especially since the quest for egalitarianism (social and economic justice) pursued as a fundamental goal over the past four decades will likely find fewer and fewer advocates. The attractions of marketization, mobility, and cultural freedom are everywhere difficult to resist. In addition, economic development will continue to create regional disparities that may well breed resentments and ultimately political tensions; some of these will likely have ethnic aspects to them. Moreover, the countryside, despite making a relatively easy transition from collectivized farms to household contracts, is still the China of most people and is beset by widespread poverty, inadequate services, an outflow of capital, deep underemployment, and environmental degradation on a massive scale (as mid-1998 official evidence corroborates). Finally, however much the party may desire to speak of "socialism with Chinese characteristics," the discrepancy between proclamations and the reality of economic, social, and political behavior will likely weaken the rulers' legitimacy further, unless Jiang Zemin's hopes for broad and deep economic achievement continue into the new century. In the end, the willingness of Jiang and his successors to pursue political reforms and institutional democratization will figure prominently in the success or failure of so much else.

As a final note bringing us back to an argument I made at the beginning of this overview of twentieth-century China, let me raise the specter of Confucius. In surprising ways, that specter has walked among Chinese throughout this century, despite attempts by many well-meaning people to cast the sage and his teachings aside. For themselves, revolutionaries are always surprised, frustrated, and disappointed at how much does not change despite all of their efforts and how survivable some ideals are even among those forced to acquiesce to gross threats over long periods of time. The power of traditions evolved over time has proved greater and more enduring than many would like to acknowledge. Thus it was that the GMD under Chiang Kai-shek recalled Confucius to serve as its ideological fount during the 1930s; that CCP portrayal of its public policy as "revolutionary" frequently appealed to the same basic human sentiments and aspirations as did the sage's words; that Mao himself used disguised Confucian wisdom to make his policies more attractive and acceptable to ordinary people, even as he used Confucius as a surrogate to condemn his own opponents and win great political debates; and that Mao's love of "the classics" is well attested, revealed all the more in photographs of his office, where such books appear most prominently.

In recent decades, especially outside of the PRC where large populations of Chinese reside, the question of Confucian teachings and ideals is of vital concern. The greater irony is that the revival of Confucian studies within the PRC has been permitted for well over a decade. If the fate of former Soviet citizens—struggling in a kind of moral and intellectual limbo in consequence of the void produced by the exorcism of Leninism—is any example, then we can fairly suggest that a similar fate awaits the Chinese as the meaning of Maoism, however modified by Deng Xiaoping, is lost. Is it implausible to expect that a neo-Confucian revival will be a significant part of Chinese lives once again? Some have said that revenge is best served cold.

NOTES

1. The phrase is from the title of a seminal work in Chinese intellectual history by the sixteenth-century scholar, Lo Qinshun.

2. Confucius, *Analects*, 2/4, quoted in David L. Hall and Roger T. Ames, *Thinking through Confucius* (Albany: State University of New York Press, 1987), vii.

3. From Zhu Xi, *Jin Si Lu* [*Reflections on Things at Hand*], quoted in Charles O. Hucker, *China's Imperial Past: An Introduction to Chinese History and Culture* (Stanford: Stanford University Press, 1975), 371.

4. A practice whereby a young girl's feet were wrapped tightly with cloth strips until the arch was broken, her toes turned under, and her feet kept at only

about half their normal size. The origins of the practice are obscure, with the earliest reference dating from the Tang dynasty (617–907). During the Song dynasty (960–1276) footbinding had become popular among the elite and wealthy. Bound feet made mobility extremely difficult and painful, at best contributing to a mincing walk and at worst to confinement. The tiny foot thus produced was, nevertheless, deemed lovely and alluring, and its idealization found reflection in poetry and other writing. The practice was finally abolished in 1911.

5. At the heart of Chinese speculation about the cosmos is the ancient notion of yin and yang: paired, complementary opposites—female/male, passive/active, negative/positive, strong/weak, cold/hot, and so forth—that animate the natural process. Unlike Western speculation that views nature in static terms, yin and yang reflect an appreciation of nature as dynamic, constantly in flux. One consequence of this mode of thought is that the Chinese have tended to see history in cyclical rather than linear terms.

6. Dwight Perkins, *Agricultural Development in China, 1368–1969* (Chicago: Aldine, 1969), 207–14. The consensus among scholars seeking to identify the causes of the demographic surge focuses on an improvement in the general (though not necessarily per capita) food supply, perhaps beginning as far back as the fifteenth century. In turn, the increase in food supply appears to have resulted from the effects of possible climatic changes, the reclamation of marginal lands for agricultural use, the introduction of new crops (such as the potato), and the development of new strains of rice with shorter growing seasons. Of probably equal impact was the nearly century-long domestic and international peace following the consolidation of Manchu control of China by the 1680s.

7. Over the course of many centuries, the Chinese government encouraged the elaboration of a system of examinations by which to identify the most qualified men in the empire (scholars) for access to elite status and possible public service. Qualification was determined by success in writing essays on themes drawn from the basic corpus of Confucian texts, wherein the emphases were on the fundamental importance of ethical and appropriate behavior, particularly in those who would aspire to scholar/official identity. The government never required the services of all scholars produced in any generation. Its need for administrators (bureaucrats) was limited by the division of the empire into districts, over which a single magistrate (the lowest-level official) would govern, and their placement in a hierarchy leading to the ministers and other counselors surrounding the emperor. As a result, quotas were always set for the number of examinees who could pass one or another of the examinations. When, by the mid-nineteenth century, the size of China's population had approximately doubled, the failure of the government to increase such quotas meant that many more men were "failed," were blocked from the traditional path of social advancement, and entered the ranks of a growing intellectual proletariat more and more resentful of these developments. At the same time, the administration of so many more people by an insufficient number of magistrates could contribute only further to China's social and political difficulties.

8. The most dramatic case in point is that of the notorious chief eunuch Heshen and his faction during the reign of the Qianlong Emperor (r. 1736–1799). From 1755 until the emperor's death, Heshen was the monarch's court favorite, holding many positions that he used to justify imperial pretensions and amass an extraordinary fortune for himself and his cronies. The forty-four years of his influence at court and upon the emperor left a legacy of corruption reaching far down into the administrative network that added to elite and popular demoralization.

9. Opium in modern Chinese history—its sources, distribution, patterns of usage, and impact—is a complex story involving questions of economics, politics, international conflict, and morality. From the late eighteenth century to the middle of the nineteenth, usage grew in China in conjunction with British marketing and Chinese addiction, although the plant from which the drug derives had been grown domestically for many centuries in the Middle Kingdom. British concern over their increasing imbalance of trade with China owing to the growing taste for tea led to their search for a commodity that would appeal to the Chinese in a comparable way. That search ended with opium, whose sales volume through Canton by the 1820s more than matched British purchases of tea, thereby tipping the balance of trade in British favor. Chinese economic disadvantage added a significant burden to the imperial treasury, a development that gradually took on political dimensions. When evidence of widespread use and addiction surfaced, especially among members of the elite, the imperial court had to respond. Its decision to stamp out the flow of opium from British merchants and adopt a hard line against addicts created an international conflict that led to the Opium War (1839–1842). China's defeat by a relatively small British expeditionary force had painful consequences, including the inability to prevent importation of opium. In the decades following, China was left with protestations rooted in moral argument alone. These did little to alter circumstances until British opinion, long indifferent to opium use at home, itself changed.

10. The history of Catholic missionary activity in China began in the sixteenth century, just as it was engaging many other parts of the non-European world in the trail of explorers and adventurers. Particularly successful, if not in the number of converts, then in their influence over elites of indigenous societies, were the Jesuits. Beginning with Matteo Ricci (in China from 1583–1610), Jesuits brought to the Celestial Kingdom a perspective that focused upon its leaders, hoping for a trickling down of Catholic theology and European culture to lower social levels. Erudite, accommodating of religious belief to Chinese culture, and willing to fit into Chinese society by learning the language, adopting clothing and hair styles, and acceding to the authority of both emperor and his scholar/officials, the Jesuits in turn received favorite status at the court of the Kangxi Emperor (1654–1722). They were allowed to practice their religion in the capital and the provinces, were placed in charge of the astronomy bureau, and were designated as advisers with regard to cartography and engineering. In 1692 the emperor decreed toleration to the Christian religion. However, religious and political controversy in China and Europe—particularly over the "rites controversy" whereby Jesuit accommoda-

tion to Chinese culture was deemed fatal to the integrity of the Christian faith, and that pitted Jesuits against Dominicans and Franciscans and involved the Pope, the Chinese emperor, and sundry political figures—ultimately unravelled these positive developments, led to the expulsion of Catholic missionaries, and foreclosed a promising relationship between China and Europe.

11. Most of these matters were included in the list of requests that Lord George Macartney brought with him on his embassy to China that began in September 1792 and culminated in a meeting with Heshen and the Qianlong Emperor a year later. A fascinating look at this initial confrontation between two expansive empires is James Hevia's *Cherishing Men from Afar: Qing Guest Ritual and the Macartney Embassy of 1793* (Durham: Duke University Press, 1995).

12. The phrase is from John K. Fairbank and Albert Feuerwerker, in the preface to volume 13 of *The Cambridge History of China* (Cambridge: Cambridge University Press, 1986), xviii.

13. The older transliteration system known as Wade-Giles renders this party's name as Kuomintang and its abbreviation as KMT. Readers are likely to find these other renderings in many books and articles not written in the last decade or so.

14. A phrase used to describe the series of nineteenth- to early twentieth-century treaties between China and one or another of the European powers and Japan. These treaties were consistently one-sided: advantageous to China's opponents and profoundly disadvantageous and costly to China.

15. Recently some have challenged the common view that Mao was generally and actively involved in party factionalism. They argue instead that he was more often above the fray, allowing others in the leadership to compete with one another for his favor and support. This is a finely nuanced argument that deserves consideration, and can be followed in two books by Fred Tiewes: *Politics at Mao's Court: Gao Gang and Party Factionalism in the Early 1950s* (Armonk, NY: M. E. Sharpe, 1990), and *The Tragedy of Lin Biao: Riding the Tiger during the Cultural Revolution, 1966–1971* (Honolulu: University of Hawaii Press, 1996).

16. Khrushchev's commitment to peaceful coexistence, particularly with the United States, was revealed in his decision not to provide China with a prototype atomic bomb or to respond with little more than rhetoric to U.S. activities, such as the dispatch of the Marines to Lebanon. Likewise, when the Chinese began bombarding the offshore island of Quemoy, where troops of Chiang Kai-shek were still stationed, the Soviet Union was conspicuous for its lack of support.

2

Basic Features of
Mao Zedong Thought

When Mao Zedong stood atop the Gate of Heavenly Peace (Tiananmen) on October 1, 1949, to proclaim the creation of the People's Republic of China, he already had shown the consummate skill reserved for only the most successful twentieth-century revolutionaries, including Vladimir Ilich Lenin in Russia, Ho Chi Minh in Vietnam, and Fidel Castro in Cuba. Mao's career as a revolutionary began in 1912. During the subsequent decades, he repeatedly proved politically adroit, tenacious in pursuit of his goals, and able to adjust to changing circumstances and opportunities. A student of Chinese history, its traditions of statecraft, and the close relationship between power politics and warfare, he turned his youthful idealism and extraordinary ambition for the Chinese people into a force that eventually swept the CCP into power. In doing so, he weathered challenges at every turn, both inside and outside his party.

The personal characteristics that helped the modern revolutionaries attain power and devote their lives to transforming their societies—unquenchable drive, unflinching conviction in their own ideas, unrelieved disdain for those of others, and a limitless willingness to sacrifice countless people to the Revolution—were what also made their revolutions more tragic and unfulfilled than they needed to be. Mao was no different from the others who hoped to see a Marxist revolution overcome their countries' weaknesses, make them competitive in the global political and economic arena, and ensure that the masses—"the People"—would not only share more fully in the rewards of their own labors but actually control their own lives and societies. Nor was he different in his failure to recognize the troubling tension between governance and revolutionary change, or the trap of assuming that people can be transformed by leaders committed to destroying centuries of organic social and cultural development in the name of generating a "new world" filled with differently thinking men and women.

Mao's revolutionary ideas, like those of his intellectual compatriots elsewhere, drew inspiration from both experience (observing and doing) and intellectual exercise. They were a response to the genuine plight of large numbers of poor, illiterate, and exploited people, although they were also the result of profound romanticization and sometimes willful ignorance of who and what the people really were. They reflected a strong inclination to distrust complex patterns of administration and governance—in a word, bureaucracy—because these only served the interests of ruling elites; and they relied upon popular enthusiasm and passion as substitutes for technical expertise and intellectual sophistication, and too frequently as a means for mobilizing (and manipulating) the masses. Moreover, they displayed an inconsistency born of a human inability to divorce oneself completely from one's cultural environment, with its heavy baggage of traditions, habits, and customs. Thus, rebellion against the decrepit and defeatist past of China was accompanied by appeals—sometimes disguised, sometimes not—to the social virtues, modes of discourse, and general spirit of that same past.

Much has been written about Mao that seeks to understand the dynamics of his personality and the interrelationship between his life's experiences in China and the powerful tenets of Marxism, a theory derived essentially from analysis of European history but proclaiming universal applicability. That interrelationship produced a fundamental tension in Mao as it has during the last 100 years in all revolutionaries finding themselves in non-European settings but desirous of sharing in Marxism's promise. The nature of the tension is quite simple: As enunciated by Karl Marx, the "truth" of the theory that bears his name is predicated upon a number of interrelated conditions that must be in place for the socialist revolution that it predicts not just to occur but survive against its opponents and fulfill its promise of liberating people from all forms of exploitation.

What those conditions are is complex, but they can be summed up by noting the answers to three simple questions: When will the socialist revolution occur, where will it occur, and who will lead it? For Marx, the answers to these questions were determined by the logic of his theory. The socialist revolution will occur when socioeconomic conditions in a society have emerged that are consistent with the possibilities of a socialist order. That demands a dominating capitalist system that has developed fully and is in the declining phase of its history, no longer capable of finding ways to handle its own inherent contradictions or the rising expectations and power of the one force—the industrial working class—that can overthrow it and forge the first truly free and egalitarian society since the beginning of human history. Explicit in Marxism, then, is the notion of the socialist revolution occurring only in a mature capitalist system that has given birth to an industrial proletariat now possessing a revolutionary consciousness, and that counts within its ranks the majority of the population.

Where is such a place? In Marx's own time, the answer was in capitalist western Europe, principally in England and Germany, and probably the United States. The rest of Europe lagged behind, as by necessity did all other human societies, including the Russian Empire, where the first "successful" Marxist revolution was nevertheless launched in 1917 and enshrined during the next seventy-five years. Lenin's intellectual gymnastics, undertaken to compensate for Russia's lack of "ripeness" for a socialist revolution, served not to align theory with reality but rather to force reality into a theoretical straightjacket that made a mockery of the very aspirations with which the revolution presumed to identify. So too did his organizational principles that gave rise to a type of revolutionary party bearing significant antidemocratic characteristics that dismayed even Marxists of the time. By seizing power in poorly developed Russia, then, Lenin emerged triumphant as both a revolutionary practitioner and theorist, whose approach acquired a legitimacy that inspired would-be revolutionaries elsewhere for nearly the remainder of the twentieth century. As a consequence, Marxist revolutions were pursued in all the wrong places, and succeeded only where they ought not to have.

If from a classical Marxist standpoint Lenin was wrong to represent Russia as an appropriate site for a Marxist revolution, Mao erred in proclaiming the same for China despite his disingenuous contention in 1942 that "Marxism-Leninism has no beauty, no mystical value; it is simply very useful." Much evidence existed, of course, to sustain an argument that China needed fundamental changes in its economic, social, and political order. Chinese had been debating this for many decades. It was also clear that foreign powers had an enormous impact on China's development, fostering it in some ways, but distorting and exploiting it in others. Mao's writings reveal that he understood quite well that his country's vulnerability to external aggression resulted largely from internal weaknesses, and that this relationship lay at the heart of his analysis and his demand for revolution.

The rules of classical Marxist revolution had no foreseeable application to China. The consequences of ignoring that fact and insisting that the revolution depended not on socioeconomic conditions but on ideology (right thinking) and the ideological education of the people meant that the revolution would have to be made by a relatively few able to awaken, guide, and manipulate the many. The commendable strain of egalitarian aspiration that one can find in Mao's writings ends up having little substance when it came to popular participation in decision making, either before 1949 or after. Even the doctrine of the "mass line," which encouraged party cadres to maintain direct contact with the masses so as to understand better their concerns, was fundamentally manipulative because it presumed that those "above" the people, with their better appreciation of history and theory, would be able to reach the decisions best suited to the people's interests. Mao summed up the process as "from the masses, to the masses," but he conveniently ignored the role of leadership, especially his own, that was always independent of popular control. The mass line was valuable in leading many to believe that their views made a difference; it was even valuable as a technique for pressuring cadres and bureaucrats to "learn from the masses" and for punishing them by sending them "down to the masses" to be rectified. Whatever its intent, the mass line was ultimately frustrating of genuine popular initiative. The CCP's coming to power in 1949 only made matters worse because, in fact, everything about the party and its leading role in China was dictatorial.

The doctrine of the mass line did not develop in isolation but reflected what was arguably the most fundamental of Mao's attitudes: voluntarism. Like Lenin, whose successes must have been instrumental in showing Mao the value of seizing the moment, Mao was a committed voluntarist—a believer in the ability of human will to overcome virtually any obstacle, despite the essential irrelevancy of human motivation to Marx's revolutionary theory. By seeking to foster revolution in places unsuitable theoretically for such a process, both Lenin and Mao had to relinquish Marxist principle and emphatic determinism (the revolution *will* follow under the right, organically evolved, socioeconomic conditions) in favor of willful action (the revolution *will* occur under whatever conditions we can take advantage of). For the sake of possibly seeing the revolution transpire in their own lifetimes, they had to impose their own wills on circumstances and equate volition with accomplishment. Marxism's attraction was, thus, also its weakness. The theory was supposed to ensure that revolution would occur, but it never promised that it would occur to suit the timetables of revolutionaries. For tremendously egotistical men like Lenin and Mao, Marxist determinism had to be balanced by a voluntarist spirit, men and women had to help make the revolution by whatever means they could be sold on, and time had to be made an ally and not an enemy.

Mao's commitment to voluntarism tied his revolutionary legacy to a series of approaches—a strategy—that included the mass line and an insistent egalitarianism, but also an argument for seemingly endless struggle against "contradictions" within society and among the people. Whipping up enthusiasm, even mass hysteria, became a well-honed Maoist method for overcoming the obstacles that kept the country poor and vulnerable to foreign exploitation. Taking the form of campaigns that typically had a narrow focus and relied upon mass mobilization, the method had the primary goal of changing the way people thought as a critical adjunct to the longer-term sociopolitical transformation of the country and its economic development. From 1950 virtually to the moment of Mao's death in 1976, nationwide campaigns were declared almost annually. Running their course over no more than a few years each, they followed a pattern that quickly developed and led from a mass mobilization phase to attacks on the party and state bureaucracies, specific social, economic, and political groups, as well as individuals.[1] Many of the latter were publicly humiliated and brutally treated. In practice, the method provided Mao with a means for criticizing and dismissing his less radical opponents and challengers, while strengthening his personal leadership role in the eyes of the multitudes.

Implicit in Mao's use of mass mobilization techniques was a belief that struggle was good for the people and their cause. The obstacles barring the way to genuine revolutionary progress would prove too formidable and unmovable, without frequent recourse to struggle involving the masses, because at their heart was a web of social relationships involving many people. Owing to residual but still powerful Confucian influences, people remained reluctant to disturb what seemed to ensure social harmony and the normal workings of society, however repressive harmony and "normalcy" may have been in their lives. Because direct confrontation was neither feasible, practical, nor likely to produce the desired results, some other means had to be found to weaken those obstacles. Mao's solution was to disrupt the social networks by encouraging wide-ranging violations of social conventions. Getting peasants to struggle against their landlords who frequently were relatives, or workers against their supervisors, or students against their teachers meant challenging profound taboos about authority and social identity. Giving the people the "right" to struggle was meant to empower them in their relations to authority, impress upon them the rewards of doing so, create a sense of self-reliance in them, and suggest to them that their active involvement in the revolution was critical. In abstract terms, Mao's theories about struggle were attractive to many; in practice, their consequences were often economically disastrous and humanly tragic.

Mao's voluntarism possessed one additional feature that further defined his worldview and enhanced his relationship to ordinary people: anti-intellectualism. Scholars commonly acknowledge that Mao was disdainful of intellectuals, perhaps because he was only marginally one himself, perhaps because the traditional Chinese social and political order was so linked to the interests and fate of a powerful class of scholars. It is likely, too, that Mao felt as he did because intellectuals were identified with an urban culture quite divorced from the much larger world of the peasants. Whatever the roots of his sentiment, it affected much of his thinking and many of his policies. He was openly contemptuous of intellectuals. He saw them as weak and indecisive, blamed them for many of China's problems, and distrusted their self-interest. He was clearly uncomfortable with the ambiguity, as he saw it, of their usefulness to Chinese society. On the one hand, they were the experts in technical and scientific fields that made them seemingly essential to China's economic development. On the other hand, their expertise threatened to turn them into a new elite enjoying privileges unattainable by workers and peasants. Moreover, many intellectuals were in fields—history, literature, philosophy, and the social sciences—that were particularly dangerous in a political environment that explicitly reserved authority and definition of truths to a single source: the CCP.

Mao's concerns about intellectuals were translated into the group's harassment, repression, and humiliation. Some mass campaigns, including the Thought Reform campaign of 1951–1952, the Hundred Flowers campaign of 1957, and the Cultural Revolution of 1966–1976 were aimed directly at them and their role in Chinese society; others, invoked for different purposes, had distinctively anti-intellectual aspects to them. Many intellectuals have been harmed irreparably since 1949, physically and in terms of their careers, and Chinese society has suffered immeasurably in the process of losing both their expertise and creativity. Forcing many of them to go down to the countryside, learn from the peasants, and engage in manual labor gave Mao a certain perverse satisfaction, and he never showed the slightest concern for the social cost of his policies. Education at all levels, but especially in the universities, has had much to overcome since the early 1980s because of what was carried out with regard to intellectuals under Mao, and except for key military projects, highly trained specialists were virtually eliminated from decision-making influence.

The kind of revolutionary that Mao Zedong was is revealed best by his own words and deeds. Especially illustrative are the phrase "poor and blank," which he wrote in 1958 and repeated many times, and his reaction, in 1967, to the establishment by workers in Shanghai of a commune independent of party or state encouragement. Mao's thesis on "poor and blank" offered a justification for the Great Leap Forward then underway. It attributed special revolutionary virtues to the Chinese people and evoked the image of a preindustrial China as being able to move forward rapidly toward socialism and communism without waiting for the fulfillment of modern capitalist economic development:

Apart from their other characteristics, China's 600 million people have two remarkable peculiarities; they are, first of all, poor, and secondly blank. That may seem like a bad thing, but it is really a good thing. Poor people want change, want to do things, want revolution. A clean sheet of paper has no blotches, and so the newest and most beautiful words can be written on it, the newest and most beautiful pictures can be painted on it.[2]

The "poor" aspect of this thesis is clear if unimaginative, though it reflects a fundamental principle of Mao's thought. It speaks to China's backwardness not as an obstacle to the possibility of change but as rendering the Chinese people especially amenable to that possibility. Backwardness—being "poor"—is a virtue. This particular notion is consistent with Mao's general theory of underdevelopment as an advantage that was also reflected, for example, in his views on military organization, weaponry, and preparations.

The second part of Mao's thesis, that the Chinese people are "blank," is more problematic and disturbing. On the one hand, being "blank" can be seen as just a complement to China's being "poor," and as such is a virtue that ensures, in Mao's mind, the success of his revolutionary enterprise. Because the Chinese have so little, they have virtually nothing to lose and everything to gain by seizing the moment. Yet, declaring the Chinese to be "blank" bears a frightening aspect as well that, given the history of Mao's behavior, deserves attention. It implies a limitation in the people that is also manipulable, particularly by someone like Mao for whom the people's will stalls if not in keeping with his own. Who, it needs to be asked, writes the beautiful words or draws the beautiful pictures on the blank peasants?

The answer can be seen in the playing out of dramatic events in Shanghai in 1967 during the height of the Cultural Revolution. By that time, workers in China's most populous metropolis had taken to heart many of the slogans that the Cultural Revolution had embraced, such as "Boldly arouse the masses" and "It is justified to rebel." Many were attracted to the reorganization of society according to principles different from the Leninist concept of the vanguard party—principally, the ideal of the Paris Commune as described by Marx, whereby cultural revolutionary committees and groups would become permanent, standing mass organizations truly shaping society. Mao underestimated the spontaneous social and political radicalism of the Shanghai working class, which as 1967 unfolded began to behave as if it really represented a people in revolution. Though there was little unity among these workers, they did share, as historian Maurice Meisner has written,

a general antipathy to an overbearing bureaucratic apparatus that controlled their lives but over which they had no control, latent hostilities that were released when the Cultural Revolution temporarily brought them the freedom to establish their own organizations and throw off old organizational restraints. Even relatively privileged workers harbored deep resentments against the often oppressive and arbitrary practices of party cadres and factory managers, and they were particularly resentful of the official trade unions, which functioned less as representative institutions than as bureaucratic appendages of party and state to control workers and spur productivity.[3]

When the Shanghai workers actually took local power and formally proclaimed the Shanghai People's Commune on February 5, 1967, the supporters of the Cultural Revolution were initially pleased. But as the reality of their intentions reached Mao with their demands for self-government and elections, Mao's response was patently dictatorial: "This is extreme anarchism, it is most reactionary. . . . In reality there will still always be heads [in charge]."[4] At that point, the Commune's demise was ensured by the demands of one man and his "thought."

Like others who have found themselves at the center of great power and who eventually came to dominate that center, Mao gradually lost touch with the realities that framed ordinary Chinese lives. Like others who are in power for long periods of time, he grew arrogant toward society generally and colleagues in the party hierarchy particularly, presuming that truth was his personal possession. Blaming others—particularly opponents and subordinates—for policy failures, as he did toward the end of the Great Leap Forward, became an inevitable feature of Mao's politics. Threats against critical Politburo members in 1959 and during the early stage of the Cultural Revolution reflected both Mao's authority but also his willingness, in the name of his own utopian vision, to forsake those who long had worked with him. He also became increasingly intolerant and seemingly paranoid, abusing his authority on a large scale and turning foolishness into tragedy for many. Thus, his encouragement of the "backyard steel campaign" in 1958 was matched by his unleashing of "red guards" a half decade later; the closing of schools nationwide in order to mobilize China's youth; and the harassment, degradation, and physical torment of millions of ordinary people. The recently published memoirs of Mao's personal physician offer disturbing evidence of these and other actions having severely negative consequences in both his public and private life.

In the end, Mao epitomized one of the basic failings of dictatorship: the extreme difficulty of turning leaders out of office, even when they have become useless, and the uselessness of dictators who continue to think in terms of notions and practices formulated when they were younger and not yet in power.

NOTES

1. The major campaigns included Land Reform (1950–1952), Three Anti and Five Anti (1951–1952), Hundred Flowers (1957), Anti-Rightist (1957), Great Leap Forward (1958–1961), Four Cleanups (1963–1965), Cultural Revolution (1966–1976), Anti-Lin Biao and Anti-Confucius (1973–1974), and Criticize Deng Xiaoping (1976).

2. An English translation of Mao's text that contained this passage is in *Peking Review*, June 10, 1958.

3. Maurice Meisner, *Mao's China: A History of the People's Republic* (New York: The Free Press, 1977), 319–20.

4. Quoted in ibid., 323.

3

Redirecting the Revolution: The Reform Ideology of Deng Xiaoping

Of those who helped shape the Chinese Revolution over its hundred-year history, few have had the kind of influence as had Deng Xiaoping. Next to Mao Zedong, Deng likely will be remembered as the Revolution's most pivotal figure, particularly in its late twentieth-century phase. Deng was remarkably successful in weathering the vagaries of decades of political struggle within the CCP, and he outlived Mao to become the man most responsible for reversing the direction of China's development that had dominated until Mao's death in 1976. Deng proved to be a consummate politician, adept at forging networks of relationships with important and useful people (including Mao and Zhou Enlai), but his political skills were increasingly associated with reform that has transformed China since the late 1970s by means that Mao long struggled against. China's Revolution, then, is in significant ways a reflection of the tension between Mao and Deng over theory and practice (work style), despite the extremely close, supportive, and trusting relationship between the two men for most of the decades since the mid-1930s.[1]

The basic features of Deng Xiaoping's thought, canonized in the early 1990s by the CCP's leadership, are distinguished by a pragmatic concern for material results (development before socialism), the forces rather than relations of production, and maintenance of a strong state dominated by a single-party system (the Leninist vanguard party). For Mao, theory (socialism) took precedence over development. This prompted him to pursue policies—as during the Great Leap Forward and the Cultural Revolution—that frequently seemed irrational and proved disastrous to the country's economic well-being. Deng saw socialism as a long-term goal that could be reached only after equally long-term development of China's economic infrastructure and an incremental but persistent rise in the standard of living for the general population. Moreover, Deng typically pushed for more-rapid rather than slower growth in the economy and was willing to accept the negative consequences of such growth—including high levels of inflation and other signs of an overheated economy—that raised concerns in the minds of others, such as Li Peng and Chen Yun.

Two episodes reveal Deng's thinking on this score. Over a five-week period from January 18 to February 21, 1992, Deng made what was termed a "southern tour," visiting Guangzhou, Shanghai, Wuchang, and the special economic zones of Shenzhen and Zhuhai. The tour followed implementation, under Li Peng's direction, of cautious economic policies in place since the autumn of 1988. Impressed by the free-wheeling market practices (capitalism) in Guangzhou, which was in the forefront of such developments, Deng declared that "low-speed development is equal to stagnation or even retrogression" and repeated the principle that the sole criterion for judging the worth of all policies should be economic results. By May 1992 Deng's "southern tour" comments had become the basis of policy, and in October, at the Fourteenth Congress of the CCP, were hailed as a "great theoretical breakthrough." The congress ratified Deng's prescription for "enlivening the economy," thereby substituting a "socialist market economic system" for the Maoist "socialist planned market economy."

In October 1993 Zhu Rongji, recently appointed governor of the central People's Bank of China and thereby in control of the country's financial policy, faced the task of reducing inflation in an economy that had become supercharged. He pushed for cutbacks in spending to cool inflation, but his choice of a more moderate pace to development was rejected by Deng, who declared succinctly that "slow growth is not socialism." A subsequent visit to Shanghai in February 1994, which was rapidly surpassing Guangzhou as the country's chief financial center, further affirmed Deng's position and ensured that Zhu's austerity program would be scrapped. The push for rapid growth confirmed Deng's startling dictum that "to get rich is glorious."

Relations of production, linked to a deep concern for class contradictions, antagonisms, and struggle, had figured prominently in Mao's theories of revolution and revolutionary development. Perhaps foremost in Mao's thinking was fear of the consequences of capitalist economics and a desire to avoid introducing any measures that would leave control of the relations of production in the hands of a relative few (capitalists), a not uncommon sentiment among twentieth-century revolutionaries in China and elsewhere. At the heart of this fear was an ethic of egalitarianism that, in its most expansive form, envisioned a society free from social tensions precisely because significant property (land, equipment, finances) would be private no longer.

For Deng, the propertyless society, for all its appeal, was at best distant and left to future generations to witness. In the short and intermediate term, placing property in the hands of as many as possible seemed the best means by which to ensure the personal responsibility required to develop the economy, raise the standard of living, and thereby create the material base for a meaningful socialist society. Deng rejected the notion of the "iron rice bowl" that had promised cradle-to-grave security to China's population regardless of productivity. Instead, he sanctioned the pursuit of profit and tolerated the temporary—it was hoped—material inequities that would result from diminished state control over economic activity. "Some must get rich first," he declared, whether as individuals or regions, or all would remain poor.

The evidence is clear that the fate of the Soviet Union and its eastern European satellites in the late 1980s and early 1990s provided important lessons to Deng. For him, the collapse of the Soviet system resulted primarily from the failure of Mikhail Gorbachev, in his eagerness to reform his country and improve its productive competitiveness, to maintain the reins of politics and authority in the hands of the Communist Party of the Soviet Union (CPSU). By attempting simultaneously to pursue *glasnost* (openness), *demokratiia* (democracy), and *perestroika* (restructuring), Gorbachev succeeded only in dismantling seventy years of institutional and infrastructural development and leaving the country leaderless, directionless, confused, and nearly overwhelmed by economic, political, and social drift that threatened anarchy and civil war. The creation of a parliamentary body and the inexorable movement toward multiparty politics meant more than just the diminution of the CPSU's role. It meant leaving the successor states of the USSR to embark upon a process of transition that produced as many problems as solutions, stalled economic development of many republics even as it enriched individuals, dramatically increased unemployment and underemployment, significantly reduced the standard of living for the majority of people, and pushed the region to the level of less-developed status.

These developments confirmed for Deng what he had long believed: The success of the revolution in China depended primarily on the leading role of the CCP, unchallenged in its "responsibility" to control the commanding heights of authority. In this narrow respect, Deng's thinking was no different from Mao's. Both men had worked together for decades to produce a party organization that could provide just such leadership, but ultimately they differed over the full significance of the party and the principles of or-

ganization and bureaucracy. For Mao, excessive organization and bureaucratic work methods threatened to stifle the ultimate goals of the revolution,
thereby leading him to embrace the politics of mass mobilization. Going
around the party directly to the people, even encouraging actions that might
temporarily upset the party's ability to function efficiently and effectively,
became hallmarks of Mao's revolutionary method that found expression
most fully, but hardly only, during the Great Leap Forward and Cultural
Revolution.

For all of his basic loyalty to Mao, Deng sorely distrusted such methods.
He criticized them as "leftist excesses" and consistently voiced the contrary
viewpoint that placed clear emphasis on the need for a strong party/state.
The energy and will of the people, though indisputably important, were
only the raw material with which the CCP could work to transform the
country. Without organization and discipline consistently and persistently
applied, without party rule that was purposeful, focused, and unified, and
without a sound program of structured socialization, China's development
would be haphazard and fitful in its progress, and the revolution ultimately
discredited. To attack the CCP and government as Mao did was to foster
confusion, undermine the very authority that Deng deemed so vital, and
weaken the relationship between party and people. Nothing could substi-
tute for party rule in Deng's mind, as his words and actions repeatedly
showed. He led the Anti-Rightist campaign in 1957 because the party's
unity was threatened, and thirty-two years later in 1989 he ousted Zhao Ziyang for attempting to split the party during the Tiananmen affair. In between
he struggled against the leftists for essentially the same reasons.[2] Even economic modernization, so dear to Deng, would have to give way to the principle of party rule if necessary in the short term.

Over the long term, however, the vanguard role of the CCP was only justified by success in fostering the material development of China. The nexus
between party and popular welfare, between the growth of the socialist state
and the development of productive forces and the people's living standards,
was from Deng's perspective defining. In a view reminiscent of the obligation that Confucius once placed upon the emperor and his officials, the party
could earn and maintain its right to rule only by demonstrating the correctness of its policies through tangible evidence of the people's betterment.
Without such betterment why would the people follow the party? On the
other hand, the benefits of an economic boom and waves of consumerism,
as has occurred in the 1990s, can go a long way toward muffling popular
discontent over other matters. Or so Deng and his supporters dared assume.

To assist with achieving the economic modernization that Deng believed
was at the heart of the revolution and that one day would result in the exis-

tence of an egalitarian (socialist) and rich nation, a reversal of Mao's international approach was needed as well. That approach had been decidedly isolationist, much as Joseph Stalin's had been for the Soviet Union until his death in 1953. The reasons behind it are complex but reflect a combination of concerns that were both theoretical—including a deliberate division of global politics between forces of light (revolution) and forces of darkness (capitalism)—and practical—fear of the influences that might arrive from abroad to corrupt or distract the revolution. Deng's "open-door" initiative that dominated the 1980s was designed to bring China more fully into the family of nations, thereby creating opportunities for Chinese students to study abroad and for foreign technology, business practices, and investment to enter China and help further the goals of economic modernization. It is ironic that Deng should have had to resort to this policy, because he was not unconcerned about the negative effects of "bourgeois pollution." But the benefits clearly outweighed the dangers for him, and despite momentary pauses, the policy continued until his death in 1997 and shows no sign of being reduced or reversed by his successors.

For all of his innovations, Deng was in many respects quite conservative. Much like the early Mikhail Gorbachev, he did not proceed from a radical critique of his country's problems but proposed to return to the traditions that he believed had once guided the party and country properly and effectively, as during the mid-1950s and early 1960s. These traditions, drawn from the party's experiences over the decades before 1949, included party democracy (the sharing of authority among leaders, the importance of cadres at all levels, and the practice of the "mass line" that linked party work with popular input), an efficient political system that provided orderly leadership and direction for social development, and economic modernization. These reflected conventional ways of doing things that respected order and discipline while restraining radical experiments. Many of the policies that Deng introduced after 1976 had been conceived much earlier and often by others, only to be set aside time and again by Mao in his pursuit of ideological correctness and his own preeminence.

In popular lore, both Chinese and foreign, Deng is frequently associated with advocacy of the "four modernizations" (agriculture, industry, national defense, and science and technology). But on December 5, 1978, a young man named Wei Jingsheng put up a "big-character" wall poster in Beijing that he entitled "The Fifth Modernization." Whereas Deng and the party had declared the four modernizations sufficient for transforming China, Wei insisted that a fifth—democracy, popular not party—was even more critical, without which the other four would falter. Rejecting the Leninist notion that democracy would flow from socialism (therefore, the ends justify the means), an idea that helped define the Chinese revolution as well, Wei argued that the achievement of a socialist society required democracy as a condition (in effect, the means justify the ends). Persecuted for his views, Wei has spent many years since 1978 in prison (he was allowed to leave China for the United States in 1997 for "humanitarian" reasons), suffering enormously but remaining unrepentant.

During his prison years, Wei developed the habit of writing letters to Deng Xiaoping (never delivered, apparently), continuing to question and challenge the leader and his policies while identifying some of the most fundamental flaws in the latter's thinking. In Wei's opinion, Deng's most significant error remained his failure to incorporate democratic and human rights principles in either theory or practice. Thereby, argued Wei, the Chinese people were "enslaved" to the dictates of their masters who, like the former emperors, dwell in halls of power to which the people are forbidden.

Deng had critics within the CCP itself, in top leaders such as Li Peng, the Soviet-educated bureaucrat for whom the label "Stalinist" would not be inappropriate, or in Yang Shangkun, one of the party elders linked closely to the military. Their criticisms were generally muted in the face of Deng's authority and the popularity of his policies, but they were not without purpose or consequence. Differences of opinion, debate, and even factionalism in the history of the CCP have been common, at times leading to compromise, at others to the party's purging of "incorrect thought," and still others to serving the larger interests of the preeminent leader, first Mao then Deng. Frequently, Mao and Deng "allowed" their opponents to test alternative policies either to create possibilities for their denunciation or to provide respites to policies in place and likely to continue. Deng, for example, when faced with an inflationary spiral and an overheating economy around 1989, had to entertain measures contrary to his own thinking, but he never intended to establish their permanence. Rather, he used them for the moment before moving on.

Deng's roughly two decades in power coincided in part with the last phase of Leonid Brezhnev's position as head of the CPSU and of the Soviet bloc. Given long years of bitter relations between the USSR and China, Deng's reformist initiatives and rejection of Maoist thought injected new reasons for modest polemics. However, as the Soviet Union itself under Mikhail Gorbachev began to move in the direction similar to and then beyond Deng's initiatives, conditions emerged that encouraged reconciliation between the two countries and prompted Gorbachev's visit in summer 1989. By then the conception of communism as an international force had lost much of its glamour, and within a few more years, following the collapse of the Soviet Union and its satellites in eastern Europe, the world ceased to be primarily a politically bipolar place and the end of the Cold War became imminent.

However much he chastised Mao for succumbing to a "personality cult" that placed him above all others and turned the party into a personal reflection, Deng was prone to fall into the same trap, giving up party, government, and military offices but retaining the authority that comes from being recognized as "paramount leader." After 1989, Deng's own personality cult became more pronounced with the publication of increasing numbers of his speeches, "private" conversations with other party leaders and foreign visitors, and a biography written by his daughter in 1993. In addition, Deng's heir apparent, Jiang Zemin, and others began to speak more frequently of "Deng Xiaoping Thought," thereby raising Deng's ideas to the pinnacle of theoretical respectability and unassailability. This has continued since Deng's death, serving as the basis of the consensus upon which Jiang relies to legitimize his own authority and to sustain the fundamental direction for the country that Deng set.

Political reform for Deng was, at best, very narrowly defined and aimed at little more than making party cadres "better educated, professionally more competent, and younger." Such goals serve the interests of state efficiency and effectiveness but do little to devolve power to the people. Neither do they dilute the authority of the one party permitted to function. Deng's distaste for democracy manifested itself continually during his life, whether in the crackdown against intellectuals during the Hundred Flowers campaign of 1957, or that against the democracy movement in 1979, 1986, and 1989. This is perhaps understandable of someone so committed to state power, but it leaves China with the question of political modernization unanswered. Signs of further loosening of political restraints under Jiang Zemin are encouraging but tentative and unlikely to do more in the near future than whet the appetites of the relatively small number of democratic advocates.

What may help accelerate changes within the political realm is something that has been happening within the past two decades in China. A subtle and occasionally public debate has been unfolding concerning the merits of socialism as a philosophy of social justice and a program of national development. Thus, accompanying the grand experiment with market-based reforms that has challenged Marxist-Leninist-Maoist dogma on economic policy has been a profound reexamination of China's socialist theory and practice. At its core, this debate centers on the question of whether many of the root problems that China continues to face are the consequence of Chinese socialism in particular and Marxism in general. The direction of policy under Deng and his successor is clear evidence that the debate is leaning to one side. As the American political scientist Yan Sun has argued in an important recent book, the fate of socialism in China and China's future will mean the decline of "ideological monopoly and hence a singular view of social order and development." Both inside the party and outside (especially among intellectuals), a pluralistic conception of socialism has meant a significant moderation of ideological labeling and concern for deviation. Instead, the leadership seems more attentive to doctrinaire and destructive tendencies on the Left (the general position associated with Mao), the "reconceptualization" of socialism, and the search by the public itself for "new solutions to new problems."[3] More than market-based reforms, this may be Deng Xiaoping's most important legacy.

NOTES

1. We should note that Deng's views as most fully articulated from the late 1970s were not unique to Deng but were espoused in many of their aspects by others, particularly in the 1950s, who included, most significantly, Liu Shaoqi, Mao's erstwhile heir apparent.

2. At Zhou Enlai's state funeral on January 15, 1976, Deng delivered the eulogy. Following a lengthy summation of his colleague's accomplishments, Deng offered a more personal note laced with criticism of Mao. Among other observations, he stressed how much Zhou had done to unite the masses of party cadres and uphold the party's unity and solidarity.

3. Yan Sun, *The Chinese Reassessment of Socialism, 1976–1992* (Princeton, NJ: Princeton University Press, 1995), 269–70. Professor Sun also notes that among the results of this development are greater roles for intellectuals in political and other important posts. Many of them have been pushing "the official parameters toward deeper reassessment, which has in turn often been incorporated into the official platform."

4

One Nation, Many Peoples: Han and Non-Han in the People's Republic of China

China is not what it seems. Mythmaking, politically inspired public relations, and just plain ignorance have conspired to create the impression in many minds, both abroad and at home, that the country is ethnically homogeneous (Han Chinese) except for scattered small groups remarkable only for their exotic character and troublesomeness. That same impression finds support from a historiography that, until recently, consistently relegated the role of such groups to the margins of China's historic and current development. Why this is so requires a complex answer beyond the scope of this essay. Some of it, however, results from an infatuation with a society whose core weathered the centuries as did no other; that generated and sustained a sophisticated political and cultural order for nearly two thousand years; that produced a philosophical tradition rich in its conceptualizations and diversity; that influenced neighbors such as Japan, Korea, and Vietnam profoundly; and that built the Great Wall. These achievements and much more have made it easy for the serious as well as casual observer of China's history to focus on that which seems eminently Chinese; to adopt a Middle-Kingdom perspective that defines civilization as moving from a center (China) outward, but seldom in the opposite direction; and to favor the Chinese over those "Others" who have always dwelled along China's frequently changing frontier.

China is more than it seems. Although the overwhelming majority of its people are ethnic Chinese (known also as Han, or Han Chinese), more than 8 percent are not. These belong to various ethnic communities—55 recognized officially—that in a land of 1.2 billion persons collectively account for roughly 100 million non-Chinese, more than enough to match the population of many an existing country.[1] (See Table 4.1.) Not only are the non-Chinese numerous in absolute terms, but they occupy more than 60 percent of the country's land mass, much of it rich in natural resources such as oil and other minerals.

They also are settled preponderantly along China's northern, western, and southwestern borders, in a horseshoe pattern hemming in China Proper (the heartland of "Chinese" China), and helping to limit direct contact with the outside world except by sea along the eastern coast or in the deep south, or by land through Southeast Asia. Finally, these minorities enjoy differential growth rates, largely owing to higher fertility, that are allowing them to increase their numbers even as the Chinese population reaches stasis.[2]

Ethnic diversity is accompanied by religious diversity, though the latter is more difficult to observe owing to the insistent, at times brutal, antireligious stance of the CCP. Organized religion has had an unusual and subdued role to play all through Chinese history, with the absence of any official, institutionalized church reflecting a cultural order that typically stressed the secular and mundane. Nevertheless, China has had its religions, above all popular cults, but also more elaborate faiths reflecting much larger, international forces. Thus, Buddhism began to penetrate China along the Silk Road from India as early as the first century A.D., enjoying a remarkable heyday during the Tang dynasty (618–907); then Islam arrived with Arab armies in the eighth century; and Christianity made its debut with Catholic missionaries in the fifteenth. Each has left its legacy to Chinese thought, art, and literature, and continues to attract adherents under difficult conditions.

The twentieth century has seen a continuation, under revolutionary circumstances, of an imperial mind-set. This has meant that non-Han peoples incorporated into the former Chinese Empire over the centuries—whether Kazakh, Uygur, Kyrgyz, Tibetan, Mongol, Manchu, or Miao, to name a few—have been prevented from determining their own fates by a dominating Han interest in preserving the self-defined integrity of a China whose territory was shaped by the last dynasty.[3] The policy of the CCP toward the so-called national minorities was cut from the same cloth as that of Lenin as he sought to bring down the Russian Empire. For both Lenin and Mao, the right of self-determination was unequivocally reserved for the minorities as an inducement to lend their support to revolution, and that right entailed the possibility of complete separation from China and the formation of independent states. Although enshrined in the 1931 CCP constitution, to which Mao repeatedly referred, the right of self-determination was ignored after 1949, as it had been repeatedly during the history of the Soviet Union. Indeed, self-determination has been the victim of revolutionary idealism's

Table 4.1
Non-Han Ethnic Groups in the People's Republic of China

Ethnic Name	Primary Locations of Settlement	Population as of 1990 (in descending order of size)
Zhuang	Guangxi, Yunnan	15,489,630
Manchu	Liaoning, Jilin, Heilongjiang	9,821,180
Hui	Ningxia, Gansu	8,602,978
Miao	Guizhou, Hunan, Yunnan	7,398,035
Uygur	Xinjiang	7,214,431
Yi	Sichuan, Yunnan	6,572,173
Tujia	Hunan, Hubei	5,704,223
Mongol	Inner Mongolia, Liaoning	4,806,849
Tibetan	Tibet, Sichuan, Qinghai	4,593,330
Bouyei	Guizhou	2,545,059
Dong	Guizhou	2,514,014
Yao	Guangxi, Guangdong	2,134,013
Korean	Jilin, Liaoning, Heilongjiang	1,920,597
Bai	Yunnan	1,594,827
Hani	Yunnan	1,253,952
Kazakh	Xinjiang, Qinghai	1,111,718
Li	Hainan	1,110,900
Dai/Thai	Yunnan	1,025,128
She	Fujian	630,378
Lisu	Yunnan	574,856
Gelao	Guizhou	437,997
Lahu	Yunnan	411,476
Dongxiang	Gansu	373,872
Va/Wa	Yunnan	351,974
Sui	Guizhou	345,993
Naxi	Yunnan	278,009
Qiang	Sichuan	198,252
Tu	Qinghai, Gansu	191,624
Xibe	Xinjiang	172,847
Mulam/Molao	Guangxi	159,328

Table 4.1 (continued)

Ethnic Name	Primary Locations of Settlement	Population as of 1990 (in descending order of size)
Kyrgyz	Xinjiang	141,549
Daur	Inner Mongolia, Heilongjiang	121,357
Jingpo	Yunnan	119,209
Salar	Qinghai, Gansu	87,697
Blang/Bulang	Yunnan	82,280
Maonan	Guangxi	71,968
Tajik	Xinjiang	33,538
Primi/Pumi	Yunnan	29,657
Achang	Yunnan	27,708
Nu	Yunnan	27,123
Ewenki	Inner Mongolia	26,315
Gin/Jing	Guangdong	18,915
Jino	Yunnan	18,021
De'ang/Benglong	Yunnan	15,462
Uzbek	Xinjiang	14,502
Russian	Xinjiang	13,504
Yugu	Gansu	12,297
Bonan/Baoan	Gansu	12,212
Monba	Tibet	7,475
Orogen	Inner Mongolia	6,965
Derung/Dulong	Yunnan	5,816
Tatar	Xinjiang	4,873
Hezhen	Heilongjiang	4,245
Gaoshan	Taiwan	2,909
Lhoba	Tibet	2,312

Source: A Mosaic of Peoples: Life among China's Ethnic Minorities (Beijing: China Nationality Art, 1992), 9–13.

perversion for the sake of power. In the name of an ever narrowly defined revolution, unity not difference became the unalterable marker of China's future.

To a large extent, the fear of disunity that could derive from granting genuine regional autonomy is historically and psychologically rooted. Experience repeatedly has shown the Chinese the threat that regionalism can pose to the country's territorial and political integrity. So, too, the overarching search for harmony, as most fully articulated in the philosophy of Confucianism, has lent its own weight to an unwillingness to give up centralized control over territory and people. For these and other reasons, the CCP has sought to encourage the development of cultural uniformity throughout the country by doing what modern states do: establish transportation and communications networks, a nationwide school system, a common spoken and written language, a complex body of public ritual, and an extensive civil service. But it has done more by being able to manipulate economic development and reserve politics for a single party, its own.

If the goal with regard to national minorities has been to render their identities ultimately meaningless in the public sphere, then much that has been fostered by the CCP since it came to power ought to be part of a success story. It is not. Rather than diminishing, cultural differences as expressed through religious preference and practice, social custom, administration of local resources (including the fate of tax revenues), and family planning are growing. Observers of the world scene in recent years will recognize this development as virtually universal, but the fact that it has occurred in China in the face of conscious and powerful efforts to the contrary is testimony to the difficulties inherent in such attempts to shape cultures.

The fate of the former Soviet Union, whose leaders shortly after its creation devised the general prescription for solving tensions within a multiethnic society that China has followed, ought to provide a warning to its one-time ally. Though the Soviet Union collapsed for myriad reasons, certainly one of the most significant was growing ethnic strife where none, in theory, was to exist at all. Marx and many other nineteenth-century thinkers argued against the survivability and desirability of nationalism in the modern age, a sentiment that inspired the Bolsheviks and those who would follow them elsewhere. Developments in the twentieth century, however, have proved such thinking incorrect and likely to be so well into the next millennium. Rather, ethnic identity is strengthening, even being created, around the world, particularly in smaller independent communities and those still within larger multiethnic societies.

China's ethnic realities are a case in point. Of the nearly 350 groups that are not recognized officially as separate ethnic entities, many have re-

quested such status. This reflects not only internal efforts at identity formation but also the benefits to be gained from being designated an "official
minority." Opportunities to practice their indigenous languages, religions,
arts, and popular cultures, permission to have more children, and allowance
to pay fewer taxes, are affirmative-action privileges in many cases denied to
the Han Chinese. As the anthropologist Dru Gladney has written recently,
"one might even say that it has become popular to be 'ethnic' in today's
China," not only among ethnics themselves but among Han Chinese who
find the cultures of others fascinating and attractive, whether for their cuisi-
nes, clothing styles, artistic motifs, or spiritual tendencies.[4]

Several of the larger groups, including the Uygurs, Mongols, and Tibetans, have taken advantage of the general atmosphere of greater liberality,
whether in economics, education, local governance, or international expo-
sure, to use their historical identities as a means to separate themselves increasingly and more firmly from the Han Chinese. True separatist
movements, underground for obvious political reasons, have sprung up in
all three regions, at times taking on violent forms. This phenomenon is of
major concern to the Chinese leadership, who deny publicly that such activity is significant. The seriousness of potential separatism is accentuated because the three regions are located where they can have contact directly with
the outside world. In the case of the Mongols, that contact is with peoples of
their own ethnicity who live in independent and sovereign circumstances.
For the Uygurs, compatriots inhabit newly independent states beyond the
Tian Shan and Pamir mountains in the former Soviet Union, who inspire
many of the Chinese Uygurs to note that their kind is "free over there." For
the Tibetans, the authority of the Dalai Lama in exile and the presence of a
significant number of Tibetans in India represent an extremely "unpleas-
ant" and dangerous circumstance for the CCP. The international sympathy
for the Tibetan plight adds an important element of support for continued
resistance.

More commonly, the typical small ethnic group adopts more-subtle
forms of resistance by pushing the limits of the possibilities that the CCP itself has opened up. If ethnic integration of the country has been an aspect of
the party's vision since the 1920s, its strategy ultimately has borne devilish
fruit. By devising various levels of at least nominally autonomous administration to take account of ethnic diversity in the country (five regions,
thirty-one prefectures, ninety-six counties, and many villages), and by placing control of this administration in the hands of carefully selected and loyal
minority leaders, the CCP sought to maintain central control and submerge
ethnic autonomy under the guise of nominal respect for ethnic identities. On
the one hand, it would garner significant public relations benefit from seem-

ing to support genuine ethnic difference; on the other, it would minimize the fallout from such difference in actuality. In this case, however, the means have not led to the CCP's expected ends. Nominal respect for ethnic identities has led to a more logical and predictable end: the demand for genuine respect that presses toward the greater autonomy and beyond.

China is less than it seems. Among the majority Chinese, a diversity exists that the casual observer can easily miss. It begins with language but is also reflected in some physical distinctions (northern Chinese tend to be taller than their southern compatriots), a range of cultural practices involving birth, marriage, and death rituals most significantly, and culinary tastes (from use of different condiments to the choice of key consumables—noodles or rice, pork or lamb, meat or fish), let alone attitudes about life generally and aspirations. Language differences are extreme. Linguists identify eight mutually unintelligible forms of Chinese, but even these possess marked diversity. In earlier times, the northern dialect (Mandarin) was the standard language of the educated and administrative elite, thereby helping to unite a frequently sprawling empire, and it has become the national language of the schools, the media, and official work in the twentieth century. But in many regions it is rarely used in day-to-day affairs, taking second place to the local speech.

A personal experience in the southern city of Guangzhou a few years back offers an extreme but pointed illustration of the problem. At a major international hotel a small group of Chinese from Shandong province in the north were having a late evening dessert, when one of the party had to leave and asked the waitress (in Mandarin) for his bill. She failed to understand his request, offering her own response in Cantonese that the hotel guest found equally incomprehensible. For twenty or thirty seconds the two attempted to communicate in their respective "Chinese," but to no avail. In desperation, finally, the young waitress exclaimed in English, "Oh, you want your bill!" To which, in English, the guest answered: "Yes, that's what I've been trying to say!"

Although such linguistic and cultural diversity is hardly unique to China, the CCP's efforts to portray all ethnic Chinese as Han has been part of basic ideology, so "understood" as to not require much direct discussion. The regime simply assumes—and expects ethnic Chinese throughout the country to assume as well—that this is the case, and any effort to "complicate" the category is taboo. The result has been an exaggerated appeal to ethnic unity that is wearing thin. In an ironic twist, groups within the Han majority have begun to discover, invent, and assert presumed differences in relation to other Han. According to the 1990 census, 14 million people formerly registered as Han have reregistered as members of minorities, with at least another 5 million also trying to do so.

The greatest evidence of challenges to Han unity seems to be accumulating among southerners, who in recent years have shown a tendency to insist on their cultural separateness from and even superiority over northerners. This has taken the form of comedic routines that poke fun at those "other" Chinese for their speech patterns, eating habits, and lack of sophistication (particularly in the marketplace). It also is reflected in a more insistent use of the local language and in the assertion that the origins of Chinese history are to be found in the south and not in the north, with the bronze culture of the southern Chu kingdom (sixth century B.C.E.) providing the stimulus and model for subsequent developments in the north along the Yellow River. There also has been some interest in articulating arguments for the separate racial origins of southerners and northerners.

Analogous developments in other parts of the world suggest that these Chinese trends hold the potential for contributing to the fragmentation rather than integration of the country. Ethnic and linguistic divisions do not need economic crisis, political collapse, or social disorder to become transformative factors in China's development. On the contrary, the country's very economic vitality shows every sign of enhancing those divisions both between national minorities and the majority Han, and within the majority Han as well. Moreover, economic growth brings other pressures and dislocations, from the creation of a large underemployed population (perhaps as many as 100 million people today) to efforts by local and provincial leaders to ensure that the wealth and productivity of their regions benefit their people, and not others in far off parts of the country. Economic growth also has compounded social circumstances by adding to and expanding class differences, making a heady mix of class and ethnic interests.

To become rich is good, proclaimed Deng Xiaoping, but becoming rich does not happen to everyone or every region at the same time, at the same pace, or at all. The inequities thus produced have encouraged resentments and added their own weight to rising crime and other social ills. Statistical evidence from minority regions has long revealed disparities with the Chinese heartland, including educational achievement, economic performance, industrial investment, and political involvement at the higher levels of party and government institutions. During the 1980s this evidence strengthened long-held minority attitudes that the Han majority was exploiting them.

Partly as a response to genuine grievances and partly to support his economic reforms by encouraging minority involvement, Deng Xiaoping began in 1978 to loosen restrictions on minorities significantly, allowing them to establish free markets, trade across foreign borders where possible, and seek foreign investments and tourism. The CCP also allowed previously forbidden religious practices, such as the pilgrimage to Mecca by Muslims, and subsidized the restoration of Muslim, Buddhist, and Christian religious structures and statuary, many of which had been damaged or destroyed during the Cultural Revolution. Despite government subsidies of many minority regions and the fact that advancements have occurred, much of the rest of the country still appears to be moving ahead more rapidly. This may have been brought home to the central party apparatus following a lengthy tour of a number of minority areas in 1991. As reported, Jiang was surprised, even astonished, by what he saw, including the widespread lack of electricity and the terrible poverty in some regions.

On the eve of the twenty-first century, China faces happy prospects but also many problems. Many of the prospects themselves are likely to exacerbate tensions between minorities and the central government, and push the latter into a deeper and deeper dilemma: how to make the minorities feel as equals to the Han Chinese in an integrated China, even as they are emboldened by those efforts to resist such integration and seek their own paths to the future. We may be seeing something of this dilemma already. "Fight against regionalism and divisions" is a slogan that has found prominence recently in the official media. Certainly the Democracy Movement of 1989 explains something of the leadership's concern for stability in the country and its ability to control things. But radical antigovernment, anti-Chinese activities by ethnic dissidents in communities as distinct as the Uygurs, Tibetans, and Mongols are obvious causes for concern as well. What is overt, however, like the approximately thirty reported bombings in 1994, and more in 1996 and 1997, by Uygur nationalists seeking an "Independent Turkestan," is merely the tip of the ethnic iceberg, most of whose force is below the surface, unseen, moving slowly, but likely to cause great distress to the system that the CCP has developed in the name of revolution.

NOTES

1. Many hundreds of groups have applied for official recognition, but all the others have been lumped together with either the Chinese or another of the minority communities.

2. Between 1982 and 1990, minority populations increased by 35 percent while the Chinese grew by only 10 percent. In part, this increase resulted from a willingness by some to be reclassified as non-Chinese, but much stems from the application of the one-child-per-family policy to Chinese but not to minorities, although the government has been trying to limit births among the latter, particularly in urban areas.

3. In an ironic twist, that dynasty, the Qing, was founded by Manchu warriors, only the last of numerous invaders from outside the Han community to establish rule over China.

4. Dru Gladney, "China's Ethnic Reawakening," *Asia Pacific Issues: Analysis from the East-West Center*, no. 18 (January 1995), 5.

Empress Dowager Cizi, the power behind the throne of the emperor Guangxu. Probably early twentieth century. Courtesy of the Freer Gallery of Art

Student demonstration outside the Forbidden City in Beijing during the 1919 protest movement sparked by Japanese demands upon China and the perceived betrayal of China by the Versailles settlement ending World War I. Courtesy of the Kautz family, YMCA of the USA Archives, and University of Minnesota Libraries

Chiang Kai-shek, 1935. Courtesy of AP/Wide World Photos

Deng Xiaoping speaks at a meeting in Beijing in March 1978. Deng, China's paramount leader, died Wednesday, February 19, 1997, from an advanced stage of Parkinson's disease with complications of lung infections, the Chinese government said. He was 92. Courtesy of AP/Wide World Photos

Portrait of Mao Zedong overlooking Tiananmen Square faces off with a statue erected in the square on May 30, 1989. The statue was dubbed "The Goddess of Democracy" by students from Central Academy of Fine Arts, who modeled it after the Statue of Liberty. Courtesy of AP/Wide World Photos

A Chinese man blocks a line of tanks heading east on Beijing's Cangan Blvd., Monday, June 5, 1989, in front of the Beijing Hotel. The man, calling for an end to the recent violence and bloodshed against prodemocracy demonstrators, was pulled away by bystanders, and the tanks continued on their way. Courtesy of AP/Wide World Photos

5

Enemies and Friends: China, the Soviet Union, and the United States

A number of countries have played significant roles during the course of China's revolutionary history since the 1920s. But the United States and the Soviet Union have been almost continually at the center of China's concerns. Each was born in revolution, though more than a century apart, and each developed a claim to a legacy that was supposed to have universal significance and applicability. In twentieth-century China, both found avid admirers, drawn by the belief that the ideological foundations, values, and experiences of one or the other offered answers to their country's terrible problems. That both became superpowers, the recognized leaders of blocs of nations, and the principal voices/models for particular (and opposed) types of societies accentuated their importance for a China that for so long sought its own modern identity and, especially after 1949, struggled to find an appropriate place for itself within global politics.

Relations between China and its would-be friends have been and still are uncertain. At times, relations have been warm, cooperative, and understanding, but at others rife with impatience, suspicion, and even contempt. There have been significant periods during which China's leaders had little or no contact with those in the United States—from 1949 to 1972, China and the United States were unquestioned foes—only to be matched by similar periods of alienation with regard to the Soviet Union, particularly from the late 1950s to 1989. On occasion, matters deteriorated so much that military conflict erupted: with the United States, most notably during the Korean War, and with the Soviet Union, during the border crisis of 1969. In sum, "friends" have found themselves at such odds at times as to make the term "enemy" more appropriate.

For revolutionary China, a large part of the "problem" with the United States and the Soviet Union has been ideological. Marxism-Leninism provided not just a theory for analyzing socioeconomic realities and their relationship to revolutionary possibilities, but offered an equally analytical prism for viewing international relations and world events. Because the Soviet Union was a primary conduit through which Marxism-Leninism infiltrated China, one would expect that Moscow would hold a decided advantage over Washington policymakers in their respective efforts to influence matters in Beijing. But that has not always been the case, before or after 1949. Ideology turns out to have been a double-edged sword, obviously dangerous to the clear antagonist (the United States), but subtly so to the complacent or arrogant ally (the Soviet Union).

As a tool for internal (domestic) social analysis and revolutionary action, Marxism-Leninism, however modified by Mao Zedong and other Chinese, has been at the core of China's twentieth-century history. Several parts of this book, including sections of the Overview and the chapter on Mao's thought, point clearly to this fact. But there has been another dimension to Marxism-Leninism's impact—Lenin's theory of imperialism—that needs comment, particularly because it has been equally important in the story of China's revolution, while helping to explain much of that country's relations with both the Soviet Union and the United States.

By 1919 Lenin had discovered the East and begun courting Asian nationalism. The immediate result was a program that linked the communist cause to so-called oppressed nations beyond Europe and its advanced capitalist development. These oppressed nations were overwhelmingly agrarian in their economies, with the vast majority of their populations pursuing agriculturally related livelihoods and living under the control of "feudal" exploiters. As such, they were, from a strict Marxist perspective, not good candidates for socialist revolutions. They first needed to pass through the long phase of capitalist development and a bourgeois revolution before generating the appropriate conditions—including a politically conscious industrial proletariat—necessary for the passage to socialism. Ever the Marxist revisionist, however, Lenin now argued that European imperialism, with its colonial domination of Asia and other parts of the world, held the key to keeping the European proletariat and Asian bourgeois nationalists weak and underdeveloped, and thereby unable to further their historic roles. If the stranglehold of imperialism could be broken, the forces favoring socialism could be unleashed and world revolution would triumph.

That, he argued, was one of the opportunities created by the success of the Russian revolution of October 1917. It not only represented the first working-class revolution in human history, but it created the possibility of being allied with Asian nationalism in the task of breaking the chains of imperialism, shortcutting the capitalist phase in the East, and liberating oppressed peoples everywhere. Communist parties would have to be created in the Asian societies to provide leadership for the peasant masses who would gradually be turned into proletarians. Those parties in turn would draw upon the experience of the socialist motherland (the Soviet Union), its leading party, and the various organizations under its aegis, such as the Communist International (Comintern), to move the local liberation movements to their proper conclusions.

The nexus between imperialism, revolutionary success in capitalist Europe, and revolutionary hope in Asia inspired the work of the Comintern in places like China and, by extension, significantly shaped the character of relations between China and the Soviet Union. Over the decades, the Soviet Union transformed the Comintern into an organ of Soviet power and interests. In doing so, it almost inevitably played out the role of elder brother, presuming unchallenged leadership in the international communist movement, providing advisers and advice on many theoretical and practical matters, and making available loans, munitions, equipment, and even factories to its Chinese disciples. However much revolutionary idealism prompted this behavior, as time passed and the Soviet Union itself evolved into an increasingly totalitarian system under Joseph Stalin, the guiding principles behind its relationship with China became more and more nationalistic. In the process, the line between what was good for international communism and what was good for the USSR blurred and eventually disappeared.

Not surprisingly, tensions developed between Soviet presumptions and the Chinese leadership's resentment at being treated as revolutionary neophytes. The failure of Soviet-imposed policies, beginning with the united front strategy with the GMD party that nearly led to the demise of the CCP in the late 1920s, helped gradually to undermine trust in the wisdom of its leaders. At the same time, the evolving circumstances in China itself through the 1930s and 1940s reinforced a sense of difference that further weakened the perceived usefulness of Soviet experience. Ironically, that difference was rooted in the very character of China—its overwhelming agrarian economy, its residual feudal system, and its vulnerability to foreign manipulation—of which Lenin believed Soviet leadership could take advantage. To men like Mao Zedong, however, this difference encouraged a feeling of independence that only grew with time, and raised a barrier that became harder and harder to ignore. Once the People's Republic of China was declared in October 1949, the writing was likely on the wall. Despite Soviet willingness in Stalin's last years to assist, even generously, with the reconstruction of its immense neighbor, and despite Chinese willingness to accede to Soviet leadership in the international setting, national differences of experience, style, and needs, as well as leaders' egos, made the Sino-Soviet split by the early 1960s likely and fully understandable.

Relations between the United States and China have a longer history, dating from when the first American merchant ship, the *Empress of China*, arrived in Guangzhou from New York to purchase tea and other Chinese commodities in 1784. Like that with the Soviet Union, the Chinese-American relationship has been colored in the twentieth century by the Marxist-Leninist ideology, but before then the United States represented for old regime China a culture that was, in many ways, the antithesis of the Confucian value system that had dominated Chinese life for centuries. Being of the West, the United States was part of the enormous challenge that Western civilization posed for China, even though it was a less important political player until the beginning of the twentieth century than were Great Britain, France, or Germany. American interest in the China trade involved it with the commerce in opium as well as tea, a fateful business that contributed a powerful emotional aspect to the growing Chinese conviction about the evils of imperialism. None of the Western powers ever colonized China, and collectively Western imperialism victimized China much less than occurred in many other countries. Yet, perhaps because the Chinese were forced, after nearly two millennia, into a profound reconsideration of who they were, they came to view their experiences with the West as extraordinarily humiliating, and commonly believe, even to this day, that they were grossly and cruelly mistreated. Much of the public spectacle surrounding the return of Hong Kong to China in 1997, including Chinese production of a big-budget film on the Opium War, was heavily tinged with this burden of humiliation and an accompanying level of self-righteousness that, for all their passion and sincerity, seemed silly and puerile to many outsiders.

The American presence in Qing China also bore the mark of missionaries, Catholic and Protestant, but heavily the latter. The close link between spreading the Christian faith among the Chinese and spreading an entirely new way of life cannot be underestimated. When the Chinese government was forced to allow missionaries into the country's interior in 1858, a veritable army of mostly dedicated and well-intentioned men and women invaded the Middle Kingdom braced by budgets raised from small and large donations each Sunday in churches across the United States. Despite all the good works performed by these soldiers of Christ, including building schools, hospitals, and orphanages, the basically subversive nature of missionary activity—the substitution of Christian for Confucian teaching, with its other-worldly focus—soon posed disturbing questions about identity for the Chinese. To make matters worse, Christianity became associated with the disastrous Taiping Rebellion of the 1850s and 1860s, a massive outbreak that affected at least sixteen of China's provinces and took the lives of more than twenty million people before being suppressed.

Radically new religious ideas accompanied radically new political, so-cial, and economic ideas, all of which contributed immensely to the crisis of self-confidence that beset China at the beginning of the twentieth century. By the 1930s, half of the 3,000 missionaries in China were Americans. In-creasingly, as historian Michael Schaller has written, "spreading Christian-ity meant spreading progress and the 'American way of life.' "[1] What this may have meant for U.S.-Chinese relations is impossible to gauge, though the evidence of Chinese displeasure with Christian advocacy is ample and took many forms, many of which were violent. Christian missionaries may have claimed to serve God, but to many Chinese, their loyalties seemed more mundane and national. Inevitably, Christianity remained hinged to its foreign origins and alien to the Chinese spirit. To many Chinese, Christian-ity was just another aspect of Western imperialism.

Observers have frequently noted that Americans have a propensity to see the rest of the world as somehow unable to do without American assistance or leadership. This point of view, different in its ethnocentricity only for its content, has had a particular influence on U.S.-Chinese relations. Quick to see China as a friend and the Chinese as wanting and needing American pa-tronage in its long effort to modernize, many Americans have participated over the last century and a half in various aid projects—in technological, commercial, and industrial areas, but especially in medicine and education. The paternalism that this behavior reflects, however, has been notably am-bivalent, so that Chinese failure to respond commensurately or to seem to appreciate American beneficence has led to disenchantment, disillusion-ment, and anger in the United States. In effect, Americans are largely polar-ized between those inclined to romanticize China and be generous in their assessments of Chinese behavior and those who stigmatize it and find deep fault in the political system that continues to defy so many cherished Ameri-can values, particularly those relating to issues of human rights, democratic process, and freedoms of speech and religion.

For their part, many Chinese harbor an equal ambivalence toward the United States and Americans. That tens of thousands of Chinese students are in the United States continuing their education, with many tens of thou-sands of others wishing to do so, is testimony to the perception of American capability and achievement in precisely those areas most associated with modernization. This is balanced by frustration with other major aspects of American life, including wide gaps in standards of living, high rates of crime, a seeming indifference to familial values, and the unsavoriness of extravagant public sexuality. Ironically, the materialism of American life is not one of the points of criticism, except in some government and party circles. On the contrary, that materialism, reflected within China by advertisements for American (and more broadly, European) products, styles, and materialist values sits well with many young Chinese who show every sign of being similarly concerned. Chinese leaders understand this very well and have repeatedly railed against the rising tide of reckless consumerism, excessive individualism, and other evidence of "capitalist pollution," even as they encourage the development of a market economy and the practical abandonment of socialism.

When the Chinese communist movement triumphed in 1949, it did so in a world increasingly being shaped by the competing interests of the Soviet Union and the United States. The ideological sparring between the United States and the Soviet Union, temporarily quieted by the economic depression in America and the great conflicts in Europe and Asia between 1937 and 1945, assumed center stage during the late 1940s when the Cold War dominated global politics. The West and the communist "East" squared off to create blocs of competing nations seemingly one step away from clashing militarily or, worse, destroying the world in an atomic catastrophe. The new People's Republic of China joined the coalition of socialist states under Soviet leadership (under a "lean-to-one-side policy") but did so differently from nearly all the others (the notable exception being Yugoslavia). Unlike the communist governments in eastern Europe, which had been created with Soviet assistance if not outright Soviet force, China established communism largely on its own. China had carried out its revolution without the need for Soviet troops and with a native leadership that had operated essentially independently of Soviet control for many years. For several decades by 1949, the Soviet Union had been pursuing a policy of "socialism in one country," whereby its national interests took precedence over proletarian internationalism. This policy did not make the USSR indifferent to the possibilities of spreading the revolution or influencing its advancement elsewhere—witness its ongoing interest in China from the 1920s onward—but it did make its leaders understandably cautious about provoking hostile reactions to such developments and thereby jeopardizing the security of its own state.

New China, braced by its extraordinary success in routing the Nationalist forces of Chiang Kai-shek, and now embarked on a monumental process of socioeconomic transformation, saw the world differently, though during the early 1950s reliance on the Soviet Union increased because of China's immense material needs. Under Mao Zedong's influence, internationalizing the doctrine of revolution and seeking to seize opportunities wherever they might arise, particularly in the so-called underdeveloped countries, gradually became a near staple of Chinese international behavior, especially between 1957 and 1969. Whether it was Mao's dictum that "the East wind was prevailing over the West wind," his pronouncement that a nuclear war would benefit revolutionary forces more than capitalist/bourgeois ones, or his arguments and policies that urged China's self-sufficiency (economically and militarily), the repercussions on the international setting were clear: China was not only socialist in its commitment and development, but its form of socialism and the ways the Chinese were achieving it were exportable as a model better suited to the bulk of the world's peoples than was the Soviet version. Failing to prod the Soviet Union into greater global militancy, China assumed an ever more aggressive posture on its own: against Taiwan, India, and, finally, even its erstwhile ally, the Soviet Union.

The Sino-Soviet split that ensued and lasted until 1989 resulted from many causes, some rooted deep in the relationship—for example the united-front and many other "unwise" policies that the Soviet leadership sought to have their Chinese counterparts pursue. But others were of more recent vintage and had a great deal to do with ideology and the proper interpretation of Marxism-Leninism.

Especially significant were developments in the Soviet Union during the late 1950s and early 1960s when Nikita Khrushchev, prompted by a combination of political cynicism and genuine good will, led an assault on Stalin and Stalinism that would astonish many in his own country and abroad and would forever change the international communist movement. At the Twentieth Congress of the Communist Party of the Soviet Union in 1956, Khrushchev delivered, ostensibly in secret, a scathing denunciation of Stalin that rambled on for hours. He revealed information little known or widely repressed about Stalin's behavior and that of many of his closest comrades, admitted that the Stalin years had witnessed a gross deformation of the revolution, and placed a great deal of blame for all the horrors on the "cult of personality" that Stalin encouraged to be developed around his own person. By attacking Stalin, Khrushchev opened the door to a kind of inner party self-criticism that had been carefully avoided since the mid-1920s and challenged a style of leadership that was practiced commonly within communist movements everywhere, including China.

Denunciation of Stalin and his cult of personality was read by many Chinese, especially Mao, in just this way. Even though there were some who would have preferred that Mao's preeminence be reduced and that his policies, such as the Great Leap Forward which Khrushchev publicly ridiculed, be abandoned, Mao was able to deflect the potential political disaster and turn it against the Soviet Union and his domestic opponents. The unity of the communist bloc, from that moment, ceased to exist.

Although Mao seemed to side with Stalin in the face of Khrushchev's revelations, in fact Mao and Stalin had a strained relationship since the later 1920s that involved a fundamental difference of interpretation over the very nature of revolution in Asia and, by extension, in the developing world generally. The Soviet Union claimed to be the product of a classical Marxist revolution, pursued in the name of the industrial proletariat and enjoying the unlimited support of that class. Whatever the truth of these assertions, the "party line" insisted on their validity not just in the Russian case but globally. When Mao began arguing for a mass-based rural revolution following his tour of Hunan in 1927, and continued to do so through 1949, he was implicitly challenging the emerging Stalinist theory and its proclaimed universal applicability. He was also claiming a status for himself within the pantheon of nearly deified revolutionary theoreticians comprising Marx, Engels, Lenin, and an aspiring Stalin.

During the 1950s, after the devastation of the Sino-Japanese War and the ensuing Civil War, the CCP was compelled to accept extensive Soviet support for economic recovery and development, and protection from possible military attack by the United States. The fear of overreliance on their northern "elder brother," however, became a source of Chinese anxiety that reinforced a natural desire for independence. Khrushchev's anti-Stalin speech added fuel to the smoldering fire, especially in Mao's thinking.[2]

Throughout the 1960s, Sino-Soviet relations deteriorated, as both sides sought to deal with regional and global events from different perspectives and to jockey for influence in places such as India, Indochina, and Indonesia. Mutual distrust generated acrimonious mutual name-calling, and finally military clashes in 1969 along the lengthy border between the two countries. Deeply concerned about subsequent Soviet military buildup on that border, Mao began exploring avenues of contact with the United States as a counterweight to what appeared to be a Soviet menace. Those explorations culminated in President Richard Nixon's visit to China in February 1972 and a reorientation of China's foreign policy increasingly toward the United States. By that time, the Chinese began seeing the "social imperialism" of the Soviet Union as a much greater threat than the "bourgeois imperialism" of the United States.

Prior to Nixon's visit, however, even as relations with the Soviet Union were deteriorating, the United States remained China's chief antagonist. Refusing to recognize the PRC, taking sides with Chiang Kai-shek's government settled in Taiwan, leading the United Nations' resistance from 1950 to 1952 to North Korean attacks on South Korea, and continuing as the capitalist bloc's key player, the United States could hardly have defined itself in a way more hostile to PRC interests. A decade and a half later, as the Cultural Revolution drew to an end, China's dramatic isolation from the international community began to ease, and the break with the Soviet Union hardened, Mao and the dominant faction within the CCP came to see the United States as the less dangerous of the two superpowers. Herein lay the opening that would lead to an easing of relations between the two countries, a lifting of the "Bamboo Curtain" dramatized by a tour of China by the American table-tennis team in 1971 (dubbed "ping-pong diplomacy" by the media), the even more significant trip to Beijing by President Nixon, and the opening of full diplomatic relations in 1979.

Over the next two decades, despite continuing disagreements over Taiwan, trade practices, human rights issues, and the treatment of the democracy movement, China and the United States have found themselves able to lean toward one another, linked above all by the paramount need of China to modernize and the equally formidable need of the United States for China's market and for balancing China against the Soviet Union. Left out of this equation for nearly twenty-five years, the Soviet Union, during the last phase of its existence, managed to reestablish normal relations with China, highlighted by Mikhail Gorbachev's visit to Beijing in May 1989, ironically during the height of the student demonstrations in Tiananmen Square. The visit climaxed a decade of mutual probing for a Sino-Soviet détente and was made possible by Soviet willingness to concede to three demands of Beijing: removal of Soviet troops from Mongolia and their reduction along the Sino-Soviet border, withdrawal of Soviet troops from Afghanistan, and pressure on Vietnam to end its occupation of Cambodia.

By 1991 the Soviet Union no longer existed, breaking up into a multitude of successor states, though Russia remains by far one of the greatest concerns to China because of its size, proximity, political instability, and potential competition in northern and east Asia. In October 1995 Jiang Zemin was scheduled to visit Moscow, but that event was postponed owing to Russian president Boris Yeltsin's hospitalization. The month before, the two countries had agreed to stop aiming nuclear weapons at one another, and two months later, in December, they resolved the last of their long-standing border issues to China's satisfaction. In November 1997, Yeltsin met with Jiang in Beijing. The two renewed a goal of $20 billion in annual trade by the year 2000 and agreed to final demarcation of their 2,500-mile eastern border, where armed clashes had occurred in 1969.

By 1998 China's relations with its two most important protagonists during the twentieth century were still plagued by disagreements, but none of these seems likely to raise any formidable obstacles to the continuation of normal dealings. The waning of Marxism and Marxist rhetoric as principal ingredients intersecting these relationships surely helps, leaving the three countries in the future to forge their ties based less on ideology than on perceived national interests. The most significant evidence of this can be seen in Yeltsin's 1997 visit to China and the nine-day visit by American president, Bill Clinton, in August 1998. Though lacking in any breakthroughs, the Clinton trip did lead the American president to utter some statements that distinctly altered U.S. diplomatic posture when he became the first president to accept Beijing's formulation on the future of Taiwan.[3] Clinton's trip was filled with symbolism and atmospherics. Both he and Jiang asserted success, and the consensus was that relations between the two countries are at least getting better and not worse. The "debate" between the two men following a state dinner was itself a first, principled but not hostile, insistent but not dismissive, and above all devoid of any of the bitter ideological polemics common in the past.

NOTES

1. Michael Schaller, *The United States and China in the Twentieth Century* (New York: Oxford University Press, 1979), 16.

2. Ironically, the antagonistic situation between the Soviet Union and China would be replayed in the mid-1970s when China's relations with Vietnam deteriorated. More than any other factor, national interest and pride on both sides took center stage. With regard to the Asian and larger developing world, the Chinese had presumed to possess the correct line concerning revolution that all should follow. For its part, after a lengthy, hard fought, and costly anticolonial conflict with the French and later the United States on the side of the South Vietnamese, the North Vietnamese looked with skepticism at China's presumption, and insisted that they could find their own path to communism without the help of an "elder brother" to the north if it meant limiting independence.

3. Clinton caused some consternation on Taiwan and back in the United States when he declared the "three noes": The U.S. does not support independence for Taiwan, or two Chinas, or one Taiwan-one China, and then added that Taiwan ought not be a member of any organization for which statehood is a requirement. The president's remarks prompted the U.S. Congress to resolve with near unanimity that U.S. policy on this matter had not changed.

6

Greater China: The People's Republic of China, Hong Kong, and Taiwan

In recent years, the merits of China's breakup into separate countries or reorganization along federal lines has been the topic of conversation and writing within a small circle of Chinese. Talk of this kind is shaped invariably by sentiments favoring such a development. Chinese who think this way are not unpatriotic, though they tend to come from those regions of the country that have greater natural resources, have traditions of high productivity (whether in agriculture, industry, or commerce), and/or have been in the right spots during the last century or so to take advantage of developmental opportunities. Such "critics" worry about the cost of continuing to seek the "four modernizations" nationally when, as they see it, some parts of the nation are paying a disproportionate share of the bill and are being held back from what they could accomplish if untethered from the remnants of centralized planning, Beijing politics, and the socialist commitment to equal welfare. Similar talk could be heard in the waning days of the Soviet Union and can be found, in fact, in all large countries where regional inequalities exist, including the United States.

Although this sentiment is the preserve of a small minority and has no likelihood of becoming a major public issue in the near future, its existence and logic will not go away. It offers a contrast to the much more powerful and public enunciation of the notion of a "Greater China," with its appeals to overseas Chinese and its vital concern for two key territories on the margins of the People's Republic of China: Hong Kong (and Macao), and Taiwan. (See Map 6.1.)

Map 6.1
The People's Republic of China

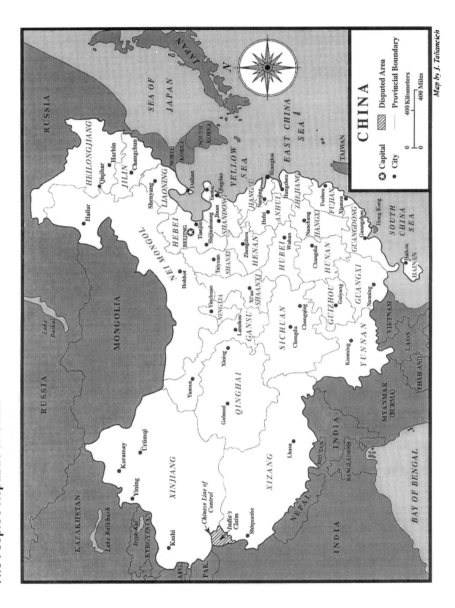

Map by J. Taliancich

As an idea, Greater China is not of recent vintage. One can identify a variant of it in the empire-building and empire-maintaining that have been part of Chinese experience for centuries, and another in the CCP's self-view as a revolutionary model for other countries. But the nineteenth and twentieth centuries, as a stretch of time that has brought China face-to-face with the modern age, have provided a different context within which the concept has flourished. Socioeconomic developments native to China, the results of which can be seen beginning in the late eighteenth century, created enormous pressures on the traditional infrastructure of the old empire that encouraged significant mobility not only within the country but also abroad. The extensive Chinese presence in places such as Singapore, Thailand, and the United States is testimony in large measure to these developments. On the other hand, the fates of Hong Kong and Taiwan are linked more to modern forces of another, primarily external kind: the intrusion of European power with its distinctive forms of social, economic, political, and intellectual experiences. European imperialism and investment further upset China's ability to conduct its own affairs and shape its own directions in ways with which it had grown comfortable through centuries of experience. The Western presence directly made Hong Kong and Taiwan what they are today, separately and in their relationships to the PRC. How was this so?

Located on the southeastern edge of China, the territory (or, under British rule, colony) of Hong Kong is both a peninsula (Kowloon) and a collection of large and small islands, one of which is Hong Kong itself. (See Map 6.2.) Covering 658 square miles (1,062 square kilometers) of land, it is roughly twice the size of New York City, providing about 5.5 million people with an overwhelmingly urban environment within which to live and work. Ethnically that population is 98 percent Chinese, essentially Cantonese, with the remaining 2 percent comprising people of European or Vietnamese descent. Since 1898 Hong Kong was a British Crown Colony, a key factor in the territory's twentieth-century development. As such, it has experienced an odd combination of a tightly controlled, highly structured political system along with a laissez-faire economy. The result was that Hong Kong residents enjoyed many of the benefits of a Western civil society (but not true democracy or representative government) and a remarkably high level of per capita income. Hong Kong means "fragrant harbor," and as a harbor it has been able to take advantage, under British guidance, of the rewards of international as well as regional commerce.

For Hong Kong, 1997 witnessed one of the most dramatic and ironic events of the twentieth century. On July 1, it reverted to Chinese control, ceasing to be a British colony and becoming a Special Administrative Region (SAR) within the PRC. It will, many presume, also become an integral

Map 6.2
Hong Kong

PEOPLES REPUBLIC
OF CHINA

TAI PANG WAN
(MIRS BAY)

Sha Tau Kok ●

HAU HOI WAN

San Tin ●

TAP MUN
CHAU

Yeun Long
Kau Hui ●

Tai Po ●

Sai Kung ●

Tsuen Wan ●

Sha Tin ●

LEUNG SHUEN
WAN CHAU

TSING
LI

Ho Chung ●

(HIGH ISLAND)

Hong Kong
Airport

KOWLOON

Hong Kong
Harbor

Sulphur
Channel

VICTORIA

TAI YUE SHAN
(LAN TAO)

HONG KONG ISLAND
● Aberdeen

Tai ●

SHEK KWU
CHAU

Cheung
Chau ●

Stanley ●

Hok Tsui

Stanley
Peninsula

SOKO
ISLANDS

POK LIU
CHAU

PO TOI

SOUTH CHINA SEA

N

HONG KONG

● City   ✪ Capital

----- City Limits

0   40   Kilometers

0   40 Miles

Map by J. Taliancich

part of the booming Special Economic Zone that centers on Shenzhen, just over the northern border of Hong Kong. The transferral of Hong Kong occurred peacefully with much official and popular fanfare. For many Chinese, the event carried strong emotional overtones. After all, it represented a long-delayed closure to British imperialism that began nearly two centuries ago. On the other hand, in the face of the collapse of international communism, the Soviet Union, and the Berlin Wall, the transferral of a relatively free society to the control of one of the last totalitarian political systems was ironic indeed.

By Chinese decree issued in 1757, Canton (now Guangzhou) was made the sole site for British and other European activity in China. The decree reflected the centuries-old Chinese practice of controlling the frontier against non-Chinese intrusion and limiting access to the interior. Keeping the Europeans confined to Canton, Hong Kong Island, and the Island of Macao made eminent sense. After all, from the Chinese perspective, the Europeans were people of low culture whose interest in commerce, let alone their physical appearance and strange customs and attitudes, proved the perception of their inferiority. Unlike other peoples with whom the Chinese previously had dealt, the Europeans since the sixteenth century were undergoing a radical transformation of their world, leading them by the beginning of the nineteenth century to become much more technologically capable than the Chinese could imagine initially. Part of that transformation was a growing belief that the rest of the world ought to abide by rules of interrelationship and engagement devised by the Europeans themselves, and ought to open itself up to the wishes of those inhabiting the westernmost portion of the Eurasian continent. The Europeans, particularly the British, found the Canton System too restraining, and they kept pressuring the Chinese to expand the number of harbors wherein Europeans could conduct commerce, to accede to European diplomatic practices, to permit Europeans committing legal infractions on Chinese territory to be safe from Chinese prosecution (extraterritoriality), and to open China's interior to economic and cultural/religious penetration.

The clash of Chinese belief and interest with European demands took several forms. One was war. The military conflict later known as the Opium War (1839–1842) was precipitated by the Chinese decision no longer to permit importation of the drug by the British and other foreigners. The contest was a war in only the most minimal sense, and its focus on the selling of opium served mostly to disguise the more significant underlying disagreements between the belligerents.[1] The war's consequences, nevertheless, were major. Chinese defeat led to the Treaty of Nanjing (1842), which gave the British much of what they wanted, including the right to trade with the

Chinese from five ports instead of one, a moderate tariff, extraterritoriality, an indemnity, and the cession of Hong Kong "in perpetuity." Eight years later, in 1850, following another British military victory, the Chinese were forced to cede additional territories (also "in perpetuity"), the most important of which was Kowloon Peninsula (roughly 3.5 square miles in size). Finally, by the second Anglo-Chinese Convention of Peking (1898), the British acquired the so-called New Territories, but under a lease arrangement and not "in perpetuity." An extension of the Chinese landmass with Kowloon at its tip, the New Territories makes up nearly 90 percent of what is known commonly as Hong Kong. The lease was to run for 99 years (until July 1, 1997). Theoretically only the New Territories had to be returned to China on the date, with Hong Kong island itself and Kowloon able to remain legally in British hands. With the New Territories providing greater Hong Kong's food and water supplies, however, and with the deep integration of the New Territories with the entire life of Hong Kong and Kowloon, return of the entire package to the PRC was unavoidable.

As a result of nineteenth-century diplomatic settlements signed under duress, then, Hong Kong became a British colony. For a brief period (1942–1945) during World War II, Japan occupied the territories. That they returned to British rule once the war ended was the result of an odd confluence of circumstances. On the one hand, the United States pressured Great Britain to relinquish its control and grant sovereignty to Hong Kong consistent with the more general process of decolonization that gained momentum in the post-1945 world. On the other, the Chinese Communist Party in the late 1940s and subsequently as leader of the PRC had ample opportunity either to seize these territories outright or force the British to withdraw. The CCP, despite occasional complaints and a special antagonism toward Britain, never did. Moreover, neither the CCP nor the people of Hong Kong had much sympathy for the notion of territorial sovereignty, the former because it would make reclaiming Hong Kong more difficult, and the latter because it worried that sovereignty would be a prelude to a communist takeover. In any event, time was on China's side. Because everything in the New Territories was leased to individuals or businesses, the British colonial government found it more and more difficult to grant land leases that could only be held—regardless of when issued—until three days before July 1, 1997. As a result, pressure built up for the negotiations that began in the early 1980s. In 1984 agreement was reached by which restoration of the entirety of Hong Kong to the PRC was ensured. The next thirteen years were spent defining the details of Hong Kong's future and ensuring a long transition during which the territories could be eased into the framework of the PRC while retaining elements of Hong Kong's "special status." The slogan, "One nation, two systems," proclaimed by Deng Xiaoping became the leitmotif of the transition. The Basic Law approved in April 1990 gives the Hong Kong Special Administrative Region a substantial degree of autonomy, except in matters of foreign policy and defense, which Beijing will control.

The concern for Hong Kong's fate beyond 1997 is in many respects out of all proportion to its size. Part of the explanation can be found in the twentieth-century evolution of the territories under British rule. Hong Kong became a major commercial and financial center. As such, it was identified increasingly (as has been Singapore) with a Chinese prosperity unavailable to the mainland and naturally associated with the very kind of economic order—capitalism and a free market—that has been antithetical to the Chinese revolution as defined by the CCP.[2] This factor was certainly more important decades ago than it is today, when China itself is rushing headlong to a future that is at least "capitalist with a Chinese face." Yet Hong Kong's commercial and public relations value to the PRC remains a major reason for Beijing's gingerly handling of this otherwise insignificant territory. The fallout from events in and around Hong Kong cannot be underestimated for another reason: their effect on China's intentions for another "Chinese" territory that has long escaped the PRC's grasp—the Republic of China on Taiwan (ROC).

Situated just 90 miles off the coast of China (see Map 6.3), the island of Taiwan has had Chinese settlers since the seventh century, although the first major settlement from the mainland occurred in the late sixteenth century as a result of growing commerce along China's southeast coast. It became a province of China only in 1885. Defeated in the Sino-Japanese War (1894–1895), China ceded Taiwan to Japan. Because the Taiwanese people refused to accept Japanese rule, they declared the island a republic, forcing the Japanese to use military force to establish a colonial administration that survived until 1945.

To this day, approximately 80 percent of the Chinese inhabitants of Taiwan are descendants of settlers who arrived before the twentieth century and mostly from the mainland's southern provinces (particularly Fujian). Just 20 percent are related to Chinese supporters of the Guomindang party who fled the mainland from many different regions in the late 1940s and after. The distinction between Taiwanese Chinese and Mainlander Chinese living in Taiwan is significant, not just because their roots tend to be in different parts of China proper, but because the Taiwanese Chinese think of themselves as Taiwanese first and linked to China only incidentally. To the contrary, the Mainlander Chinese have insisted since their arrival that China and Taiwan are one and that they, the Mainlanders, are the legitimate heirs to the mantle of power that should rule over both. Moreover, owing to their

Map 6.3
Taiwan

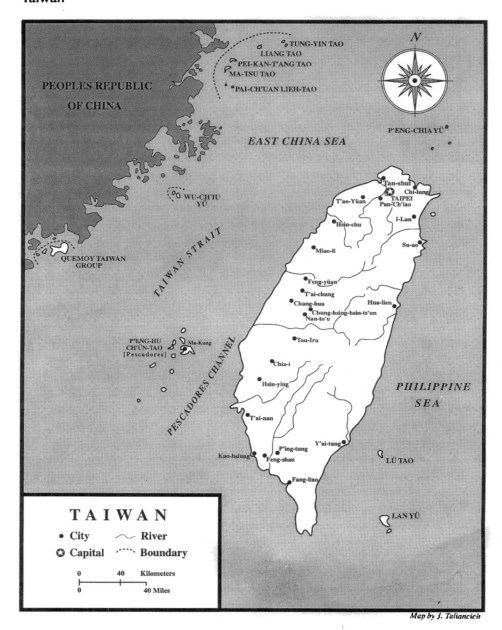

TAIWAN
• City   ～ River
✪ Capital ⋯ Boundary

0   40   Kilometers
0   40 Miles

Map by J. Taliancich

military power and political organization through the Guomindang and the charismatic leadership of Chiang Kai-shek, the Mainlanders have dominated Taiwan's political elite and system—except at the local level—to the virtual exclusion of Taiwanese interests and participation until the late 1980s. The Mainlander cause was bolstered by support from the United States as a natural corollary to the Cold War that dominated and shaped international politics in the decades following World War II. The Korean War (1950–1953) and the presence of the U.S. Seventh Fleet in the Taiwan Strait prevented Beijing from reclaiming Taiwan by force when its chance was best, though it always has insisted that the issue of Taiwan is an "internal" Chinese matter.

Until 1971, U.S. support ensured that the Republic of China would represent "China" in international organizations. In that year, however, more than two-thirds of the countries represented in the United Nations voted to withdraw the ROC's right to represent China in favor of the PRC. That vote as well as the ROC's continued insistence since then that there is one China and Taiwan is merely one of its provinces has meant that the ROC has had no independent representation in any international organization. It enjoys representation in a few such organizations (the Olympic Games, for example) as "Taipei-China," but only at the sufferance of the PRC, which generally resists letting this happen. Moreover, since the late 1970s the PRC has used its growing international clout as an emerging economic and military power in East Asia to keep the ROC under wraps and insist that any country wanting normal relations with China must accept Beijing's "principled stand" on Taiwan.

For nearly forty years after May 1949, Taiwan remained under martial law. Dominated by the GMD party (the only party legally allowed to function), the island's political life was shaped by conditions of political authoritarianism, however "soft" or limited. By the mid-1980s, however, socioeconomic modernization and the growing strength and maturity of the political opposition had created conditions favorable to political liberalization. Under presidents Chiang Ching-kuo (1978–1988) and Lee Teng-hui (1988–   ), major steps along the road to democratization have been taken, beginning in 1986–1987 with the lifting of martial law and the removal of the ban on organizing new political parties. In January 1989 Lee promulgated the Civil Organizations law setting rules for the formation of new parties, with laws enacted the following month that lifted many restrictions on campaign activities. Another important step came in 1990 when Taiwan's Council of Grand Justices (the nation's highest judicial organ and arbiter of constitutional questions) forced the retirement of the senior legislators elected to the Legislative Yuan and National Assembly on the mainland in the late 1940s. In the aftermath of a political crisis resulting from factionalism within the GMD over the forthcoming presidential election, as well as the rising temper of opposition and student activism, the GMD leadership encouraged the National Assembly to pass constitutional amendments in April 1991 providing for a total renewal of the three parliamentary bodies comprising the central government (the National Assembly itself, the Legislative Yuan, and the Control Yuan). Over the next three years, elections for each of these bodies were scheduled. In 1994 mayoral elections for the island's largest cities (Taipei and Kaohsiung) were likewise held, the first since 1967, with Taipei's voters putting the opposition candidate into office. Finally, in November 1997, the opposition Democratic Progressive Party (DPP) delivered a stinging defeat to the GMD in elections for county magistrates and city mayors, winning twelve out of twenty-three seats. Moreover, the DPP gained a slightly larger percentage of the total votes cast—43.32 percent to the GMD's 42.12 percent. The extent of the DPP's victory suggested that it could make further gains in the December 1998 elections for the Legislative Yuan, perhaps giving the opposition control of the legislature for the first time. Voters, however, provided the GMD a comfortable victory (123 seats out of 225), thereby frustrating any hope for a realignment of party politics. All in all, the transition from authoritarianism to democracy, though still incomplete, has made remarkable headway since 1991.

Much of the impetus for this political trend comes from a second major development in Taiwan over the past fifty years: the island's own version of an economic miracle. As a result of consistently high rates of growth in GNP and foreign trade since the 1950s, Taiwan became second only to Japan among East Asian nations in terms of industrialization, foreign currency reserves, and quality of life. By 1989, per capita income had risen to $7,512, nearly triple what it was in 1980; even with modest growth, that figure should at least double again by the end of the century. Although small and resource-poor, Taiwan has benefited from its leaders' sound economic strategy that until the 1970s gave priority to agriculture and light industry, in sharp contrast to the approach taken by the Chinese communists in Beijing, under the influence of the USSR. For two decades, land reform and agricultural diversification, along with labor-intensive and export-oriented consumer industries, stabilized and improved the domestic economy while allowing Taiwan's products to penetrate foreign markets and create larger and larger currency reserves. Beginning in 1973 with the announcement of the Ten Major Projects (including a north-south freeway, an international airport, a modern steel mill, a petrochemical complex, and a giant shipbuilding corporation), development emphasis shifted to more sophisticated and heavier industry. The trend was maintained into the 1990s by the launching of other large-scale, high-tech, and capital-intensive industrial projects.[3]

Forty years of economic development and growth, accelerated by American, European, and especially Japanese investments, has meant the transformation of the Republic of China from a predominantly agricultural society to a major industrial power, one with increasingly democratic practices and institutions. As such, it has become something of a model, or at least an alternative, to the socioeconomic and political system that has developed not far away in the People's Republic of China. The ROC's evolution and achievements, coupled with the PRC's own policy shifts since the death in 1976 of Mao Zedong, also have contributed to a diminishment of hostility between the two countries and a significant improvement in interstate relations as well as rapidly increasing economic interaction, tourism, sports and cultural exchanges, and people-to-people contacts. Even though the issue of reunification of the two Chinas, left over from the long and bitter Civil War, is still far from resolved, the two sides are now dealing with one another at many levels.

Still, the relationship between the PRC and the ROC is troubled by an underlying tension that stems from the "one China" policy. The PRC refuses to budge on an issue to which the ROC itself had steadfastly adhered since 1949. Recently, however, the ROC has begun to move away from this policy in favor of one that seeks international recognition of Taiwan's statehood. Part of the reason for doing so is Taiwan's isolation and the discrepancy between its "official" international position, which is embarrassingly tiny, and its actual regional economic and political role and achievements. Moreover, the process of democratizing Taiwan's internal politics, of reducing the power of the GMD party, and of respecting more fully the interests of the Taiwanese over the Mainlanders has led inevitably to a weakening of the "one China" theory on the island in favor of a Taiwanese nationalism. The election of Lee Teng-hui as the first Taiwanese-born and first directly elected president has further encouraged this development. In Lee, Taiwan found a leader willing to speak publicly about "two Chinas" or "one China-one Taiwan"—a new policy of "pragmatic" or "flexible" diplomacy— thereby all but severing the long-argued link between the two countries. Lee's diplomatic gesture has resulted in only minor gains in Taiwan's official status, but it has led to an improvement in the island's relations with many developed nations, who now regularly send high-level officials for discussions. "Creeping officiality," as Beijing described the trend, seemed to be creating an implicit recognition of Taiwan's sovereignty.

When Lee campaigned for reelection in 1996, he boldly included in his platform the demand for greater international recognition of Taiwan as an independent state. Beijing's response was swift and dramatic: a military buildup of some 200,000 troops in Fujian Province across from Taiwan and the "testing" of missiles in waters around the island. Designed to intimidate the Taiwanese on the eve of their presidential election, PRC maneuvers probably helped secure Lee's reelection and the 30 percent hold on seats in the Legislative Yuan by the Democratic Progressive Party, which continues to call for independence to be decided by popular self-determination.[4]

U.S. reluctance to support Lee fully and unambiguously was balanced by deployment of two aircraft carrier battle groups near Taiwan that helped ease the immediate tension. Once the election passed, both Beijing and Taipei sounded conciliatory notes, with Lee reaffirming his commitment to the reunification of China and announcing his willingness to meet with PRC leaders. Subsequently, however, likely emboldened by American concern for the China trade and continuing normalization of relations, and by Hong Kong's uneventful return to the PRC, Beijing has trumpeted its intention to pay close attention to the "Taiwan issue." Changes now being implemented in the way that Taiwan is governed that amount to administrative simplification, a revision in power sharing, and further erosion of one-party rule are worrisome to Beijing because they ensure Taiwan's further democratization. If a formal declaration of independence from Taipei is not likely in the foreseeable future, Taiwan is nevertheless drawing further away from the PRC and its insistence on authoritarian politics.

Work continues by both sides to extend and consolidate economic and cultural ties, but some movement toward political accommodation only began in 1998. A four-day meeting between the highest-ranking of Taiwan's ruling party ever to talk with Chinese officials took place in Shanghai beginning on October 14. In the months leading to the meeting, both sides conceded something significant: The PRC dropped its demand that the talks focus on reunification, and the ROC gave up its insistence that the talks deal only with "practical issues." The talks were a positive development, but without any breakthroughs, they revealed just how far the road will be to a settlement of Taiwan's identity.

NOTES

1. In the context of late twentieth-century concerns with the spread of illicit drugs globally and changed sentiments concerning Europe's former global power that are reflected in a growing post-colonial perspective, it may seem apologetic of the opium trade to suggest that it was not really the heart of the problem between Britain and China but a symptom. Yet we must keep in mind that attitudes toward drug use were quite different in early Victorian England than they have become, and many British subjects (including working-class people) were them-

selves avid users of a variety of substances. Selling them elsewhere did not yet raise the moral outrage then that it has more recently, not even among the Chinese whose concerns about opium addiction were more focused on its economic, political, and social impact.

2. It is a commonplace to note that another Chinese city, Shanghai, offered a much greater likelihood of achieving what Hong Kong has. One of the world's great ports before 1949, Shanghai saw its importance eclipsed following the creation of the PRC. That Shanghai has been recovering since the early 1980s with the country's reopening to world trade suggests how the city might have developed had the CCP pursued other policies under Mao Zedong.

3. The relationship between agricultural and manufacturing productivity, and hence emphasis in economic policy, can be seen in percent-of-gross-domestic-product statistics over the past forty years: Agriculture's percentage share of GDP has declined from 32 in 1952 to 4 in 1989, while manufacturing's has risen from 13 to 36 in that same period.

4. The question of independence for Taiwan is a thorny one for most Taiwanese. Polls and other data suggest that large majorities of the island's citizens prefer the status quo to either unification or independence. The logic here is that doing nothing is less threatening to Taiwan's economic and other accomplishments.

7

Interpreting China's Revolution: Impact and Consequences

The twentieth century has witnessed the appeal of powerful secular ideas to the deepest sentiments of people in virtually every society around the world. The two most significant of these have been the ideologies of Marxism and nationalism, both of which emerged in Europe but then spread across the globe to affect communities of people nearly everywhere. Essentially products of the nineteenth century, both owe much to the intellectual trajectory of European culture from the High Middle Ages of the eleventh and twelfth centuries through the Renaissance and the Enlightenment, with major contributions from the remarkable developments in scientific method and practice that have helped transform the way people do things and lead their lives. Though sharing in this legacy, Marxism and nationalism have little else in common. Their visions are antipodal (diametrically opposed). The one anticipates a borderless world in which all are equal economically, socially, and politically; the other speaks of a world filled with borders dividing humanity according to identities rooted in ethnic or other culturally derived norms. So different are they that Karl Marx saw nationalism as a fundamental, though temporary, obstacle on the way to universal socialism and declared its disappearance, as a creature of bourgeois culture, to be inevitable and praiseworthy. For their part, nationalists have tended to decry the Marxist indifference to the strength of cultural differences, and have resisted subsuming identity to Marxism's explicit internationalism.

Despite the tensions that exist between Marxism and nationalism, many have found it difficult to accept one or the other to the exclusion of its nemesis. More often than not, the two have been brought together in the service of revolution, each playing leading roles at times and then retreating into the background at others. It is incontestable, in fact, that all the revolutions of the past one hundred years carried out in Marxism's name have relied upon nationalist sentiment to rally support for their cause, and have frequently suppressed Marxist theoretical principles for the sake of short-term gains. It is at least arguable that without nationalist appeals, Marxist movements would have had a more difficult time in their struggles to achieve and hold on to power.

In China's case, the introduction of Marxist theory into the intellectual world of the early twentieth century occurred when the formulation of nationalist ideals already had a substantial history and nationalist sentiment was beginning to penetrate Chinese society across social and occupational lines. Despite the heated debates and ideological clashes that had typified efforts to address China's problems since the late nineteenth century, the underlying aspiration of growing numbers of thinking Chinese was nationalist: to restore the country's wealth, power, and dignity and to do so by fostering political change that would limit central authority in relationship to the people. By the time of the formation of the Chinese Communist Party in 1921 it was difficult for Chinese Marxists to resist the temptations and emotional power of nationalism. As time passed and the task of revolutionizing the country unfolded, the difficulty grew. In the 1990s echoes of those earlier years can still be heard. Even as the government continues to try to define the meaning of patriotism—witness the CCP's issuance of the "Outline for the Implementation of Patriotic Education" in 1994—in an effort to use nationalism as a unifying ideology in the face of communism's weakening, important cultural figures (writers, cinematographers, and painters, among others) use their creativity to foster forms of patriotism rooted in a passion for national independence and strength that is outside the bounds of official culture. The goal of building a modern nation has, arguably, won out over Marxism, and so, it would seem, has capitalism.

What, then, of the impact and consequences of the Chinese Revolution? Let's begin with some easy observations before turning to others that are more complex and subtle. It is probably safe to argue that the revolution has proved successful (or did so for much of its history) as a result of the kind of political order that was gradually created in the decades before 1949 and became more fully developed subsequently. That order was (and is) highly centralized and authoritarian, with the ability under a single-party leadership to mobilize national resources—material and human—often on a large scale, thereby compensating for deficiencies in investment capital, human skills, and other ingredients seemingly necessary for modernization. It was also a political order that defined its goals in terms of a socialist vision within which all would share equally in society's burdens and rewards. That vision was not only inspiring for its emphatic egalitarianism, but also for its nationalistic appeals, promising to lift China from its embarrassing depths of inadequacy and eliminate its vulnerability to foreign exploitation. A China with restored national status, sufficiently productive for the needs of its people and powerful enough to ensure independence of action, promised basic material security along with something more intangible but no less significant: dignity.

The other side of China's political reality is less appealing and, many would say, both inconsistent with fundamental revolutionary goals and subversive of the revolution's most important promise: liberation from forces and people that exploit the many by controlling society's means of production and their supporting institutions. More than authoritarian, the political order produced by the revolution in China was, like that in the Soviet Union, totalitarian. This is a term whose use has engendered much controversy, but it seems appropriate as a means to distinguish those regimes that seek to control not just politics but economics, social relations, culture, and human psychology in ways that at least aspire to monopolize influence unchallenged by any competition. Monopolization of politics and economic resources gives to such regimes extraordinary power, and so confounds society as to render it nearly helpless vis à vis the state. Promoting collectivist policies, though consistent with socialist ideology, only serves to weaken society further in the absence of genuine popular governance (democracy) and the existence of legal norms that would protect individuals.

Under these circumstances, it ought not be surprising that, for all their differences, the two most dominant leaders in China since 1949, Mao Zedong and Deng Xiaoping, were believers in the socialist vision and remained convinced that its fulfillment depended upon strict control over society. Both ruled as dictators, handpicking successors, purging opponents, ultimately defining what can and cannot be discussed. For Mao, the Great Leap Forward and the Cultural Revolution are particularly revealing of how he kept trying to turn the revolution into a reflection of his own changing vision, determined to force society (and its leaders) to follow paths that in practical terms were irrational. For Deng, the events in Tiananmen Square in 1989 are telling, because the massacre shows how little he was willing to tolerate in the political sphere, even as he had been seriously reforming the economic system to make it more rationally organized and striving to bring China into the mainstream of international life.

One of the ironies about these two men is that Mao disdained capitalism because he understood that its means and ends are not easily separated, whereas Deng leaned toward capitalism believing that its means and ends could be easily separated. For Mao, were China to follow the capitalist path with its offer of greater developmental possibilities, the country would have to accept more than just a way of organizing production. It would have to tolerate the encouragement of individual initiative, a stress on expertise, inequalities of reward, and the likelihood that a new elite would emerge to dominate. For Deng, the capitalist path was unavoidable as a means to a socialist end. Its path may be strewn with dangers (clearly identified by Mao), but these were manageable and would eventually give way, as more and more people enjoyed higher and higher living standards, to the reassertion of socialist norms and values. The path to socialism required development that could only come through capitalist means, a point that Marx would have appreciated. The problem for China, as it had been for the Soviet Union, was that capitalism had not developed fully before the revolution as it should have: under the auspices of a native bourgeoisie committed to all of what capitalism entailed. Because this did not occur, the work of capitalist construction would have to be borne by those at heart ill disposed to it but willing to pretend that it did not matter. Like late Qing intellectuals who, arguing that cultures possess *ti* (essence) and *yung* (superficial features), also proposed that the two are separable and can be interchanged, so did Deng believe that a China with socialist identity could emerge with the assistance of capitalist means.

In the name of socialism, capitalist development was undercut and then stifled by the CCP until the death of Mao in 1976. In the name of socialism, but also of national needs, capitalist development has been encouraged since the late 1970s, largely at the insistence of Deng. Both Mao and Deng are now dead, and so too, it would seem, is the debate over which path China should follow. For all the continued pronouncements in official circles of socialism as China's goal, or of "socialism with a Chinese face," the truth after nearly fifty years of extraordinary events and profound sacrifices is that the socialist dream is itself nearly dead. For all the economic, and in its wake, social inequity that have crept back into Chinese society; the increased burden upon the peasants to produce ever more without the safety net of social security that they had once had; the expanding un- and underemployment that one now finds in rural areas especially; the evidence of an emerging underclass of low-paid and temporary workers serving the needs of an equally new urban bourgeoisie that has too much money to bother with a whole range of occupations; the regional differences in wealth and opportunities; the ravaging impact of rampant development upon the environment; and the remarkable commodification of labor, property, and culture—for all that, capitalism has triumphed. Rather than ask how the political system will deal with these and other negative consequences of that triumph, it might be more prudent to ask what it would do if economic growth slowed significantly and for a long period, if the opportunities for making money dwindled seriously or dried up, and if those not yet the main beneficiaries of the spectacular economic gains of recent years perceive that those gains will not reach them?

Through it all, China's revolutionary leaders have succeeded in building an increasingly modern and an independent nation whose economy now ranks with the most productive in the world. Some socialist survivals likely will linger for the foreseeable future, including the heroic tradition of revolutionary struggle, the expectation by many of a social safety net, and cooperative and egalitarian values. But once people do not have to "eat out of the same big pot," as opponents of Mao's egalitarian approach protested they would if they followed his path, how is the single big pot brought to the table once again? If one looked to today's modern urban youth for an answer, one would likely get a snicker, reflecting an unnerving absence of either socialist or bourgeois values. As one Chinese intellectual wrote several years ago: "The pendulum has swung from the extremism of the Maoist age to the extremism of the current period, from moral absolutism to nihilism, from radical collectivism to radical individualism, from the suppression of all desire to its indulgence."[1] As in many modern parts of the world on the eve of the twenty-first century, a specter stalks China, and it is rampant materialism.

NOTE

1. Liu Zi'an, "China Calls for Morality," *China Focus*, 2, no. 4 (1994): 5, as quoted in Maurice Meisner, *The Deng Xiaoping Era: An Inquiry into the Fate of Chinese Socialism, 1978–1994* (New York: Hill and Wang, 1996), 509.

Biographies: The Personalities Behind the Chinese Revolution

Chen Duxiu (Ch'en Tu-hsiu, 1879–1942)

Leader of the cultural and literary revolution that culminated in the May Fourth Movement of 1919, and head of the Communist party from 1921 to 1927, Chen was born on October 8, 1879, in Huaining county, Anhui province. Shortly after Chen's birth, his father, a holder of the first degree in the civil service examination and a military official in Manchuria, died. Under the tutelage of his grandfather and elder brother, he received a traditional education in the Chinese classics, taking and passing the examinations for the first and second degrees in 1896 and 1897. During the next several years, Chen pursued a modern education, studying French, English, and naval architecture in Hangzhou and then traveling to Japan for further education. There he met several ex-patriot revolutionaries who were members of the Tongmenghui party headed by Sun Yat-sen, but refused to join the movement on the grounds that it was too narrowly based. Nevertheless, inspired to social activism, he returned to China in 1903, forged an alliance with a group of friends he had made in Japan, and founded a revolutionary newspaper in Shanghai called the *National Daily News (Guomin ribao)*.

He became active in the republican movement following the revolution of October 1911. In the summer of 1914, in association with another political fugitive, Zhang Shizhao, Chen became the junior editor of *Tiger Magazine (Jia yin za zhi)*, published in Japan. Liberal in political orientation, *Tiger Magazine* survived less than a year before being suppressed by Japanese authorities. Returning to China in the summer of 1915, Chen began to publish *Youth Magazine (Qingnian za zhi)*, which quickly became one of China's most influential publications.

Over the next two years, Chen sought to raise Chinese awareness of the utility of Western ideas (individualism, social and economic equality) while also condemning traditional Confucian social teaching. Using vernacular Chinese rather than the classical language for literature, Chen and his magazine, renamed *New Youth (Xin Qingnian)*, were in the forefront of what became known as the Chinese literary renaissance. In his writings, he popularized the characters "Mr. Democracy" and "Mr. Science," who were used as voices of classical nineteenth-century European liberalism and faith in material progress.

Political developments in China, particularly Beijing itself in 1918 and 1919, encouraged Chen to create a new publication called *Weekly Critic (Meizhou pinglun)* with Li Dazhao, a professor at Beijing university. The journal was explicitly political, publishing articles that commented critically on the domestic and foreign policies of the Beijing government. By arousing their young readers to the relationship of politics to China's future, Chen and Li were instrumental in providing the inspiration for the May Fourth Movement of 1919.

Radicalized by the events of 1919, Chen became involved with young intellectuals who were reading and discussing the theories of European anarchists and socialists. He had begun the study of doctrines espoused by Karl Marx and Vladimir Ilich Lenin as early as 1918, and already had published articles on Marxism in his journals. By the summer of 1920 he concluded that China's hope lay with socialism. Although never a complete follower of Marx and Lenin, Chen believed that the former's ideas and the latter's strategies were useful to China's cause, leading him to propose the creation of a communist party in China. The nucleus of the party was established in Shanghai with other cells to follow in the country's major cities. A Youth League was organized in August to train future members of the party. A school of foreign languages was also created largely to teach Russian to youth who would then travel to the Soviet Union for additional education. To assist these efforts, Chen transferred *New Youth* to Shanghai to serve as an organ of the communist group. When the First National Congress of the Chinese Communist Party was held in July 1921 in Shanghai, Chen was unanimously elected secretary of the party's Central Committee.

Despite his founding role in the history of the CCP, Chen was attacked at the party's Fifth National Congress in April 1927 by those increasingly dissatisfied with Comintern policies. Difficulties within his own party increased when Joseph Stalin began blaming Chen's leadership for Comintern blunders in China. At a secret emergency conference on August

7, 1928, Chen was replaced as CCP head and censured for his "opportunism" in advocating a conciliatory line toward the GMD. In mid-December 1927 he issued an open letter to CCP members in which he rejected all charges against him; five days later, he joined in publishing a statement that sharply attacked Stalin and the current CCP party line, and vigorously supported Trotsky's call for a continuously advancing world revolutionary process. In 1931 Chen's new direction contributed to the formation of the Chinese Communist Party Left Opposition Faction.

The remaining decade of Chen's life saw his political influence wane almost completely. He was imprisoned from 1932 to 1937, and following his release he devoted his attention largely to study of the ancient Chinese language. He died in his home county on May 27, 1942.

Chiang Kai-shek (Chiang Chieh-shih, 1887–1975)

Successor to Sun Yat-sen as military and political leader of the Guomindang party, head of the Nationalist government in China (1928–1949), and leader of the Nationalist government in exile on Taiwan (1949–1975). Born on October 31, 1887, to a modestly prosperous farmer/salt-merchant family in the coastal province of Zhejiang, Chiang was educated, following primary school, largely in preparation for a military career. He enrolled first at the Baoding Military Academy in north China (1906), and then continued his military education (1908–1911) in Japan, where he even served for two years in the Japanese army. His experience with the modern Japanese military had a significant influence on him, as did his contacts with Chinese students studying in Tokyo, who typically held anti-Qing sentiments and advocated the replacement of the monarchy with a republic.

As news reached Japan in 1911 of spontaneous Chinese uprisings against the dynasty, Chiang returned home to join in the fighting that would overthrow the Qing before the year was out. From 1913 to 1916, he participated in the struggle against Yuan Shikai, who served as president of the newly formed Chinese Republic but had aspirations of restoring the monarchy under his domination. From 1916 to 1917 Chiang lived in Shanghai where he apparently joined a secret society known as the Green Gang. In 1918 he reentered public life by joining the Guomindang party and beginning an association with its leader, Sun Yat-sen.

In the midst of reorganizing the GMD on the pattern of the Communist Party of the Soviet Union, Sun dispatched Chiang to the USSR in August 1923 to study the Soviet military system, the political indoctrination of Red Army troops, and the Bolshevik party's methods of discipline. Upon his return to China four months later, Chiang was named superintendent of the newly created Whampoa Military Academy near Canton. Soviet advisers began to arrive in China in growing numbers thereafter.

When Sun died in March of 1925, the party's military authority rested with Chiang who was responsible for developing an officer corps that would staff the new revolutionary force. The academy's cadets already had become a significant military factor in regional developments prior to Sun's death, principally in challenging various of the southwestern warlords seeking to expand their powers. On June 25, 1926, the Nationalist government appointed Chiang commander-in-chief of the National Revolutionary Army that consisted of 6,000 Whampoa cadets and 85,000 troops. The following month Chiang set out on a major campaign against the northern warlords (the Northern Expedition). The drive ended in 1928 when his forces entered Beijing. A new central government, with Chiang at its head, was then established at Nanjing.

Meanwhile, relations between the GMD and CCP, always tenuous despite the alliance encouraged by Sun and the Soviet government, collapsed. Ever suspicious of the communists whose growing strength he feared, but needing Soviet support, Chiang had followed a fine line between cooperation and subversion. In 1927, however, he decided to end the alliance by launching a surprise assault on communist strongholds, expelling the communists from the GMD, and suppressing the labor organizations that they had been most responsible for organizing.

As head of the Nationalist government and unifier of the country, Chiang enjoyed wide popular support. But he faced exceptional difficulties in trying to carry out reforms that would have placed the country on a new, more stable, and more prosperous track. To start with, some of the warlords remained to dispute his authority. Secondly, the communists were momentarily neutralized but were not crushed. In fact, they withdrew to rural strongholds and formed their own army and government. Third, war with Japan seemed certain following the latter's seizure of Manchuria in 1931. Hoping to deal with the communist problem first, thereby having a free hand to face the Japanese later, Chiang continued to apply military pressure against communist bases. In 1934 he forced the communists to abandon their stronghold and undertake a trek known as the Long March that lasted a year.

When war with Japan broke out in 1937, Chiang opted to follow a policy of strategic withdrawal in the face of superior forces with better weapons and training, giving up territory in the hopes of extending the Japanese supply lines beyond their limits. But nationalist sentiment forced Chiang to reconsider his policy. As a result of the so-called Xi'an Incident, wherein Chiang was "kidnapped" by some of his own officers and held until he agreed to a united-front alliance with the CCP against the Japanese invaders, more-aggressive handling of the Japanese and less attention to suppressing the communists followed.

The war's end reestablished the centrality of the struggle between the GMD and CCP for political control of China. Much had changed over the preceding eight years, however, to alter the balance between the two sides. Whereas the CCP had made remarkable gains in popular support by following a policy of social reform rather than radical politics and by taking advantage of the social rewards of pursuing guerrilla military tactics, the GMD was saddled with governmental responsibilities and with a growing authoritarian and corrupt image. By the summer of 1946 when the civil war recommenced, the advantage, with hindsight, clearly lay with the communists. Increasingly pushed to the southeast of the country, Chiang's forces lost China to its opponents by summer 1949. As the People's Republic of China was being proclaimed on October 1, Chiang already had led his followers to the island of Taiwan. There he formed a new government in exile and declared the creation of the Republic of China on Taiwan until such time as he could retake the mainland from the communists. Chiang ruled over Taiwan for two decades, during which time, with substantial U.S. aid and protection, he set the island on the road to modern economic development. Political reform, however, would have to wait until after Chiang's death on April 5, 1975.

Deng Xiaoping (Teng Hsiao-p'ing, 1904–1997)

Long-time political officer in the CCP who rose to become its top leader and reordered the PRC following the death of Mao Zedong in 1976. Deng was born on August 22, 1904, in Guang'an, Sichuan, the eldest son of a landowning family. Little is known about either his family background or his own early life, though rumors have persisted that the Dengs were Hakka (a Chinese subgroup). The nature of his primary and middle-school education is unclear, although we know that he attended classes in Chongqing before going to Shanghai and then Europe in 1920. In 1922 he joined the China Socialist Youth League and first became acquainted with Zhou Enlai. At some point in 1924, he joined the CCP. Following his sojourn in France, he went to Moscow where he spent several months attending classes at Sun Yat-sen University.

When he returned to China, possibly in August 1926, his first CCP assignment was as instructor at the Xi'an Military and Political Academy. In 1928 he was assigned by the Soviet Communist Party to assist Li Lisan, then CCP head, in Shanghai. He was involved in development of the party's military wing, including the Seventh Red Army, and joined Mao Zedong's forces in their retreat to Jiangxi province (1928–1934). In 1932 he began serving in the propaganda department of the communist military headquarters and became editor of the army newspaper *Red Star* (Hongxing). In 1934, at the beginning of the Long March, he was director of the First Army Corps Political Department, then under Peng Dehuai; by 1936 he was its deputy political commissar. He was elected to the CCP's Central Committee in 1945 and served as one of the most prominent military leaders during the final stage of the Chinese Civil War (1946–1949).

Until the Cultural Revolution, Deng was one of the top six leaders of the CCP. In 1966 he was accused of collaborating with Liu Shaoqi, Mao Zedong's primary target in his assault on the party, and was purged. That he had previously criticized the personality cult of Mao and had proposed "liberal" agricultural policies was held against him. Vilified as a "capitalist roader," Deng was publicly humiliated by Red Guards who paraded him wearing a dunce cap through the streets of Beijing in a jeep. First spending two years in Beijing in solitary confinement, he was subsequently sent with his wife and stepmother to an abandoned military school near Nanchang (Jiangxi province). There he worked in a tractor factory under strict supervision.

In early 1973, with Zhou Enlai's recommendation, Deng was rehabilitated, and between 1973 and 1976 he was restored to the vice premiership and the Politburo Standing Committee. He was purged once again, however, in 1976 following the April Tiananmen Incident and Zhou's death, but recovered following Mao's death later that year to begin the process of becoming the most powerful political figure in China until his own death in 1997.

In November 1987, he retired from all official posts except the Military Commission, a position he finally yielded in November 1989. Despite these moves, he remained the unchallenged "paramount leader." Dispensing with the radicalism of Mao, Deng long advocated consensus building and compromise to ensure China's economic development. He was the key figure in the post-Maoist reform of virtually all aspects of China's economic and political life, introducing decentralized economic management and rational and flexible long-term planning in industry. His policy of giving peasants greater responsibility for their production and profits led to remarkable increases in agricultural production that further stimulated the economy as a whole. In foreign affairs, Deng sought to expand China's trade, encourage foreign investment, and create opportunities for Chinese students to study abroad. His remarkable record, however, will be marred by his unwillingness to institute political reform and his responsibility for the Tiananmen massacre in June 1989. He died on February 19, 1997, in Beijing.

Hu Yaobang (Hu Yao-pang, 1915–1989)

Long a member of the CCP, Hu served as general secretary of the CCP from 1981 to 1987. Born in November 1915 (the exact date is unknown) in Liuyang, Hunan Province, Hu joined the CCP as a teenager and spent his career prior to the Cultural Revolution focused on youth work. A veteran of the Long March, he served in the Eighteenth Army Corps from 1941 to 1948, worked briefly in Taiyuan city administration, and then rejoined the army to serve in Sichuan Province from 1950 to 1952. He was on the CCP Central Committee from 1949 to 1964 and the Sino-Soviet Friendship Association's executive board from 1949 to 1954. From 1952 to 1957 he led several international youth delegations.

Hu was purged during the Cultural Revolution, then rehabilitated in 1975–1976. He did not return to high office until 1979 when he was elevated to the Politburo, with Deng Xiaoping's support, where he remained until his death. Hu was appointed to the Politburo Standing Committee in 1980, the post of chairman of the CCP in 1981, and then secretary-general of the Central Committee in 1982. He served in the latter position until 1987 when he was dismissed for "bourgeois liberalization" and for having supported student protests in December 1986.

Along with Zhao Ziyang he was instrumental in carrying out the reforms associated with Deng Xiaoping's policies. His death on April 15, 1989, sparked student-led pro-democracy demonstrations that ended in tragedy in Tiananmen Square in early June.

Hua Guofeng (Hua Kuo-feng, b. 1921)

Hua rose to the top rank of the Chinese leadership to serve as chairman of the CCP (1976–1981) and premier of the PRC (1976–1980). He was born in 1921 in Jiaocheng, Shanxi province, into a family of poor peasants. He completed primary school but is not known to have had any further education. In 1935, when communist forces reached his area following the Long March, he joined their ranks.

He made his early career in Hunan province where he held many posts, was involved in carrying out land reform in the early to mid-1950s, and eventually served as party secretary beginning in 1970. During the Cultural Revolution, with the blessing of Zhou Enlai, he was named to the preparatory group for the establishment of the Revolutionary Committee of Hunan province, and then was designated its vice chairman. At the Ninth Party Congress (April 1969), he was elected a member of the CCP Central Committee and later confirmed in that position in 1973, 1977, and 1982.

Following his election to the Central Committee, Hua moved to Beijing and the center of national politics. In 1973 he became a member of the Politburo, then was appointed deputy prime minister and minister of public security (1975–1976). In February 1976 he was identified as acting premier, in April as premier, and in October as chairman of both the CCP Central Committee and its Military Commission. From 1978 to 1980, he was increasingly involved in foreign affairs, heading delegations abroad. Personally designated by Mao Zedong to succeed him as party chairman, Hua served as a transitional figure between the death of Mao and the emergence of Deng Xiaoping as China's new leader. Hua was responsible for ordering the arrest of the Gang of Four, thereby preventing Mao's widow and her colleagues from seizing power. He hoped to consolidate his own position in the aftermath but was outflanked by the more adroit and connected Deng at the Third Plenary Session of the Eleventh Party Congress in December 1978 and gradually saw his authority reduced. He resigned the premiership in 1980 in favor of Zhao Ziyang, a protégé of Deng, and was replaced as party chairman in September 1982, although he retained his position on the Central Committee. He has been in virtual political retirement since then.

Jiang Qing (Chang Ch'ing, 1913[?]–1991)

Third wife of Mao Zedong and the most influential woman in China during the Cultural Revolution and until Mao's death in 1976, she was the head of the "Gang of Four" that sought to usurp power in Mao's name. Jiang Qing was born in Zhucheng in 1913 or 1914, under the name Li Yunhe. Upon completing elementary school, Jiang enrolled in an acting school in Tai'an, becoming involved with an avant-garde theatrical group in 1929. She moved to Qingdao in 1930, began to associate with the Communist party, and in 1931 became a member. Her activities led to her arrest and brief imprisonment in 1933.

Returning to Jinan, she met the film critic Ma Jiliang, whom she married in 1934. For several years thereafter, Jiang acted under the name of Lan Ping in several films produced in Shanghai. All were minor roles. She divorced Ma Jiliang in 1937 following an affair with a film director; the entire matter was scandalous and was widely publicized in the Shanghai press.

With the outbreak of the Sino-Japanese War that same year, Jiang fled to Chongqing where she worked for the Nationalist-controlled Central Movie Studio, although shortly she headed for Yan'an and the central base of the CCP. At Yan'an she found work at the Lu Xun Art Institute, met Mao Zedong, and within less than a year married the party leader. Their affair met strong resistance from old party cadres because Mao was still married to He Zizhen, a woman who had shared with him some of the worst trials in the history of the CCP, including the Long March. A compromise was worked out eventually by which Mao's divorce from He Zizhen and marriage to Jiang Qing were approved, so long as Jiang stayed out of politics and restricted her role to that of housewife.

Despite the compromise, Jiang began to assume more-public roles by the early 1960s. In 1962 she embarked on an ambitious project to reform the Beijing Opera by instilling revolutionary content into its classical form. Mao encouraged her in this undertaking. In 1966 she was identified as a cultural adviser to the People's Liberation Army and as one of the leading advocates of the Cultural Revolution.

In April 1969, as the Cultural Revolution wound down and order was being restored throughout the country, Jiang was elected member of the Politburo and the Central Committee. She was reconfirmed in these positions in 1973. Plotting to seize power, she and her closest comrades comprising the "Gang of Four" were purged in October 1976, not long after Mao's death. She was sentenced to death with a two-year reprieve and permanent deprivation of political rights in January 1981; two years later, her death sentence was reduced to life imprisonment under house arrest. She died on May 14, 1991, rumored to have committed suicide.

Jiang Zemin (Chiang Tse-min, b. 1926)

Named general secretary of the CCP in 1989 and president of the PRC in 1993, Jiang is dedicated to continuing the policies and directions of Deng Xiaoping. Born in 1926 in Yangzhou, Jiangsu province, Jiang was trained as an electrical engineer, graduating from a Shanghai university in 1946. That same year he joined the CCP. His party work began when he was appointed director of the Northeast Military Region's Military Engineering Department in 1950 and then commercial counselor at the Chinese embassy in Moscow from 1950 to 1956, where he was also a trainee at the Stalin Automobile Factory. He held an array of posts in automotive, machine building, and electronics industries from the 1950s to the mid-1980s.

Jiang was elected to the Twelfth Central Committee in 1982 and the Thirteenth Party Congress's Presidium and Politburo in 1987. From 1985 to 1988, he was mayor of Shanghai. Following the student pro-democracy demonstrations of 1989, the suppression of which he supported, he moved to Beijing and replaced Zhao Ziyang as CCP secretary-general and Deng Xiaoping as chairman of the CCP Central Military Commission (1990). In the process, he was proclaimed by Deng as the "core" of the third generation leaders. Jiang also has become president of the PRC. As the most prominent figure in Chinese politics since Deng's death, he has maintained his predecessor's general policies: encouraging economic relations with the

West but remaining tough on dissent, and continuing free-market economic reforms while preserving the CCP's monopoly on political power.

Li Dazhao (Li Ta-chao, 1888–1927)

A major influence on China's youth at the time of the May Fourth Movement and founding member of the Chinese Communist Party. Born on October 6, 1888 in Loting, Hubei province, Li was orphaned when quite young and reared by his grandparents. He enrolled in middle school in his home town at age sixteen, and two years later moved to Tianjin to attend the Beiyang School of Law and Government, from which he graduated in 1913. To continue his education, Li was sent to Japan where he enrolled in Waseda University in Tokyo and began writing articles on political and economic themes for a Chinese magazine. He became an outspoken opponent of Yuan Shikai's regime and of Japanese pressure on China, calling on students to resist the Twenty-One Demands that Japan issued in 1915.

Following his return home in 1916, he joined other progressives in an association devoted to constitutional research. Under its auspices, Li became editor of a newspaper that soon acquired a reputation for liberalism. He also became a member of the editorial staff of *New Youth*, the major periodical of the literary and cultural movements sweeping China. In February 1918 he accepted an offer to serve as head of Peking University's library. Subsequently, he served the institution as professor of history, economics, and political science.

In October 1918, a year after the Bolshevik seizure of power, Li wrote an essay in which he declared his support for the Marxist experiment in Russia. That same year he founded a Marxist research society, and in May 1919 edited a special issue of *New Youth* devoted exclusively to Marxism. His own introduction to that issue made clear his sympathy for Marxism's aims, though he remained unconvinced of its general validity. By mid-1920, however, he had lost his doubts and seems to have accepted the Marxist viewpoint fully. Convinced that further study was needed, Li created the Society for the Study of Marxism in the summer of 1920, at whose meetings he and other professors gave lectures to interested university students.

Li believed at that time that Marxist study was more important than actual political organization, but his view gradually changed under the influence of Chen Duxiu. Having moved to Shanghai, Chen was actively engaged in organizing a communist party cell, with plans to establish a network of nuclei in major cities as a prelude to formal organization of a communist party. To organize Beijing, Chen turned to Li.

During the winter of 1920–1921, Li brought together a group of students to deliver the Marxist message to railway workers in northern China. Working with colleagues in Shanghai and Canton, he helped plan the congress of communists that met in that city in July 1921. Unable to attend that first congress or its second a year later, he was nevertheless elected to the party's Central Committee and participated in a special plenum of the organization that met in Hangzhou in August 1922 to discuss the Comintern's new policy of cooperation with the GMD. Li's position accorded with that of the Comintern, leading him to play an active role in implementing the policy that dominated CCP-GMD relations between 1922 and 1926. His view was important in persuading Sun Yat-sen to accept the entente, and his personal prestige made him a prominent leader in both parties.

Li continued to direct CCP activities in north China into early 1927, when the Manchurian warlord, Zhang Zuolin, raided the Soviet embassy, seized Li, and placed him under arrest. Along with nineteen comrades, he was hanged on April 28.

An early martyr to the communist cause, Li was much more of a theoretician than an organizer. Despite his ultimate commitment to Marxist doctrine, he did not believe that China's small proletariat could by itself lead the revolution that China needed. Instead, he favored broadening the revolutionary social base to include as many as possible, especially the Chinese peasants. In the end, his nationalism remained more significant than his Marxism in shaping his worldview and revolutionary consciousness.

Li Lisan (Li Li-san, 1900–1967)

One of the leading labor organizers in the early history of the CCP, and Mao Zedong's chief rival for leadership within the CCP before 1930. He became de facto head of the party in 1928. Born in 1900, Li's family background is obscure, although we know that his father was a poor rural teacher in Hunan province. The boy, whose original name was Li Longzhi, received some secondary schooling in Changsha. Around 1919 Li went to France on the work-study program popular among Chinese youth at the time, but information is sketchy about his early activities while abroad. By 1921 he was in Paris, joining Zhou Enlai and others in organizing the Chinese Communist Youth party. His work involved heading the party's propaganda department and editing its newspaper.

Following his expulsion from France for engaging in a demonstration protesting a French loan to the Beijing government, Li returned to China, arriving in Shanghai to take up work as a labor organizer. Not long after, he was sent to Jiangxi province to work among coal miners. That work ended in 1924 following troop suppression of a strike that he had helped organize.

Returning to Shanghai, Li continued to work as a labor agitator for about a year before fleeing to Canton in September 1925. The following March he was sent to Moscow to attend the fourth session of the Communist International Federation of Trade Unions. Upon returning to China, he was elected vice president of the All-China Federation of Labor (May 1926). His attention soon turned to organizing an unsuccessful uprising in August against the GMD in Nanjing. Leaving the city with communist forces, Li then took part in an equally unsuccessful attempt to seize Shantou (Swatow). In the aftermath, along with Zhou Enlai and others, he fled to Hong Kong.

Rising rapidly in the CCP, Li began to develop a series of policies that later became known as the "Li Lisan line." Believing that conditions were ripe for revolution in China, he argued that the key to its success would be large-scale uprisings in major cities (beginning with Wuhan) by organized labor, supported by the Red Army and even peasants, but not led by them. While Li's argument about the role of the proletariat was classically Marxist, it contradicted that increasingly articulated by Mao Zedong, who was placing his emphasis on rural China and guerrilla warfare from the countryside. By insisting also that events in China would lead to "world revolution" and the final phase of global class struggle, Li put himself at odds with the Comintern.

By September 1930, efforts to implement Li's views proved unsuccessful. Attacks on Nanjing were repulsed and seizure of Changsha lasted little more than a week. In light of these developments, the CCP Central Committee met to reconsider Li's policies. Li was criticized, particularly by Zhou Enlai, for deviating from Comintern tactics, though not in aims. Following the meeting, Li was sent to Moscow to face accusations that he had also violated Comintern doctrines. Acknowledging his guilt, Li was subsequently expelled from the CCP Political Bureau, and spent the next fifteen years in exile in the USSR. Although he enjoyed a modicum of political rehabilitation in the late 1940s (he served as minister of labor for several years after 1949), he never returned to the level of influence he held before 1930. Further conflict with other party leaders led to his resignation from the ministry in 1954. Reports are that he committed suicide in 1967 when he was subjected to public attack by supporters of the Cultural Revolution.

Li Peng (Li P'eng, b. 1928)

A ranking member of the CCP, whose conservative views have offered some balance to the reformist positions of Deng Xiaoping and Jiang Zemin.

Li was born in October 1928 in Chengdu, Sichuan province, the son of the writer Li Shuoxun who was executed by the GMD in 1930. From age eleven, Li Peng was the adopted son of Zhou Enlai. Li received part of his education at the Moscow Power Institute in hydroelectric engineering during the late 1940s and early 1950s, and spent much of his subsequent career in the power industry until the 1980s. In that decade he began to assume broader political responsibilities, including being elected to the CCP Central Committee in 1982 and vice premier in 1983. He was elevated to the Politburo in 1985 and became premier in 1988 (replacing Zhao Ziyang after the crushing of the pro-democracy movement), a position he retained until 1994.

Following the crackdown of the pro-democracy movement in 1989, Li led China's efforts to restore its international reputation by heading delegations to India, Europe, Japan, Vietnam, and the United Nations. His experiences in the USSR have made him a key player in relations with Russia and the countries of eastern Europe. He has been a strong proponent of the controversial Three Gorges Dam project. In early 1998 he was replaced as premier by Zhu Rongji, who also is responsible for economic development, but Li remains the second most important figure in the CCP.

Lin Biao (Lin Piao, 1907–1971)

Rose to prominence within the CCP as a Red Army field commander, eventually holding many high government and party posts. A key figure during the Cultural Revolution, Lin was for a time Mao Zedong's heir apparent, before being implicated in a plot to remove Mao. He was born on December 5, 1907, in Huanggang, Hubei province. His family was of peasant stock with modest landholdings. Beginning his education in a village school, Lin subsequently entered middle school in Wuchang in 1921. There he became interested in socialism and began to participate in radical student activities. Following graduation in 1925, he joined the Socialist Youth League in Shanghai.

That same year, he moved to Canton and enrolled in the Whampoa Military Academy. There he first drew the attention of Zhou Enlai, at the time the deputy director of the academy's political department, and soon joined the Communist Youth League. Upon graduation, he was assigned to a regiment attached to the Fourth Army and participated in the first phase of the Northern Expedition launched by Chiang Kai-shek. He forsook Chiang when the latter turned on the Chinese communists. Lin joined the party in 1927.

Lin participated in the Long March in 1934–1935. At the new party headquarters in Yan'an, he once again headed the Red Army Academy.

Wounded in the summer of 1938, he was sent to the Soviet Union for medical treatment. He would remain three years occupying himself with activities that are not known. Returning to China in 1942, he served the party in a number of capacities and was elected to the Central Committee in 1945. During the late 1940s as the Civil War entered its last phase, Lin's forces were reorganized into the Fourth Field Army that played a central role in the communist victory over the Nationalists.

With the creation of the People's Republic of China on October 1, 1949, Lin was selected a member of the Government Council, and in February 1950 he received command of the entire Central-South Military Region. In 1954 he was elected a deputy to the National People's Congress and then assumed the posts of vice premier of the State Council and vice chairman of the National Defense Council. In April 1955 he was elected to the Politburo and in September 1955 was named a marshal of the PRC. By 1958 he was vice chairman of the Central Committee, thereby making him a member of the Politburo's Standing Committee and the sixth-ranking leader of the CCP. In September 1959 he replaced Peng Dehuai as Minister of Defense and held other major positions that helped determine military policy. In those positions, he began reforming the army and intensifying the political education of its soldiers.

In late 1961, as Mao Zedong was preparing the foundation for the Cultural Revolution, Lin instigated a campaign known as the "Four Firsts," consisting of four fundamental relationships—between weapons and men, political and other work, routine political work and ideological work, and theory and practice. The campaign opened the way for the PLA to be involved in political activity, just when Mao was looking for support from outside the CCP. "Learn from the People's Liberation Army" became a rallying slogan for Chinese society generally that in conjunction with the unchallengeable "Thought of Mao Zedong" was at the heart of the Cultural Revolution. Lin's support of Mao earned him a central role during the Cultural Revolution and status as the second ranking member of the CCP behind Mao himself, replacing Liu Shaoqi in August 1966 as Mao's heir apparent.

By 1971 Lin and the army had amassed more authority than Mao seemed to believe appropriate. Fearing that he and others within the high command were about to be purged, Lin apparently plotted a coup that was discovered. Fleeing to the Soviet Union, his plane was reported to have crashed in Mongolia on September 13, with all aboard killed. The truthfulness of this account has been questioned, but Lin's death remains uncontested, and with it ended a potentially dangerous power struggle.

Liu Shaoqi (Liu Shao-ch'i, 1898–1969)

Liu rose in the CCP hierarchy to become chairman of the PRC from 1959 to 1968 and be recognized as Mao Zedong's heir apparent until being purged during the Cultural Revolution. Born in 1898 in Ningxiang district, Hunan province, his parents were peasant landowners. His primary education was in the Chinese classics followed by attendance at a normal school in Changsha (1916–1918) at which Mao Zedong and Li Lisan were also enrolled. Hoping to travel to France for further education, he went to north China to study French, but for reasons not clear he changed his plans, returning to Hunan instead. The next couple of years were spent between Hunan and Shanghai with Liu joining the Socialist Youth League, making contact with Comintern operatives, being arrested, and studying Russian. In the winter of 1920, he was chosen to accompany a small group of Chinese youth to the Soviet Union where, in 1921, they were enrolled in the Communist University for Toilers of the East in Moscow. That same year Liu joined the Communist party.

The following spring he returned to China. The party assigned him to help organize labor first in Shanghai and then among miners in Anyuan, where Li Lisan was also working. In the winter of 1923, Liu went to Canton to prepare for the implementation of the GMD-CCP alliance. He managed to avoid the fate (arrest and even execution) of other labor organizers and union members during Chiang Kai-shek's anticommunist drive that began in April 1927, and he continued to rise in the CCP hierarchy. Late in April he was elected to the party's Central Committee and in May became general secretary of the All-China Federation of Labor. For the next several years, Liu worked as an underground agent in Nationalist-controlled areas.

In the autumn of 1932, he moved from Shanghai to the main communist base in Jiangxi, helping to organize rural workers in the workshops supplying communist forces. His growing status within the movement is reflected in his election to the Politburo in January 1934. He participated on the Long March from Jiangxi to Yan'an, but did not remain in the new central base. Instead, he was sent to work in areas still controlled by the Nationalists. Between 1936 and 1942, Liu served as head of several regions (north China, central plains, and central China) for the Central Committee, still in an underground capacity. In the same period, he wrote an important report, entitled "How to Be a Good Communist" (1939), that helped expand the notion of the proletariat. Liu argued that a person may acquire a proletarian outlook regardless of his socioeconomic background because proletarianism is a product of one's state of mind as shaped by self-discipline, self-examination, self-criticism, and self-cultivation. In view of the Japanese invasion of China, Liu's argument had the additional value of making nationalism—also a state of mind—as important as class struggle in rallying Chinese.

Returning to Yan'an in early 1943, Liu was named vice chairman of the People's Revolutionary Military Council and a member of the five-man Secretariat of the Central Committee (along with Mao Zedong, Zhu De, Zhou Enlai, and Ren Bishi). His work focused on problems of organization and party structure, reflected in a lengthy report, entitled "On the Party," that he delivered in May 1945. In it, he affirmed the party's commitment to the principle of "democratic centralism" that Lenin had proclaimed in 1902, while also declaring the thought of Mao Zedong to be the core of the party's ideology. Probably for his dedication, Liu became the third-ranking member of the Central Committee, behind Mao and Zhu De, as well as vice chairman of the Politburo.

At the completion of the Civil War, and with the creation of the People's Republic of China on October 1, 1949, Liu was selected as second vice chairman of the new government, adding that position to his already held post of general secretary of the party Secretariat. When the government was reorganized in 1954, Liu became chairman of the standing committee of the National People's Congress, making him the highest responsible figure over all government organs. When Mao announced in December 1958 that he intended to relinquish his governmental responsibilities, Liu was elected Chairman of the PRC the following April. This act, combined with the official description of Liu as Mao's "closest comrade in arms," seemed to ensure that Liu was being groomed to succeed Mao as chairman of the CCP as well.

Despite his growing visibility in both domestic and foreign affairs, Liu became the chief victim of the Cultural Revolution. Beginning in 1966, he was the target of increasingly severe criticism from Mao and his new-found supporters in the PLA. By August, Lin Biao had emerged as Mao's new heir apparent, and in December a document was circulated that purported to be a political confession made by Liu at a Central Committee meeting in October. Many people (including Peng Zhen and Deng Xiaoping) associated with Liu and many organizations that provided him with his base of support were purged or subjected to mounting public demonstrations. In October 1968, Liu was stripped of his party positions and declared to be a "capitalist roader" and "China's Khrushchev." Placed under house arrest, he died on November 12, 1969 in Kaifeng. Following Mao's death in 1976, the failed coup by the Gang of Four, and Deng Xiaoping's rehabilitation and emergence as China's preeminent political figure, Liu was partially rehabilitated when the Gang of Four was accused of "concocting false evidence" and subjecting him to a "political frame-up and physical persecution."

Mao Zedong (Mao Tse-tung, 1893–1976)

The principal theoretician and for many years the unchallenged leader of the Chinese communist movement. Born December 26, 1893, in the village of Shaoshan, Hunan province, Mao was the eldest child of an erstwhile poor peasant who had become modestly prosperous as a farmer and grain dealer. His early education was in the village school, which he left at age thirteen in order to work on the family farm. His father's strictness and inflexibility, however, encouraged Mao to leave the farm to live with his mother's family and enroll in the Tongshan Higher Primary School. He subsequently moved to Changsha to enter middle school.

In June 1918 he graduated from the Hunan Fourth Provincial Normal School and was encouraged to go to Beijing to the university. Upon arriving in the capital, he was introduced to Li Dazhao, recently appointed university librarian, but more important for his influence on students and, subsequently, for his evolving interest in Marxism and his role in forming the first Marxist cell in Beijing. The six months that Mao spent at the university coincided with the culmination of the May Fourth Movement. When Mao returned to Beijing in 1920 after being away in Shanghai and Changsha, Li had moved leftward in his political thought, and Mao followed him. In May he again went to Shanghai to work with students organized against the warlord controlling Hunan. There he met Chen Duxiu, a colleague of Li Dazhao and an intellectual also moving in the direction of Marxism. Mao later wrote that he considered himself a Marxist from 1920 onward.

In July 1921 Mao went to Shanghai as a representative of Hunan to attend the inaugural meeting of the Chinese Communist party. Two years later, when the party entered an alliance with Sun Yat-sen's Guomindang party, Mao was an early supporter of the alliance, joining the GMD and becoming an alternate member of its Executive Bureau. Meanwhile, at the Third National Congress of the CCP, meeting at Canton in June 1923, Mao was elected to the Central Committee and named director of the organization department. Toward the end of 1924, he became ill and returned to his native village for a rest.

Taking up party work once again in the early months of 1925, he began to organize peasant associations, thereby commencing his long involvement with the class that he soon believed was the key to China's revolutionary success. But his work attracted the attention of the authorities, forcing him to flee to Canton, the main power base of the GMD. There he became director of the Peasant Movement Training Institute, a school supervised by the peasant department of the GMD. He also served as acting head of the GMD's propaganda department, editing its leading organ, the *Political Weekly*.

In November 1926 Mao returned to Hunan, and several months later he was investigating the peasant movement that was showing remarkable vitality. His observations were compiled in a "Report on an Investigation of the Peasant Movement in Hunan" that predicted an uprising so elemental and forceful that nothing would be able to stop it. Notwithstanding Mao's prediction, other developments were about to plunge the communist movement into one of its worst experiences. In the summer of 1927 the alliance between the GMD and CCP was verging on collapse, and the CCP was nearly destroyed when its erstwhile ally turned against it. In response, Mao led several hundred followers out of central Hunan to the border region with Jiangxi to form a new base from which to direct a new type of revolutionary warfare in the countryside.

For the next three years or so, Mao worked closely with Zhu De, commander-in-chief of the army, to develop the tactics of guerrilla warfare from base areas in the countryside. In large measure, the two men had little choice, cut off as they were from the cities that seemed to be the more appropriate sites for revolutionary activity from a Marxist perspective, and left with few resources with which to further the revolution. The CCP leadership was barely sympathetic to Mao's and Zhu's strategy, continuing to believe that rural agitation was a stopgap measure until such time as the real agitation, among industrial workers in the cities, could be pursued more energetically and fully. Mao, however, also was inspired by his earlier discovery that the peasants could, if properly led, become a revolutionary force. When in the summer of 1930 he was ordered to send his troops to occupy several major cities in south central China, and the effort was proving unsuccessful, Mao disobeyed orders and abandoned the battle to return to his rural stronghold.

In November 1931 Mao was involved in the founding of the Chinese Soviet Republic in a portion of Jiangxi province and became its chairman. The focus of Mao and his colleagues now was on strengthening the movement's base areas and control of rural populations. Despite near continuous pressure from the GMD, the project was rather successful, with the Red Army growing to around 200,000 men. Chiang Kai-shek's military, however, finally was able to overwhelm Mao's defenses and force him to abandon Jiangxi in autumn of 1934 and head out with most of his supporters on a Long March that ended up a year later in Yan'an, Shaanxi province.

The trek, which later became part of the folklore of the communist revolution, was conducted under terrible conditions that left the movement with only about 8,000 troops with which to begin rebuilding. It also provided the conditions under which Mao emerged as the undisputed leader of the party, a role that he would enhance over the next several years by writing some of his most important works ("On Practice," "On Contradiction," *On Protracted War*, and *Strategic Problems of China's Revolutionary War*), by consciously working to "sinify" the revolutionary movement in China through his writings and the Rectification Campaign of 1942–1943, and by elevating himself into a recognized party theoretician.

During those same years, the relationship between the GMD and CCP once more took a major turn under the threat of Japanese invasion and encouragement from Moscow. A second united front was agreed upon, reluctantly by Chiang Kai-shek, but with pragmatic assent from Mao and other communist leaders who saw in it some value for the short term. The alliance relieved some of the military pressure that Chiang wished to continue putting on his communist antagonists and permitted Mao and his associates to focus more of their resources on disrupting the Japanese presence in north China and consolidating their own presence among the Chinese people. The latter was furthered by shifts in CCP policies that now emphasized reform to improve the lives of peasants rather than revolution, and appealed to nationalist sentiment as a means for rallying the country.

In March 1943 Mao became chairman of both the CCP Secretariat and Politburo. The Rectification Campaign, already underway, for a time became a vehicle for purging party cadres showing insufficient loyalty to Mao, in some ways establishing a pattern that would be repeated especially after 1949.

Defeat of Japan was followed in China by a breakdown of the united front policy and resumption of the civil war between the CCP and GMD. The communist triumph in that struggle reflected the greater discipline of its organization and the wider popular support that it had acquired during the Yan'an period. When Mao declared the establishment of the People's Republic of China in Beijing on October 1, 1949, the way was now open for a thoroughgoing reconstruction and redirection of the country. What had become identified with Mao—a rural-based strategy that relied upon the energy and support of the peasants—was widely recognized as the reason for the success of the communist revolution, and it was Mao who received the accolades and who garnered the popular respect.

But governing a vast country is different from being in opposition, and the CCP was faced with deep economic, social, and political problems that demanded immediate attention. The goal of building a socialist country was for a few years after 1949 put off in favor of economic and infrastructural reconstruction that would restore order and stability and set the stage for more dramatic changes. By 1952–1953 the party was ready to move into a more aggressive phase of socialist construction by following the Soviet model and introducing centralized planning in the form of the First Five Year Plan.

Mao's support for this stage was evident; he already had warned the country that although its revolution had been somewhat unorthodox in its path and had relied upon the "countryside encircling the cities," it would for the near future take the orthodox road of the cities leading and guiding the countryside. Despite its successes in achieving many of the goals scheduled for the plan, within two years Mao began having doubts about some of its aspects and their consequences.

Worried that the very success of centralized planning, with its emphasis on leadership, expertise, education, and technicalism would actually stifle the revolution and lead to a restoration of social realities that it was designed to eliminate, Mao reversed his position and began arguing that the social transformation of China could, and should, occur before its economic transformation. When mobilized for revolutionary goals, he came to believe, the people could transcend their limited material resources and lead the country in transforming social relations by dint of their will. The corrupting influences of technical progress could thus be thwarted and genuine progress toward a truly egalitarian society be made.

This represents some of the basic thinking behind a campaign that Mao launched in May 1958 known as the Great Leap Forward. It also helps explain later campaigns, such as the Great Proletarian Cultural Revolution (1966–1969), that he endorsed and that were designed to bypass party and governmental organs as a means of upsetting the "normal" trajectory of development that most expected to be followed. Much of the PRC's history down to Mao's death on September 9, 1976, is a reflection of this politics, including the ongoing tensions among the top leaders who were divided between the Maoists and the more pragmatic like Liu Shaoqi, Deng Xiaoping, and Peng Chen. Loyalty to Mao's vision became the criterion by which one's usefulness and fate would be determined. The requirement of adulation, of a personality cult, grew naturally from Mao's insistence on the correctness of his truth alone, leaving his legacy, like that of Joseph Stalin in the USSR, heavy, costly, and painful for tens of millions.

Sun Yat-sen (Sun Yixian, 1866–1925)

Sun is generally regarded by Chinese of all political persuasions as the father of modern China and its twentieth-century revolution. Sun was born November 12, 1866, in the village of Choyhung, Guangdong province, about thirty miles north of Macao. Except for a brief stint as a tailor in Macao, his father was by occupation a peasant. When six years old, Sun Yat-sen began his formal education at a village school, where he took up the Chinese classics. In 1879, however, he was sent to Hawaii to join his elder brother, who was a prosperous farmer and merchant. In Hawaii, Sun Yat-sen was enrolled in a British-sponsored school from which he graduated in 1882, having been exposed to Western-style education and Christian religious principles. Returning to his home village in China, he was disturbed by the traditional religious beliefs of the villagers, and when he defaced an idol in a village temple, he was expelled.

He then lived for a couple of years in Hong Kong, though we know little of his activities. He did continue his education and was baptized a Christian, before returning briefly to his home village to accept an arranged marriage to a local girl. Following a second trip to Hawaii, he returned to Canton and entered the medical school attached to a Western hospital. His stay was shortlived, succeeded by a move to Hong Kong and five further years of medical studies. After graduating and trying to begin a practice in Macao, Sun moved to Hong Kong in 1893 to begin his profession.

By the early 1890s Sun was involving himself in potentially subversive discussions with friends who shared an antipathy for the Manchu rulers of China and a concern for the country's ability to defend itself against international pressure. For now his approach was reformist, but when war broke out with Japan and Japanese troops threatened Beijing itself, Sun joined a secret revolutionary group (the Furen Literary Society), whose basic aim was to organize a revolt against the dynasty and establish a republican form of government. An uprising was planned for Canton in 1895, but on the day preceding the scheduled event it was uncovered by authorities. Although some of the conspirators were arrested, others, including Sun, escaped to Hong Kong and then Japan.

This episode marked the beginning of Sun's career as a revolutionary, and he would spend the next sixteen years abroad, unable to return home, pursuing his new profession. In early 1896 he was in Hawaii, but then spent the next year in the United States and especially England before returning to Japan by way of Canada in July 1897. In Japan he planned a series of uprisings relying upon the support of secret societies in central and southern China as well as collaborators in Japan itself. An uprising in the Huichou area about 150 miles east of Canton erupted in October 1900, with Sun in Taiwan, but it failed. Sun spent the next three years living quietly in Yokohama, Japan.

The influx of Chinese students to Japan in the first years of the twentieth century provided a new and larger audience for Sun's views and organizational activities. He saw these students, however, as part of a larger support group among overseas Chinese generally. Their enthusiasm and anti-Manchu sentiments prompted him to renew his efforts to extend the network of revolutionary activity among such Chinese first in Southeast Asia, then in the continental United States and Hawaii, and several countries of Europe. In each place he set up new branches of his revolutionary organization, at the time known as the Revive China Society. In 1905 he became head of a revolutionary coalition known as Tongmenghui (United League), founded in Tokyo.

The fortunes of Tongmenghui and the Chinese revolutionary movement generally were dismal despite the fervor of its participants. The party was poorly organized—in part a reflection of one of Sun's personal weaknesses—and attempted revolts hatched in various countries all failed. Increasingly, Sun found himself a *persona non grata* in Japan, French Indochina, and Hong Kong, prompting him to spend the year 1909–1910 touring Europe and the United States. Returning to Asia in 1910, he left shortly thereafter once more for the West in order to raise money for an attempt to capture Canton for the revolution. The so-called March 29 Revolution (according to the Chinese calendar, April 27 according to the Western calendar) proved as unsuccessful as previous efforts.

What did help the revolution were the consequences of reforms and other policies that the Qing dynasty has been pursuing since 1905. These affected the military, educational system, and the organization of governmental units; moreover, they led to the introduction of provincial and national assemblies that naturally drew popular support away from the monarchy. In 1911 armed rebellion broke out in Sichuan province when the Qing decided to nationalize all the trunk railways. By October a second rebellion had broken out spontaneously in Wuhan that succeeded in overthrowing the provincial government. Other provincial uprisings followed quickly.

In the United States while these events were transpiring, Sun returned to Shanghai in December and was elected provisional president of a new Chinese republic by delegates meeting in Nanking. Concerned that the revolution lacked sufficient strength to avoid a civil war, Sun relinquished his title to the military commander and imperial minister, Yuan Shikai. Within three days—February 12–14, 1912—the Qing emperor abdicated, Sun resigned as president, and Yuan was elected his successor.

What proved a marriage of convenience between Yuan and the revolution began to unravel almost immediately. Sun openly opposed Yuan in March 1913, but failing to topple him, had to flee to Japan. Several developments there weakened Sun's popular support. First, he promised the Japanese major concessions in China in return for aid (not forthcoming) to the revolution; second, he began requiring revolutionaries to take an oath of personal allegiance to him; and third, he married his secretary without divorcing his first wife.

Circumstances in China did not improve following Yuan's defeat in 1916 but increasingly were complicated by the failure of central government and the growing local/regional authority of warlords. Sun's efforts to further the revolution over the next seven years were shaped and inhibited by these realities. Meanwhile, the Bolshevik Revolution in Russia and the subsequent creation of the Soviet Union gave Sun a potential new ally just as he was growing disillusioned with the West. Conversations with the Soviet diplomat, Adolf Joffe, in 1922 and 1923 led to public declaration by the USSR that it had no territorial interest in China, that it was willing to relinquish its concessions there, and that it did not believe that a communist revolution was suitable for China. In addition, the groundwork was laid for cooperation between the Chinese Communist Party and the Guomindang (as the Tongmenghui was known since 1913). For Sun, his Soviet contacts led him in early 1924 to reorganize the GMD into a much more tightly disciplined party with a hierarchy of authority on the pattern of the Soviet Communist party as originally formulated by Lenin in 1902. To accompany his party reorganization, Sun delivered a series of lectures that contained the fundamentals of his ideology, known popularly as the "three people's principles" (nationalism, democracy, and the people's livelihood).

Despite his efforts, Sun continued to meet resistance both within the GMD and in the larger world of Chinese politics. His death from cancer on March 12, 1925, occurred before the alliance between the CCP and GMD collapsed into civil war.

Zhao Ziyang (Chao Tzu-yang, b. 1919)

Part of the generation of CCP members being groomed for top-level positions, Zhao served as secretary-general of the party from 1987 until the Tiananmen events of 1989, when he was ousted and placed under house arrest for excessive sympathy toward the student demonstrators. Zhao was born on October 17, 1919, in Hua county, Honan province, under the name Zhao Xiusheng. His father was a landlord. Zhao received an elementary education in his hometown between 1928 and 1936 and then attended middle schools in Kaifeng and Wuhan, but for only a year. Zhao joined the Communist Youth League in 1932 and the CCP in 1938. Prior to 1949 he held a variety of provincial posts, including that of CCP secretary of the third Special District in the Hebei-Shandong Border Region (1940) and CCP secretary of Luoyang District in Henan province (1948–1949).

After 1949 Zhao spent much of his career prior to the Cultural Revolution in Guangdong province, where he became first party secretary (1964) and gained renown for his role in implementing successful land reform.

During the Cultural Revolution, he was attacked sharply as a counterrevolutionary revisionist supporter of Liu Shaoqi and was paraded through the streets of Guangzhou by Red Guards. He was denounced publicly on October 16, 1967. The first sign of his political rehabilitation came in May 1971, when he was identified as CCP secretary of the Inner Mongolia Autonomous Region. In less than two years (1973) he was back in Guangdong as a party secretary and was elected a member of the CCP Central Committee. In 1975 he became first party secretary of Sichuan province, one of the country's most productive and populated agricultural regions. In that post, he introduced radical and successful market-oriented rural reforms, allowing peasants to expand their private plots. He also implemented innovative policies that rewarded workers on the basis of work performance rather than need and used material incentives to encourage individual initiative. Because factory managers were provided greater autonomy, the authority of central officials to set production quotas was undercut. These successes thrust him into national attention and led to his being named a Politburo alternate (1977), full member (1979), and premier (1980), replacing Hua Guofeng in the latter position.

In the 1980s he became the major architect of Deng Xiaoping's economic reforms (under the slogan of the "four modernizations"), effectively extending his Sichuan policies throughout all of China. Peasants were given much more control over and responsibility for their production and profits, and industrial enterprises by the thousands were provided increased self-management. The results were rapid increases in both agricultural and light-industrial production, the very areas that had long suffered from Mao Zedong's concern for political correctness rather than productivity.

Zhao replaced Hu Yaobang as secretary-general of the CCP in 1987 when the former was blamed for the student-led protests of the previous year; at the same time, Li Peng, much more conservative and cautious, was named premier. As secretary-general, Zhao continued to support economic development by loosening governmental controls over the economy and encouraging creation of special economic zones along the country's coastal regions. But he became a political casualty himself during the Tiananmen Square demonstrations in 1989 for displaying too much sympathy for the student protesters and refusing to sanction the use of force against them. Deng Xiaoping, as paramount leader, threw his support to Li Peng, who imposed martial law and then used armed forces to crush the protesters. On June 24, 1989, Zhao was formally dismissed from his party and government posts and replaced as secretary-general by Jiang Zemin. He is reported to be living under house arrest but has retained his party membership despite official investigations of his political errors.

Zhou Enlai (Chou En-lai, 1898–1976)

The leading international spokesman for the PRC, serving for many years as foreign minister and as the principal executive officer in the central government. Zhou was born in 1898 in Huai'an, Jiangxi province, where his family belonged to the local gentry and owned a small business. His father passed the traditional civil service examination but never held a government post. Following the death of the father, the family's fortunes declined. Under the more difficult circumstances, Zhou was sent to live with an uncle in Zhejiang province, where he received a primary education. He attended middle school in Tianjin. In those years he read deeply in the writings of strongly nationalist scholars of the early Qing period, such as Gu Yanwu (1613–1682), who opposed the Manchu takeover of the empire in 1644. He graduated in 1917 and the following autumn went to live in Tokyo where he studied Japanese and enrolled in Waseda University. By the next year, he had moved to Kyoto and attended lectures on economics, including the economic theories of Marx.

After the outbreak of the May Fourth Movement in 1919, Zhou was encouraged to return to China to become editor of a newspaper published by the Tianjin student association. That autumn he enrolled in Nankai University, a new institution. Over the next couple of years, he combined his studies with political activities, including joining a small Marxist discussion group at Beijing University under the guidance of Chen Duxiu and Li Dazhao. Mao Zedong was also a member of that group. A short stint in jail for participating in an anti-Japanese demonstration was followed by participation in a work study program in France. There Zhou continued to examine the range of political theories in search of one that would suit China's needs. At some point, he became a Marxist and began to devote himself totally to political work.

During 1923–1924, he worked to promote the interests of both the CCP and the GMD, then allied in a united front. Although the Chinese students in Europe held many different political views and belonged to a variety of groups, they all were advocates of a strong and unified China and were opposed both to the ineffectual government in Beijing and the foreign powers that exploited China's vulnerabilities at will.

Zhou returned to China in June 1924, settling in Canton after visiting his family. There he was appointed a secretary of the Guangdong provincial committee of the CCP and became deputy director of the political department of the Whampoa Military Academy, then under the command of Chiang Kai-shek. Tensions began to rise between the CCP and GMD during the winter of 1925 and became acute the following spring. For a brief period, Zhou was under arrest, but was released with Chiang Kai-shek's support.

He continued to work to preserve the CCP-GMD alliance, showing early on the skill at compromise that would remain with him all his life.

Zhou assisted Chiang's northern campaign against the warlords by directing a general strike of communist-controlled unions in Shanghai, thereby opening the city to GMD military forces. When Chiang struck against the communists in April 1927, barely a month later, Zhou was again arrested, but in the absence of further investigation of his case, he was quickly set free. According to some sources, he was elected to the Central Committee of the CCP for the first time in 1927 and to its military committee.

In 1928 Zhou traveled to the USSR to attend the Sixth National Congress of the Chinese Communist Party, where he was reelected to the Central Committee. He was also part of the Chinese delegation to the Sixth Congress of the Comintern meeting in Moscow, and for a short time he attended lessons in Marxism-Leninism and revolutionary strategy at Sun Yat-sen University. He did not return to China until 1929.

In January 1931 the central apparatus of the party was seized by a group of young Russian-trained Chinese communists who used their newfound authority to discredit the so-called Li Lisan line that had stressed urban uprisings rather than peasant mobilization. Although he had previously criticized Li's political policies, Zhou was now charged with having done so too leniently. He recanted and was able to retain his several positions in the party organization. Turning its attention to strengthening relations with the rural bases that Mao Zedong and Zhu De had developed in southeastern Jiangxi, the central party apparatus dispatched Zhou to the region in the spring of 1931. For the next three years, he continued to hold prominent positions in the military and political activities of the party.

Faced with renewed GMD military pressure in late 1934, the party was forced to plan for the evacuation of its Jiangxi base. Zhou was increasingly allied with Mao Zedong, becoming the latter's deputy on the military committee, and moved with him on the Long March of CCP forces that finally reached Shensi province in October 1935. Once settled in Shensi, the party adopted a united front policy against Japanese aggression, with Zhou playing a prominent negotiating role with the GMD. A compromise between the two parties was eventually worked out at Xi'an (Sian), during a major incident (December 1936) that witnessed Chiang Kai-shek being held captive by rebellious generals until he agreed to cooperate with the CCP against the Japanese. Zhou was by all accounts instrumental in saving Chiang's life and working out the details of the new CCP-GMD political alliance. During the next year, he mediated the relationship by traveling back and forth between Yan'an and Nanjing.

Zhou spent much of the wartime years serving as principal liaison officer with both the Soviet Union and the GMD. He also was involved in developing strategies to maximize political support for the CCP, particularly among Chinese intellectuals. From such work came the creation of the China Democratic League. The obverse of this work was organized, if subtle, mobilization of anti-Guomindang sentiment. The major tool that Zhou used for both strategies was the New China News Agency, the CCP propaganda center in Chongqing.

The CCP-GMD cooperative policy began to unravel in January 1941 but continued to require Zhou's attention. By the summer of 1943 he was spending more time in Yan'an with the party leadership, but was called upon occasionally to explore possibilities of strengthening what was increasingly a politically tenuous alliance. U.S. involvement in Chinese political life after the close of World War II added new pressure for a negotiated settlement of CCP and GMD differences. But CCP political and military successes by the spring of 1946 made the party leadership, including Zhou, increasingly unlikely to make concessions. In November he left Nanjing for the last time, all but closing off any further negotiations.

With the communist victory in the final phase of the civil war and the creation of the People's Republic of China on October 1, 1949, Zhou assumed a series of prominent government responsibilities while also being appointed as the party's chief spokesman for its dealings with noncommunist groups in China, a position clearly requiring the negotiating skills and experience of someone like Zhou. During the early 1950s he also was involved in campaigns designed to mobilize public support for regime policies and, following his appointment as the country's first foreign minister, became identified with the early development of PRC foreign policy institutions and practice. His work to gain U.N. recognition of the PRC, settle disputes with China's neighbors (especially Pakistan, Burma, and Nepal), and rally support from emerging nations was particularly important. By the second half of the 1950s he also was called upon to mediate frictions within the larger communist bloc and to minimize the impact of the emerging Sino-Soviet dispute, though the latter continued to deteriorate, especially after 1960.

Virtually alone among those closest to Mao Zedong, Zhou managed to survive the ebb and flow of Beijing politics from the late 1950s until his and Mao's deaths only months apart in 1976 (Zhou on January 8). He was never purged from party leadership and was frequently seen as a voice of reason and compromise within that small group. He never, apparently, lost Mao's support despite not being associated with the leader's more radical policies, whether reflected in the Great Leap Forward or the Great Proletarian Cultural Revolution. Since his death, Chinese public opinion has been uniformly positive about his contributions to the revolution and his legacy.

Zhu De (Chu Te, 1886–1976)

One of the CCP's greatest military leaders, Zhu was born on December 18, 1886, in I Long, Sichuan province, into a peasant family. Originally a physical education instructor, Zhu enrolled in the Yunnan Military Academy from which he graduated in 1911. That same year, he took part in the events that overthrew the Qing dynasty and brought an end to the Chinese monarchy. For the next decade, he served in the armies of various warlords in Sichuan and Yunnan provinces, until he grew disillusioned with warlordism and the political fragmentation of the country. In 1922 he went to Europe to study in Germany, both in Berlin and Göttingen. There he joined the CCP.

His political activities earned him expulsion from Germany in 1926, at which time he returned to China. He joined the GMD, concealing his affiliation with the CCP. In August 1927 he participated in the communist-led Nanchang Uprising against the GMD. Although suppressed, the uprising is regarded by communists as marking the birth of the CCP's Red Army. Retreating to Hunan province, Zhu linked his forces with those of Mao Zedong to form the Fourth Red Army. Establishing a base in Jiangxi province (known as the Jiangxi Soviet), Zhu achieved remarkable success in building up the Red Army to more than 200,000 men by 1933. His responsibilities included defending the base from successive GMD attacks (1931–1933) and then serving as commander-in-chief of the Red Army throughout the Long March.

During the Sino-Japanese War, Zhu commanded the Red Army northern forces, renamed the Eighth Route Army, but also had responsibility for all communist military operations directed against the Japanese between 1937 and 1945. With the end of the war and recommencement of the conflict between the Nationalists and communists, Zhu retained command of the latter's forces, renamed the People's Liberation Army (PLA). He held that command until 1954.

Although a Politburo member since 1934, he was never considered a key political figure or contender for power. He is, however, generally recognized as the major architect of the large-scale guerrilla warfare strategy that contributed most to the military success of the CCP. He died on July 6, 1976.

Primary Documents
of the Chinese Revolution

A fundamental tenet of Karl Marx's political philosophy is that the industrial working class, or proletariat, created as a necessary by-product of the emergence and development of capitalism, will lead the socialist revolution to victory against the bourgeoisie. Another is that the socialist revolution will occur organically and inevitably as capitalism matures and generates the conditions for its own demise. In practice, all revolutions thus far produced under Marxism's banner have belied these key assumptions, largely because of the revolutionaries' unyielding arrogance and basic impatience with historical developments. Socioeconomic realities in those societies that have succumbed to "Marxist" revolutions in the twentieth century have been anything but consistent with Marx's expectations and arguments, and the fact that revolutions occurred at all in those places is testimony not to the applicability of Marx's theories but to the power stemming from their being distorted to fit those realities. In sum, the latter reflected societies that were overwhelmingly agrarian with small industrial bases and tiny proletariats.

Mao Zedong proved no different as a Chinese revolutionary. That his Marxism would end up with a Chinese face proves nothing more than that, as theory, Marxism did not fit the China Mao knew and wanted to change—hence his own extensive revisions of theory to match his expectations and needs. It began very early, when still a young man in the 1920s filled with idealism, less wedded to wielding power, and more trusting of the capabilities of the people. With the CCP hewing to a traditional, orthodox Marxist line, a few cadres were working with peasants, founding associations, and providing guidance.

Their successes, coupled with the outbreak of the Autumn Harvest insurrection in Hunan province in September 1927, affirmed to Mao the
significance of peasant revolution.

The following text is from a report that Mao produced following his
on-site investigation of the Hunan events. Its obvious importance is as
evidence of Mao's final conversion to the idea of peasant revolution,
but it is also important in showing Mao's greater inclination at this
early date to bow to peasant leadership, an inclination that would
gradually recede as evidence mounted of the incapacity of peasants to
undertake a revolution, rather than merely an insurrection, without
proper leadership. For the moment, Mao is happy to regard the peasants as the "vanguard of the revolution," a role that would later be
transferred to the CCP. Finally, we cannot ignore Mao's acceptance of
violence as organic to the revolution, epitomized in his famous phrase
"a revolution is not a dinner party."

The text has been edited for inclusion here. Punctuation and spelling are as in the original.

Document 1
REPORT ON AN INVESTIGATION OF THE PEASANT
MOVEMENT IN HUNAN

THE IMPORTANCE OF THE PEASANT PROBLEM

During my recent visit to Hunan I made a first-hand investigation of conditions in the five counties of Xiangdan, Xiangxiang, Hengshan, Liling, and
Zhangsha. In the thirty-two days from January 4 to February 5, I called together fact-finding conferences in villages and county towns, which were
attended by experienced peasants and by comrades working in the peasant
movement, and I listened attentively to their reports and collected a great
deal of material. Many of the hows and whys of the peasant movement were
the exact opposite of what the gentry in Hankou and Zhangsha are saying. I
saw and heard of many strange things of which I had hitherto been unaware.
I believe the same is true of many other places, too. All talk directed against
the peasant movement must be speedily set right. All the wrong measures
taken by the revolutionary authorities concerning the peasant movement
must be speedily changed. Only thus can the future of the revolution be
benefitted. For the present upsurge of the peasant movement is a colossal
event. In a very short time, in China's central, southern, and northern provinces, several hundred million peasants will rise like a mighty storm, like a
hurricane, a force so swift and violent that no power, however great, will be
able to hold it back. They will smash all the trammels that bind them and
rush forward along the road to liberation. They will sweep all the imperial-

ists, warlords, corrupt officials, local tyrants, and evil gentry into their graves. Every revolutionary party and every revolutionary comrade will be put to the test, to be accepted or rejected as they decide. There are three alternatives. To march at their head and lead them? To trail behind them, gesticulating and criticizing? Or to stand in their way and oppose them? Every Chinese is free to choose, but events will force you to make the choice quickly.

GET ORGANIZED!

The development of the peasant movement in Hunan may be divided roughly into two periods with respect to the counties in the province's central and southern parts where the movement has already made much headway. The first, from January to September of last year, was one of organization. In this period, January to June was a time of underground activity, and July to September, when the revolutionary army was driving out Zhao Hengdi, one of open activity. During this period, the membership of the peasant associations did not exceed 300,000–400,000, the masses directly under their leadership numbered little more than a million, there was as yet hardly any struggle in the rural areas, and consequently there was very little criticism of the associations in other circles. . . . The second period, from last October to January of this year, was one of revolutionary action. The membership of the associations jumped to two million and the masses directly under their leadership increased to ten million. . . . Almost half the peasants in Hunan are now organized. In counties like Xiangdan, Xiangxiang, Liuyang, Zhangsha, Liling, Ningxiang, Bingkiang, Xiangyin, Hengshan, Hengyang, Leiyang, Zhenxian and Anhua, nearly all the peasants have combined in the peasant associations or have come under their leadership. It was on the strength of their extensive organization that the peasants went into action and within four months brought about a great revolution in the countryside, a revolution without parallel in history.

DOWN WITH THE LOCAL TYRANTS AND EVIL GENTRY! ALL POWER TO THE PEASANT ASSOCIATIONS!

The main targets of attack by the peasants are the local tyrants, the evil gentry, and the lawless landlords, but in passing they also hit out against patriarchal ideas and institutions, against the corrupt officials in the cities, and against bad practices and customs in the rural areas. In force and momentum the attack is tempestuous; those who bow before it survive and those who resist perish. As a result, the privileges which the feudal landlords enjoyed for thousands of years are being shattered to pieces. Every bit of the dignity and prestige built up by the landlords is being swept into the dust. With the collapse of the power of the landlords, the peasant associations have now become the sole organs of authority and the popular slogan "All power to the peasant associations" has become a reality. . . . Every revolutionary comrade should know that the national revolution requires a great change in the countryside. The Revolution of 1911 did not bring about this change, hence its failure. This change is now taking place, and it is an important factor for the completion of the revolution. Every revolutionary comrade must support it, or he will be taking the stand of counter-revolution.

THE QUESTION OF "GOING TOO FAR"

Then there is another section of people who say, "Yes, peasant associations are necessary, but they are going rather too far." This is the opinion of the middle-of-the-roaders. But what is the actual situation? True, the peasants are in a sense "unruly" in the countryside. Supreme in authority, the peasant association allows the landlord no say and sweeps away his prestige. This amounts to striking the landlord down to the dust and keeping him there. The peasants . . . fine the local tyrants and evil gentry, they demand contributions from them, and they smash their sedan-chairs. People swarm into the houses of local tyrants and evil gentry who are against the peasant association, slaughter their pigs and consume their grain. They even loll for a minute or two on the ivory-inlaid beds belonging to the young ladies in the households of the local tyrants and evil gentry. At the slightest provocation they make arrests, crown the arrested with tall paper-hats, and parade them through the villages, saying, "You dirty landlords, now you know who we are!" Doing whatever they like and turning everything upside down, they have created a kind of terror in the countryside.

This is what some people call "going too far," or "exceeding the proper limits in righting a wrong," or "really too much." Such talk may seem plausible, but in fact it is wrong. First, the local tyrants, evil gentry, and lawless landlords have themselves driven the peasants to this. For ages they have used their power to tyrannize over the peasants and trample them underfoot; that is why the peasants have reacted so strongly. . . .

Secondly, a revolution is not a dinner party, or writing an essay, or painting a picture, or doing embroidery; it cannot be so refined, so leisurely and gentle, so temperate, kind, courteous, restrained and magnanimous. A revolution is an insurrection, an act of violence by which one class overthrows another. A rural revolution is a revolution by which the peasantry overthrows the power of the feudal landlord class. Without using the greatest force, the peasants cannot possibly overthrow the deep-rooted authority of the landlords which has lasted for thousands of years. The rural areas need a mighty revolutionary upsurge, for it alone can rouse the people in their millions to become a powerful force. . . . To put it bluntly, it is necessary to cre-

ate terror for a while in every rural area, or otherwise it would be impossible
to suppress the activities of the counter-revolutionaries in the countryside or
overthrow the authority of the gentry.

Source: Selected Readings from the Works of Mao Tsetung (Peking: Foreign Language
Press, 1971), 23–39. Written March 1927.

Below is the partial text of a speech that Mao Zedong delivered to the
Eleventh Session (enlarged) of the Supreme State Conference, February 27, 1957. According to Chinese sources, Mao later went over the
speech and made certain additions before its publication in *Renmin Ribao* (*The People's Daily*), in June of the same year.

The background to this speech was one of high expectations for
faster economic growth and broader movement along the socialist path
(particularly in agriculture), accompanied by a growing debate among
the highest party leaders over the proper relationship between the
CCP and China's intellectuals. International events, particularly Soviet
Premier Nikita Khrushchev's denunciation in a "secret" speech in February 1956 of Joseph Stalin's "cult of personality" and numerous other
abuses of power, as well as the uprising in Hungary in October of that
same year, added to the intensity of debate at this very important juncture in post-1949 Chinese history. The issue of China's intellectuals
was framed in relationship to the country's current conditions: Could
the party relax its controls over intellectuals and allow them to criticize public policy and even the CCP itself on the argument that their
contribution to China's unity and achievement remained great, or
should they be subject to even tighter discipline because the party no
longer needed their talents and so no longer needed to consider their
morale or sensibilities?

Mao headed the group, which included Zhou Enlai, Chen Yun, Deng
Xiaoping, and Lin Biao, pushing for conciliation and arguing that avoid-
ance of "contradictions" among the people would best sustain and
further the achievements of the revolution. By early 1957, however, his
opponents, led by Liu Shaoqi, Zhu De, Peng Dehuai, and Peng Zhen—
so-called hard-liners—were in ascendance. To counter them, Mao delivered the text of "On the Correct Handling of Contradictions Among
the People" that he had been working on for more than the better part
of a year. To those arguing that the dangers of loosening controls over
intellectuals were too great, he responded that perhaps they had been
too stringent. In the months following the speech, Mao exerted all his influence to promote the Hundred Flowers campaign, encouraging intellectuals to speak out against abuses within the party as a renewed effort
to "rectify" the party of its bureaucratism and heavy-handedness.

The text has been edited for inclusion here. Punctuation and spelling are as in the original.

Document 2
ON THE CORRECT HANDLING OF CONTRADICTIONS
AMONG THE PEOPLE

Never before has our country been as united as it is today. . . . However, this does not mean that contradictions no longer exist in our society. To imagine that none exist is a naive idea which is at variance with objective reality. We are confronted by two types of social contradictions—those between ourselves and the enemy and those among the people themselves. The two are totally different in their nature. . . .

Since they are different in nature, the contradictions between ourselves and the enemy and the contradictions among the people must be resolved by different methods. To put it briefly, the former are a matter of drawing a clear distinction between ourselves and the enemy, and the latter a matter of drawing a clear distinction between right and wrong. It is, of course, true that the distinction between ourselves and the enemy is also a matter of right and wrong. For example, the question of who is in the right, we or the domestic and foreign reactionaries, the imperialists, the feudalists and bureaucrat-capitalists, is also a matter of right and wrong, but it is in a different category from questions of right and wrong among the people.

Our state is a people's democratic dictatorship led by the working class and based on the worker-peasant alliance. What is this dictatorship for? Its first function is to suppress the reactionary classes and elements and those exploiters in our country who resist the socialist revolution, to suppress those who try to wreck our socialist construction, or in other words, to resolve the internal contradictions between ourselves and the enemy. For instance, to arrest, try and sentence certain counter-revolutionaries, and to deprive landlords and bureaucrat-capitalists of their right to vote and their freedom of speech for a specified period of time—all this comes within the scope of our dictatorship. To maintain public order and safeguard the interests of the people, it is likewise necessary to exercise dictatorship over embezzlers, swindlers, arsonists, murderers, criminal gangs and other scoundrels who seriously disrupt public order. The second function of this dictatorship is to protect our country from subversion and possible aggression by external enemies. In that event, it is the task of this dictatorship to resolve the external contradiction between ourselves and the enemy. The aim of this dictatorship is to protect all our people so that they can devote themselves to peaceful labour and build China into a socialist country with a modern industry, agriculture, science, and culture. Who is to exercise this dictatorship? Naturally, the working class and the entire people under its leadership. . . .

But this freedom is freedom with leadership and this democracy is democracy under centralized guidance, not anarchy. Anarchy does not accord with the interests or wishes of the people.

Certain people in our country were delighted by the [1956] events in Hungary. They hoped that something similar would happen in China, that thousands upon thousands of people would demonstrate in the streets against the People's Government. . . . There are other people in our country who wavered on the question of the Hungarian events because they were ignorant of the real state of affairs in the world. They think that there is too little freedom under our people's democracy and that there is more freedom under Western parliamentary democracy. They ask for a two-party system as in the West, with one party in office and the other out of office. But this so-called two-party system is nothing but a device for maintaining the dictatorship of the bourgeoisie; it can never guarantee freedom to the working people. As a matter of fact, freedom and democracy do not exist in the abstract, only in the concrete. In a society rent by class struggle, if there is freedom for the exploiting classes to exploit the working people, there is no freedom for the working people not to be exploited, and if there is democracy for the bourgeoisie, there is no democracy for the proletariat and other working people. . . .

In advocating freedom with leadership and democracy under centralized guidance, we in no way mean that coercive measures should be taken to settle ideological questions or questions involving the distinction between right and wrong among the people. All attempts to use administrative orders or coercive measures to settle ideological questions or questions of right and wrong are not only ineffective but harmful. We cannot abolish religion by administrative decree or force people not to believe in it. We cannot compel people to give up idealism, any more than we can force them to believe in Marxism. The only way to settle questions of an ideological nature or controversial issues among the people is by the democratic method, the method of discussion, of criticism, of persuasion and education, and not by the method of coercion or repression. . . .

This democratic method of resolving contradictions among the people was epitomized in 1942 in the formula "unity, criticism, unity." To elaborate, it means starting from the desire for unity, resolving contradictions through criticism or struggle and arriving at a new unity on a new basis. In our experience this is the correct method of resolving contradictions among the people. In 1942 we used it to resolve contradictions inside the Communist Party, namely, the contradictions between the dogmatists and the great majority of the membership, and between dogmatism and Marxism. The "Left" dogmatists had resorted to the method of "ruthless struggle and merciless blows" in inner-Party struggle. This method was incorrect. In criticizing "Left" dogmatism, we discarded this old method and adopted a new one, that is, one of starting from the desire for unity, distinguishing between right and wrong through criticism or struggle and arriving at a new unity on a new basis. This was the method used in the rectification movement of 1942. Thus within a few years, by the time the Chinese Communist Party held its Seventh National Congress in 1945, unity was achieved throughout the Party, and as a consequence the great victory of the people's revolution was won. The essential thing is to start from the desire for unity. For without this desire for unity, the struggle is certain to get out of hand. . . .

Marxist philosophy holds that the law of the unity of opposites is the fundamental law of the universe. This law operates universally, whether in the natural world, in human society, or in man's thinking. Between the opposites in a contradiction there is at once unity and struggle, and it is this that impels things to move and change. Contradictions exist everywhere, but they differ in accordance with the different nature of different things. In any given phenomenon or thing, the unity of opposites is conditional, temporary and transitory, and hence relative, whereas the struggle of opposites is absolute. Lenin gave a very clear exposition of this law. In our country, a growing number of people have come to understand it. For many people, however, acceptance of this law is one thing, and its application in examining and dealing with problems is quite another. Many dare not openly admit that contradictions still exist among the people of our country, although it is these very contradictions that are pushing our society forward. Many do not admit that contradictions continue to exist in a socialist society, with the result that they are handicapped and passive when confronted with social contradictions; they do not understand that socialist society will grow more united and consolidated through the ceaseless process of the correct handling and resolving of contradictions. For this reason, we need to explain things to our people, and to our cadres in the first place, in order to help them understand the contradictions in a socialist society and learn to use correct methods for handling these contradictions. . . .

The basic contradictions in socialist society are still those between the relations of production and the productive forces and between the superstructure and the economic base. However, they are fundamentally different in character and have different features from the contradictions between the relations of production and the productive forces and between the superstructure and the economic base in the old societies. The present social system of our country is far superior to that of the old days. If it were not so, the old system would not have been overthrown and the new system could not have been established. . . .

But our socialist system has only just been set up; it is not yet fully established or fully consolidated. In joint state-private industrial and commercial enterprises, capitalists still receive a fixed rate of interest on their capital, that is to say, exploitation still exists. So far as ownership is concerned, these enterprises are not yet completely socialist in character. Some of our agricultural and handicraft producers' co-operatives are still semi-socialist, while even in the fully socialist co-operatives certain problems of ownership remain to be solved. Relations between production and exchange in accordance with socialist principles are still being gradually established in various departments of our economy, and more and more appropriate forms are being sought. To decide the proper ratio between accumulation and consumption within each of the two sectors of socialist economy—that in which the means of production are owned by the whole people and that in which the means of production are collectively owned—and also between the two sectors themselves is a complicated problem for which it is not easy to work out a perfectly rational solution all at once. To sum up, socialist relations of production have been established and are in harmony with the growth of the productive forces, but they are still far from perfect, and this imperfection stands in contradiction to the growth of the productive forces.

Apart from harmony as well as contradiction between the relations of production and the developing productive forces, there is harmony as well as contradiction between the superstructure and the economic base. The superstructure consisting of the state system and laws of the people's democratic dictatorship and the socialist ideology guided by Marxism-Leninism plays a positive role in facilitating the victory of socialist transformation and the establishment of the socialist organization of labour; it is suited to the socialist economic base, that is, to socialist relations of production. But survivals of bourgeois ideology, certain bureaucratic ways of doing things in our state organs and defects in certain links in our state institutions are in contradiction with the socialist economic base. We must continue to resolve all such contradictions in the light of our specific conditions. Of course, new problems will emerge as these contradictions are resolved. And further efforts will be required to resolve the new contradictions. . . .

Today, matters stand as follows. The large-scale and turbulent class struggles of the masses characteristic of the previous revolutionary periods have in the main ended, but class struggle is by no means entirely over. While welcoming the new system, the broad masses of the people are not yet quite accustomed to it. Government workers are not sufficiently experienced and have to undertake further study and exploration of specific policies. In other words, time is needed for our socialist system to become established and consolidated, for the masses to become accustomed to the new system, and for the government workers to learn and acquire experience. It is therefore imperative at this juncture that we should raise the question of distinguishing contradictions among the people from those between ourselves and the enemy, as well as the question of the correct handling of contradictions among the people, so as to unite the people of all nationalities in our country for a new battle, the battle against nature, to develop our economy and culture, to help the whole nation to traverse this period of transition fairly smoothly, to consolidate our new system and build up our new state.

Source: Selected Readings from the Works of Mao Tsetung (Peking: Foreign Languages Press, 1977), 384–421.

THE EMERGING DISPUTE BETWEEN BEIJING AND MOSCOW: CHINESE DOCUMENTS, 1956–1957

Foreign relations is an often neglected aspect of the study of China during its long revolution, despite the significance of those relations for short- and long-term developments. Chapter 5 of this book is concerned with the linkages between China and two of the twentieth-century's great powers, the Soviet Union and the United States. The following Chinese documents, long secret and only recently published in China and translated in the United States, are part of a growing number that reveal the workings of the Sino-Soviet alliance from the early days in the 1920s to the end of the Maoist era. Particularly interesting in the selections presented here is the evidence of CCP attitudes, particularly of Mao Zedong and Zhou Enlai, toward the Soviet Union and various of its leaders, from Lenin to Stalin to the latter's immediate successors.

Relations between the two neighbors—"fraternal" communist countries, as the public line went—were affirmed in February 1950 with the signing of a treaty of friendship. For the remainder of the decade, both sides extolled the alliance and proclaimed that it would last forever. The public hyperbole, we now know, masked serious problems and disagreements that gradually developed into vitriolic polemic in the 1960s over the nature of socialism and communism, which party best represented the international proletarian revolution, and which path—Stalinist or Maoist—ought to be the revolutionary model for the underdeveloped world. In 1969 the relationship had so deteriorated that a military clash erupted along the common border in March.

The documents presented here include two speeches by Mao Zedong and a report by Zhou Enlai. Dating from 1956 and 1957, they reflect Chinese views of a range of topics, but especially of the Soviet leadership, of Nikita Khrushchev's criticism of Stalin (delivered most dramatically in 1956 at a secret session of the Soviet Communist Party Central Committee), and of Chinese expectations from the Sino-Soviet alliance. Particularly noteworthy is Mao's response to Khrushchev's denunciation of Stalin's "cult of personality," a condemnation that could easily be applied to the Chinese leader as well.

The texts have been edited for inclusion here. Punctuation and spelling are as in the original.

Document 3
MINUTES, MAO'S CONVERSATION WITH A YUGOSLAVIAN COMMUNIST UNION DELEGATION, BEIJING, [UNDATED] SEPTEMBER 1956

In today's world, the Marxist and Communist front remains united, whether in places where success [of Communist revolution] is achieved or not yet achieved. However, there were times when we were not so united; there were times when we let you down. We listened to the opinions of the Information Bureau[1] in the past. Although we did not take part in the Bureau's [business], we found it difficult not to support it. In 1949 the Bureau condemned you as butchers and Hitler-style fascists, and we kept silent on the resolution [condemning you], although we published articles to criticize you in 1948. In retrospect, we should not have done that; we should have discussed [this issue] with you: if some of your viewpoints were incorrect, [we should have let] you conduct self-criticism, and there was no need to hurry [into the controversy] as [we] did. The same thing is true to us: should you disagree with us, you should do the same thing, that is, the adoption of a method of persuasion and consultation. . . .

When you offered to recognize new China, we did not respond, nor did we decline it. Undoubtedly, we should not have rejected it, because there was no reason for us to do so. When Britain recognized us, we did not say no to it. How could we find any excuse to reject the recognition of a socialist country?

There was, however, another factor which prevented us from responding to you: the Soviet friends did not want us to form diplomatic relations with you. If so, was China an independent state? Of course, yes. If an independent state, why, then, did we follow their instructions? [My] comrades, when the Soviet Union requested us to follow their suit at that time, it was difficult for us to oppose it. It was because at that time some people claimed that there were two Titos in the world: one in Yugoslavia, the other in China, even if no one passed a resolution that Mao Zedong was Tito. . . .

The Wang Ming line[2] was in fact Stalin's line. It ended up destroying ninety percent of our strength in our bases, and one hundred percent of [our strength] in the white [Guomindang] areas. Comrade [Liu] Shaoqi pointed this out in his report to the Eighth [Party] Congress.[3] Why, then, did he not openly attribute [the losses] to the [impact of] Stalin's line? There is an explanation. The Soviet Party itself could criticize Stalin; but it would be inappropriate for us to criticize him. We should maintain a good relationship with the Soviet Union. Maybe [we] could make our criticism public sometime in the future. It has to be that way in today's world, because facts are facts. The Comintern made numerous mistakes in the past. Its early and late stages were not so bad, but its middle stage was not so good: it was all right when Lenin was alive and when [Georgii] Dimitrov was in charge.[4] The first Wang Ming line dominated [our party] for four years, and the Chinese revolution suffered the biggest losses. . . .[5]

That was the first time when we got the worst of [from] Stalin.

The second time was during the anti-Japanese war. Speaking Russian and good at flattering Stalin, Wang Ming could directly communicate with Stalin. Sent back to China by Stalin, he tried to set [us] toward right deviation this time, instead of following the leftist line he had previously advocated. Advocating [CCP] collaboration with the Guomindang, he can be described as "decking himself out and being self-inviting [to the GMD];" he wanted [us] to obey the GMD wholeheartedly. . . .

The third time was after Japan's surrender and the end of the Second World War. Stalin met with [Winston] Churchill and [Franklin D.] Roosevelt and decided to give the whole of China to America and Jiang Jieshi. In terms of material and moral support, especially moral support, Stalin hardly gave any to us, the Communist Party, but supported Jiang Jieshi. This decision was made at the Yalta conference. . . .

Only after the dissolution of the Comintern did we start to enjoy more freedom. We had already begun to criticize opportunism and the Wang Ming line, and unfolded the rectification movement. Rectification, in fact, was aimed at denouncing the mistakes that Stalin and the Comintern had committed in directing the Chinese revolution; however, we did not openly mention a word about Stalin and the Comintern. Sometime in the near future, [we] may openly do so. There are two explanations of why we did not openly criticize [Stalin and the Comintern]: first, as we followed their instructions, we have to take some responsibility ourselves. Nobody compelled us to follow their instructions! Nobody forced us to be wrongfully deviated to right and left directions! . . . Second, we do not want to displease [the Soviets], to disrupt our relations with the Soviet Union. The Comintern has never made self-criticism on these mistakes; nor has the Soviet Union ever mentioned these mistakes. We would have fallen out with them had we raised our criticism.

The fourth time was when [Moscow] regarded me as a half-hearted Tito or semi-Titoist. Not only in the Soviet Union but also in other socialist countries and some non-socialist countries were there some people who had suspected whether China's was a real revolution.

You might wonder why [we] still pay a tribute to Stalin in China by hanging his portrait on the wall. Comrades from Moscow have informed us that they no longer hang Stalin's portraits and only display Lenin's and current leaders' portraits in public parade. They, however, did not ask us to follow their suit. We find it very difficult to cope. The four mistakes committed by Stalin are yet to be made known to the Chinese people as well as to our whole party. Our situation is quite different from yours: your [suffering inflicted by Stalin] is known to the people and to the whole world. Within our party, the mistakes of the two Wang Ming lines are well known; but our people do not know that these mistakes originated in Stalin. Only our Central Committee was aware that Stalin blocked our revolution and regarded me as a half-hearted Tito.

We had no objection that the Soviet Union functions as a center [of the world revolution] because it benefits the socialist movement. You may disagree [with us] on this point. You wholeheartedly support Khrushchev's campaign to criticize Stalin, but we cannot do the same because our people would dislike it. In the previous parades [in China], we held up portraits of Marx, Engels, Lenin and Stalin, as well as those of a few Chinese [leaders]—Mao, Liu [Shaoqi], Zhou [Enlai], and Zhu [De]—and other brotherly parties' leaders. Now we adopt a measure of "overthrowing all": no one's portrait is handed out. For this year's "First of May" celebration, Ambassador Bobkoveshi[6] already saw in Beijing that no one's portrait was held in parade. However, the portraits of five dead persons—Marx, Engels, Lenin and Stalin and Sun [Yat-sen]—and a not yet dead person—Mao Zedong—are still hanging [on the wall]. Let them hang on the wall! You Yugoslavians may comment that the Soviet Union no longer hangs Stalin's portrait, but the Chinese still do. . . .

Before I met with Stalin, I did not have much good feeling about him. I disliked reading his works, and I have read only "On the Basis of Leninism," a long article criticizing Trotsky, and "Be Carried Away by Success," etc. I disliked even more his articles on the Chinese revolution. He was very different from Lenin: Lenin shared his heart with others and treated others as equals whereas Stalin liked to stand above every one else and order others around. This style can be detected from his works. After I met with him, I became even more disgusted: I quarreled a lot with him in Moscow. Stalin was excitable by temperament. When he became agitated, he would spell out nasty things. . . .

Generally speaking, the Soviet Union is good. It is good because of four factors: Marxism-Leninism, the October Revolution, the main force [of the socialist camp], and industrialization. They have their negative side, and have made some mistakes. However, their achievements constitute the major part [of their past] while their shortcomings are of secondary significance. Now that the enemy is taking advantage of the criticism of Stalin to take the offensive on a worldwide scale, we ought to support the Soviet Union. They will certainly correct their mistakes. Khrushchev already corrected the mistake concerning Yugoslavia. They are already aware of Wang Ming's mistakes, although in the past they were unhappy with our criticism of Wang Ming. They have also removed the "half-hearted Tito" [label from me], thus, eliminating altogether [the labels on] one and a half Titos. We are pleased to see that Tito's tag was removed. . . .

Few people in China have ever openly criticized me. The [Chinese] people are tolerant of my shortcomings and mistakes. It is because we always want to serve the people and do good things for the people. Although we sometimes also suffer from bossism and bureaucracy, the people believe that we have done more good things than bad ones and, as a result, they praise us more than criticize us. Consequently, an idol is created: when some people criticize me, others would oppose them and accuse them of disrespecting the leader. Everyday I and other comrades of the central leadership receive some three hundred letters, some of which are critical of us. These letters, however, are either not signed or signed with a false name. The authors are not afraid that we would suppress them, but they are afraid that others around them would make them suffer.

NOTES

1. A reference to the Information Bureau of Communist and Workers' Parties (Cominform), which was established in September 1947 by the parties of the Soviet Union, Bulgaria, Romania, Hungary, Poland, France, Czechoslovakia, Italy, and Yugoslavia. The Bureau announced that it was ending its activities in April 1956.

2. Wang Ming (1904–1974), also known as Chen Zhaoyu, was a returnee from the Soviet Union and a leading member of the Chinese Communist Party in the 1930s. Official Chinese Communist view claims that Wang Ming committed "ultra-leftist" mistakes in the early 1930s and "ultra-rightist" mistakes later in that decade.

3. The CCP's eighth national congress was held in Beijing, September 15–27, 1956.

4. Georgii Dimitrov (1882–1949), a Bulgarian communist, was the Comintern's secretary general from 1935 to 1943.

5. Mao points here to the period from 1931 to 1935, during which the "international section," of which Wang Ming was a leading member, controlled the central leadership of the CCP.

6. Bobkoveshi was Yugoslavia's first ambassador to the PRC, with whom Mao Zedong met for the first time on June 30, 1955.

Source: Zhang Shu Guang and Chen Jian, trans., "The Emerging Dispute Between Beijing and Moscow: Ten Newly Available Chinese Documents, 1956–1958," *Bulletin of the Cold War International History Project*, nos. 6–7 (1995/1996), 148–54. All brackets, except one, and notes are the translators'.

Document 4
SPEECH, MAO ZEDONG, "ON SINO-AMERICAN AND SINO-SOVIET RELATIONS," 27 JANUARY 1957

[Let me] talk about U.S.-China relations. At this conference we have circulated a copy of the letter from [Dwight D.] Eisenhower to Jiang Jieshi. This letter, in my view, aims largely at dampening the enthusiasm of Jiang Jieshi and, then, cheering him up a bit. The letter urges [Jiang] to keep calm, not to be impetuous, that is, to resolve the problems through the United Nations, but not through a war. This is to pour cold water [on Jiang]. It is easy for Jiang Jieshi to get excited. To cheer [Jiang] up is to continue the hard, uncompromising policy toward the [Chinese] Communist Party, and to hope that internal unrest would disable us. In his [Eisenhower's] calculation, internal unrest has already occurred and it is hard for the Communist Party to suppress it. Well, different people observe things differently!

I still believe that it is much better to establish diplomatic relations with the United States several years later than sooner. This is in our favor. The Soviet Union did not form diplomatic relations with the United States until seventeen years after the October Revolution. The global economic crisis erupted in 1929 and lasted until 1933. In that year Hitler came to power in Germany whereas Roosevelt took office in the United States. Only then was the Soviet-American diplomatic relationship established. [As far as I can anticipate], it will probably wait until when we have completed the Third Five-Year Plan[1] that we should consider forming diplomatic relations with the United States. In other words, it will take eighteen or even more years [before we do so]. . . . I once told an American in Yan'an that even if your United States refused to recognize us for one hundred years, I simply did not believe that your United States could refuse to recognize us in the one hundred and first year. Sooner or later the U.S. will establish diplomatic relations with us. When the United States does so and when Americans finally come to visit China, they will feel deep regret. It is because by then, China will become completely different [from what it is now]: the house has been thoroughly swept and cleaned, "the four pests"[2] have altogether been eliminated; and they can hardly find any of their "friends." Even if they spread some germs [in China], it will have no use at all. . . .

At present there exist some controversies between China and the Soviet Union. . . . As far as I can see, circumstances are beyond what persons, even those occupying high positions, can control. Under the pressure of circumstance, those in the Soviet Union who still want to practice big-power chauvinism will invariably encounter difficulties. To persuade them remains our current policy and requires us to engage in direct dialogue with them. The last time our delegation visited the Soviet Union, [we] openly talked about some [controversial] issues.[3] I told Comrade Zhou Enlai over the phone that, as those people are blinded by lust for gain, the best way to deal with them is to give them a tongue-lashing. What is [their] asset? It involves nothing more than 50 million tons of steel, 400 million tons of coal, and 80 million tons of oil. How much does this count? It does not count for a thing. With this asset, however, their heads have gotten really big. How can they be communists [by being so cocky]? How can they be Marxists? . . . This time Comrade [Zhou] Enlai no longer maintained a modest attitude but quarreled with them and, of course, they argued back. This is a correct attitude, because it is always better to make every [controversial] issue clear face to face. As much as they intend to influence us, we want to influence them too. However, we did not unveil everything this time, because we must hold some magic weapons [in reserve]. Conflict will always exist. All we hope for at present is to avoid major clashes so as to seek common ground while reserving differences. Let these differences be dealt with in the future. Should they stick to the current path, one day, we will have to expose everything.

NOTES

1. China adopted the first Five-Year Plan in 1953. Based upon this, 1968 would have been the year ending the third Five-Year Plan.

2. The elimination of the "four pests" (rats, bedbugs, flies, and mosquitoes) became the main goal of a national hygiene campaign in China during the mid and late 1950s.

3. A reference to Zhou Enlai's visit to the Soviet Union, Poland, and Hungary, January 7–19, 1957. For Zhou's report on the visit, see the next document.

Source: This text was part of Mao's speech to a conference attended by Central Committee provincial, regional, and municipal secretaries. Zhang Shu Guang and Chen Jian, trans., "The Emerging Dispute Between Beijing and Moscow: Ten Newly Available Chinese Documents, 1956–1958," *Bulletin of the Cold War International History Project*, nos. 6–7 (1995/1996), 148–54. All brackets and notes are the translators'.

Document 5
REPORT, "MY OBSERVATIONS ON THE SOVIET UNION," ZHOU ENLAI TO MAO ZEDONG AND THE CENTRAL LEADERSHIP, 24 JANUARY 1957 (EXCERPT).[1]

Having already spoken considerably about the achievements of the Soviet Communist leadership in public, now let [me] illustrate again the major mistakes it has made:

(1) In my view, the mistakes of the Soviet Communist leadership arise from erroneous thinking. They often set the interests of the Soviet Communist Party ahead of their brotherly parties; they often set their own interests as the leaders ahead of those of the party. As a result, they often fail to overcome subjectivity, narrow-mindedness, and emotion when they think about and resolve problems; they often fail to link together the interests of the above-stated sides in an objective, far-sighted, and calm fashion. Although they may correct one mistake, they are not free of making others. Sometimes they admit that they made mistakes; but it does not mean that they fully come to grips with their mistakes for they merely take a perfunctory attitude toward these mistakes.

For instance, the dispatch of their troops to Warsaw was clearly interference with the internal affairs of a brotherly party by armed forces, but not an action to suppress counterrevolutionaries. They admitted that they had committed a serious mistake, and they even stated in our meetings this time that no one should be allowed to interfere with other brotherly parties' internal affairs; but in the meantime, they denied that [their intervention in Poland] was a mistake.

When we had a general assessment of Stalin, analyzing the ideological and social roots of his [mistakes], they kept avoiding any real discussion. Although they seemingly have changed [their view] in measuring Stalin's achievements and mistakes, to me such an alteration was to meet their temporary needs, not the result of profound contemplation.

We immediately sensed this shortly after our arrival in Moscow. At the dinner party hosted by Liu Xiao[2] on the 17th [of January], Khrushchev again raised the Stalin issue. Having much to say that was inappropriate, he offered no self-criticism. We then pushed him by pointing out that, given the development of Stalin's authoritarianism, ossified way of thinking, and arrogant and conceited attitude over twenty years, how can those comrades, especially those [Soviet] Politburo members, who had worked with Stalin, decline to assume any responsibility? They then admitted that Stalin's errors came about gradually; had they not been afraid of getting killed, they could have at least done more to restrict the growth of Stalin's mistakes than to encourage him. However, in open talks, they refused to admit this.

Khrushchev and Bulganin claimed that as members of the third generation [of Soviet] leadership, they could not do anything to persuade Stalin or prevent his mistakes. During [my visit] this time, however, I stressed the ideological and social roots of Stalin's mistakes, pointing out that the other leaders had to assume some responsibility for the gradual development of Stalin's mistakes. I also expressed our Chinese Party's conviction that open self-criticism will do no harm to, but will enhance, the Party's credibility and prestige. Before getting out of the car at the [Moscow] airport, Khrushchev explained to me that they could not conduct the same kind of self- criticism as we do; should they do so, their current leadership would be in trouble. . . .

It is safe to say that although every public communique [between the Soviet Union and] other brotherly states has repeatedly mentioned what the 30 October [1956] declaration[3] has announced as the principles to guide the relationship among brotherly parties and governments, [the Soviets] seem to recoil in fear when dealing with specific issues and tend to be inured to patronizing others and interfering with other brotherly parties' and governments' internal affairs.

(2) About Sino-Soviet relations. Facing a [common] grave enemy, the Soviet comrades have ardent expectations about Sino-Soviet unity. However, in my opinion, the Soviet leaders have not been truly convinced by our argument; nor have the differences between us disappeared completely. For instance, many leaders of the Soviet Communist Party toasted and praised our article "Another Comment on the Historical Lessons of the Proletarian Dictatorship." Their three top leaders (Khrushchev, Bulganin, and Mikoyan), however, have never mentioned a word of it. Moreover, when we discussed with them the part of the article concerning criticism of Stalin, they said that this was what made them displeased (or put them in a difficult position, I can't remember the exact words). . . . Therefore, I believe that some of the Soviet leaders have revealed a utilitarian attitude toward Sino-Soviet relations. Consequently, at the last day's meeting, I decided not to raise our requests concerning the abolition of the long-term supply and purchase contracts for the Five-Year Plan, the [Soviet] experts, and [Soviet] aid and [Sino-Soviet] collaboration on nuclear energy and missile development. About these issues I didn't say a word. It was not because there wasn't enough time to do so, but because [I wanted to] avoid impressing upon them that we were taking advantage of their precarious position by raising these issues. These issues can be raised later or simply dropped.

(3) In assessing the international situation, I am convinced that they spend more time and effort on coping with specific and isolated events than on evaluating and anticipating the situations thoroughly from different angles. They explicitly demonstrate weakness in considering and discussing strategic and long-term issues. As far as tactics are concerned, on the other hand lacking clearly defined principles, they tend to be on such a loose ground in handling specific affairs that they will fail to reach satisfactorily the strategic goals through resolving each specific conflict. As a result, it is very likely that some worrisome event may occur in international affairs....

(4) In spite of all of the above, however, Sino-Soviet relations are far better now than during Stalin's era. First of all, facing the [common] grave enemy, both sides have realized and accepted the necessity of promoting Sino-Soviet unity and mutual support, which had been taken as the most important principle. Second, now the Soviet Union and China can sit down to discuss issues equally. Even if they have different ideas on certain issues, they must consult with us. The articles by the Chinese Party are having some impact on the cadres and people in the Soviet Union, and even on some [Soviet] leaders. Third, the previous dull situation in which the brotherly parties and states could hardly discuss or argue with one another no longer exists. Now, different opinions can be freely exchanged so that unity and progress are thereby promoted. Fourth, the majority of the Soviet people love China, and feel happy for the Chinese people's achievements and growth in strength. Their admiration and friendship with the Chinese people are being enhanced on a daily basis.... Fifth, on the one hand, extremely conceited, blinded by lust for gain, lacking far-sightedness, and knowing little the ways of the world, some of their leaders have hardly improved themselves even with the several rebuffs they have met in the past year. On the other hand, however, they appear to lack confidence and suffer from inner fears and thus tend to employ the tactics of bluffing or threats in handling foreign affairs or relations with other brotherly parties. Although they did sometimes speak from the bottom of their hearts while talking with us, they nevertheless could not get down from their high horse. In short, it is absolutely inadvisable for us not to persuade them [to make changes]; it is, however, equally inadvisable for us to be impatient in changing them. Therefore, changes on their part can only be achieved through a well-planned, step-by-step, persistent, patient, long-term persuasion.

NOTES

1. During this visit Zhou had five formal meetings with Soviet leaders, including Nikolai Bulganin, Nikita Khrushchev, and Anastas Mikoyan. After returning to Beijing, Zhou prepared this report for Mao and the CCP central leadership.

2. Liu Xiao was Chinese ambassador to the Soviet Union from February 1955 to October 1962.

3. A reference to the "Declaration on Developing and Further Strengthening the Friendship and Cooperation between the Soviet Union and the Other Socialist Countries" issued by the Soviet government on the evening of October 30, 1956. As a response to the Hungarian crisis, the Soviet leadership reviewed its relations with other communist countries and promised that it would adopt a pattern of more equal exchanges with them in the future.

Source: Zhang Shu Guang and Chen Jian, trans., "The Emerging Dispute Between Beijing and Moscow: Ten Newly Available Chinese Documents, 1956–1958," *Bulletin of the Cold War International History Project*, nos. 6–7 (1995/1996), 148–54. All brackets and notes are the translators'.

At the Eleventh Plenum of the Eighth CCP Central Committee on August 8, 1966, the following decision was adopted that defined the basic theory and practice of the Cultural Revolution. In it, we can see most prominently the hand and thinking of Mao Zedong, a man whom the historian John King Fairbank reminds us had "two careers, one as rebel leader, one as updated emperor."[1] By acknowledging his second career, it becomes possible to understand how Mao was able to shape and carry off the Cultural Revolution, and lead many people, within and outside the party, to mass destruction. He had become the most special person in the People's Republic of China, above everyone else, the "Great Helmsman" whose guidance was unchallengeable and whose errors were always forgiven. That status enabled him once again to charge the country's leadership with pursuing the wrong policies and to win the "moral" high ground by using the masses for explicitly political purposes.

He had plenty to be concerned about. Particularly troubling were all the signs of the revolution's institutionalization, the reemergence of elitism and bureaucratic practice, the complacency of the younger generation that had no experience with revolution or the tribulations of their parents, and the reassertion of influence by intellectuals, the group that he despised the most. For several years, the intellectuals had been producing a crescendo of criticism—Aesopian in form to maintain the traditional Chinese practice of not naming names publicly—that all knew, however, was leveled at Mao and his policies. His errors were becoming subjects of public discussion and derision, as were his tactics in general and some of his most emphatic and enduring pronouncements. The temerity of some in claiming that literature need not directly serve the revolution was a huge slap in the face to Mao. It all smacked of revisionism of the kind that Mao saw unfolding in the Soviet Union under Nikita Khrushchev. The Cultural Revolution, a return slap to impudent and ultimately lesser beings, was his response.

The decision reprinted here shows Mao at his worst, the consummate demagogue. In the name of the people, with promises of allowing them to speak boldly without fear of reprisal, he sought to identify and root out those in positions of authority who disagreed with his views. They were the ones with more-moderate views about developmental policy and less inclination to see everything as politics. Castigated as "capitalist roaders," "Rightists," and counterrevolutionaries, they were to be subjected to criticism and worse should they be revealed as real enemies of the people. Education and learning became identified with experience "in the movement" rather than in schools, dominated as they were in Mao's mind by intellectuals out of touch with workers and peasants. The teachers, actual and metaphorical, needed to become learners at the feet of the people. Mao, of course, was excluded from this obligation.

The text has been edited for inclusion here. Punctuation and spelling are as in the original.

Document 6
DECISION CONCERNING THE CULTURAL REVOLUTION

1. A NEW STAGE IN THE SOCIALIST REVOLUTION

The Great Proletarian Cultural Revolution now unfolding is a great revolution that touches people to their very souls and constitutes a new stage in the development of the socialist revolution in our country, a deeper and more extensive stage. . . .

Although the bourgeoisie has been overthrown, it is still trying to use the old ideas, culture, customs, and habits of the exploiting classes to corrupt the masses, capture their minds, and endeavour to stage a comeback. The proletariat must do just the opposite: It must meet head-on every challenge of the bourgeoisie in the ideological field and use the new ideas, culture, customs, and habits of the proletariat to change the mental outlook of the whole of society. At present, our objective is to struggle against and crush those persons in authority who are taking the capitalist road, to criticize and repudiate the reactionary bourgeois academic "authorities" and the ideology of the bourgeoisie and all other exploiting classes, and to transform education, literature and art, and all other parts of the superstructure that do not correspond to the socialist economic base, so as to facilitate the consolidation and development of the socialist system.

2. THE MAIN CURRENT AND THE ZIGZAGS

The masses of the workers, peasants, soldiers, revolutionary intellectuals, and revolutionary cadres form the main force in this Great Cultural

Revolution. Large numbers of revolutionary young people, previously unknown, have become courageous and daring pathbreakers. They are vigorous in action and intelligent. Through the media of big-character posters and great debates, they argue things out, expose and criticize thoroughly, and launch resolute attacks on the open and hidden representatives of the bourgeoisie. In such a great revolutionary movement, it is hardly avoidable that they should show shortcomings of one kind or another, but their main revolutionary orientation has been correct from the beginning. . . .

Since the Cultural Revolution is a revolution, it inevitably meets with resistance. This resistance comes chiefly from those in authority who have wormed their way into the Party and are taking the capitalist road. It also comes from the old force of habit in society. At present, this resistance is still fairly strong and stubborn. However, the Great Proletarian Cultural Revolution is, after all, an irresistible general trend. There is abundant evidence that such resistance will crumble fast once the masses become fully aroused.

Because the resistance is fairly strong, there will be reversals and even repeated reversals in this struggle. There is no harm in this. It tempers the proletariat and other working people, and especially the younger generation, teaches them lessons and gives them experience, and helps them to understand that the revolutionary road is a zigzag one, and not plain sailing.

3. PUT DARING ABOVE EVERYTHING ELSE AND BOLDLY AROUSE THE MASSES

The outcome of this Great Cultural Revolution will be determined by whether the Party leadership does or does not dare to boldly arouse the masses. . . .

What the Central Committee of the Party demands of the Party committees at all levels is that they persevere in giving correct leadership, put daring above everything else, boldly arouse the masses, change the state of weakness and incompetence where it exists, encourage those comrades who have made mistakes but are willing to correct them to cast off their mental burdens and join in the struggle, and dismiss from their leading posts all those in authority who are taking the capitalist road and so make possible the recapture of the leadership for the proletarian revolutionaries.

4. LET THE MASSES EDUCATE THEMSELVES IN THE MOVEMENT

In the Great Proletarian Cultural Revolution, the only method is for the masses to liberate themselves, and any method of doing things on their behalf must not be used.

Trust the masses, rely on them, and respect their initiative. Cast out fear. Don't be afraid of disorder. Chairman Mao has often told us that revolution cannot be so very refined, so gentle, so temperate, kind, courteous, restrained, and magnanimous. Let the masses educate themselves in this great revolutionary movement and learn to distinguish between right and wrong and between correct and incorrect ways of doing things. . . .

5. FIRMLY APPLY THE CLASS LINE OF THE PARTY

Who are our enemies? Who are our friends? This is a question of the first importance for the revolution, and it is likewise a question of the first importance for the Great Cultural Revolution.

Party leadership should be good at discovering the Left and developing and strengthening the ranks of the Left, and should firmly rely on the revolutionary Left. During the movement this is the only way to isolate thoroughly the most reactionary rightists, win over the middle, and unite with the great majority so that by the end of the movement we shall achieve the unity of more than 95 percent of the cadres and more than 95 percent of the masses. . . .

6. CORRECT HANDLING OF CONTRADICTIONS
AMONG THE PEOPLE

A strict distinction must be made between the two different types of contradictions: those among the people and those between ourselves and the enemy. Contradictions among the people must not be made into contradictions between ourselves and the enemy; nor must contradictions between ourselves and the enemy be regarded as those among the people.

It is normal for the masses to hold different views. Contention between different views is unavoidable, necessary, and beneficial. In the course of normal and full debate, the masses will affirm what is right, correct what is wrong, and gradually reach unanimity.

The method to be used in debates is to present the facts, reason things out, and persuade through reasoning. Any method of forcing a minority holding different views to submit is impermissible. The minority should be protected, because sometimes the truth is with the minority. Even if the minority is wrong, they should still be allowed to argue their case and reserve their views. . . .

7. BE ON GUARD AGAINST THOSE WHO BRAND
THE REVOLUTIONARY MASSES AS
"COUNTER-REVOLUTIONARIES"

In certain schools, units, and work teams of the Cultural Revolution, some of the persons in charge have organized counter-attacks against the masses who put up big-character posters against them. These people have even advanced such slogans as: Opposition to the leaders of a unit or a work team means opposition to the Party's Central Committee, means opposition to the Party and socialism, means counter-revolution. In this way it is inevitable that their blows will fall on some really revolutionary activists. This is an error on matters of orientation, an error of line, and is absolutely impermissible. . . .

9. CULTURAL REVOLUTIONARY GROUPS, COMMITTEES, AND CONGRESSES

Many new things have begun to emerge in the Great Proletarian Cultural Revolution. The cultural revolutionary groups, committees, and other organizational forms created by the masses in many schools and units are something new and of great historic importance.

These cultural revolutionary groups, committees, and congresses are excellent new forms of organization whereby under the leadership of the Communist Party the masses are educating themselves. They are an excellent bridge to keep our Party in close contact with the masses. They are organs of power of the Proletarian Cultural Revolution.

The struggle of the proletariat against the old ideas, culture, customs, and habits left over by all the exploiting classes over thousands of years will necessarily take a very, very long time. Therefore, the cultural revolutionary groups, committees, and congresses should not be temporary organizations but permanent, standing mass organizations. They are suitable not only for colleges, schools, government, and other organizations, but generally also for factories, mines, other enterprises, urban districts, and villages.

It is necessary to institute a system of general elections, like that of the Paris Commune, for electing members to the cultural revolutionary groups and committees and delegates to the cultural revolutionary congresses. The lists of candidates should be put forward by the revolutionary masses after full discussion, and the elections should be held after the masses have discussed the lists over and over again.

The masses are entitled at any time to criticize members of the cultural revolutionary groups and committees and delegates elected to the cultural revolutionary congresses. If these members or delegates prove incompetent, they can be replaced through election or recalled by the masses after discussion. . . .

10. EDUCATIONAL REFORM

In the Great Proletarian Cultural Revolution a most important task is to transform the old educational system and the old principles and methods of teaching.

In this Great Cultural Revolution, the phenomenon of our schools being dominated by bourgeois intellectuals must be completely changed.

In every kind of school we must apply thoroughly the policy advanced by Comrade Mao Zedong of education serving proletarian politics and education being combined with productive labour, so as to enable those receiving an education to develop morally, intellectually, and physically and to become labourers with socialist consciousness and culture.

The period of schooling should be shortened. Courses should be fewer and better. The teaching material should be thoroughly transformed, in some cases beginning with simplifying complicated material. While their main task is to study, students should also learn other things. That is to say, in addition to their studies they should also learn industrial work, farming, and military affairs and take part in the struggles of the Cultural Revolution as they occur to criticize the bourgeoisie. . . .

14. TAKE FIRM HOLD OF THE REVOLUTION AND STIMULATE PRODUCTION

The aim of the Great Proletarian Cultural Revolution is to revolutionize people's ideology and as a consequence to achieve greater, faster, better, and more economical results in all fields of work. If the masses are fully aroused and proper arrangements are made, it is possible to carry on both the Cultural Revolution and production without one hampering the other, while guaranteeing high quality in all our work.

The Great Proletarian Cultural Revolution is a powerful motive force for the development of the social productive forces in our country. Any idea of counterpoising the Great Cultural Revolution to the development of production is incorrect. . . .

16. MAO ZEDONG'S THOUGHT IS THE GUIDE FOR ACTION IN THE GREAT PROLETARIAN CULTURAL REVOLUTION

In the Great Proletarian Cultural Revolution, it is imperative to hold aloft the great red banner of Mao Zedong's thought and put proletarian politics in command. The movement for the creative study and application of Chairman Mao Zedong's works should be carried forward among the masses of the workers, peasants, and soldiers, the cadres and the intellectuals, and Mao Zedong's thought should be taken as the guide to action in the Cultural Revolution.

In this complex Great Cultural Revolution, Party committees at all levels must study and apply Chairman Mao's works all the more conscientiously and in a creative way. In particular, they must study over and over again Chairman Mao's writings on the Cultural Revolution and on the Party's methods of leadership, such as *On New Democracy, Talks at the Yan'an Forum on Literature and Art, On the Correct Handling of Contradictions among the People, Speech at the Chinese Communist Party's National Conference on Propaganda Work, Some Questions Concerning Methods of Leadership*, and *Methods of Work of Party Committees*.

Party committees at all levels must abide by the directions given by Chairman Mao over the years, namely that they should thoroughly apply the mass line of "from the masses and to the masses" and that they should be pupils before they become teachers. They should try to avoid being one sided or narrow. They should foster materialist dialectics and oppose metaphysics and scholasticism.

The Great Proletarian Cultural Revolution is bound to achieve brilliant victory under the leadership of the Central Committee of the Party headed by Comrade Mao Zedong.

NOTE

1. John King Fairbank, *China: A New History* (Cambridge, MA: Harvard University Press, 1992), 385.

Source: Peking Review, no. 33 (1966), 6–11.

> Given events in China from the late 1950s until Mao Zedong's death in 1976, it is hard to imagine the existence of a text, except the Bible, Qur'an, or some other collection of religious wisdom, that has been read by more people with greater devotion and intensity than Mao's "Little Red Book." Over 300 pages in length in its first English edition (1966), and bound with its famous red plastic cover, *Quotations from Chairman Mao* was published in a format (smaller than a 3″ × 5″ card) small enough to be easily carried in one's hand, purse, or pocket, thereby encouraging its constant accessibility for reading, discussion, and veneration. Images from television and film that come from the years of the Cultural Revolution are replete with crowds, sometimes immense, holding and waving the "little red book" as they chant slogans in support of Mao's radical policies, or smaller "study groups" set up in every village and workplace intent on drawing the last drop of guiding principle from this text. A product of the evolving controversy between Mao and other party leaders over the country's direction, and compiled by Marshal Lin Biao, who temporarily would become Mao's closest ally and heir apparent until the latter lost interest in him by the early 1970s, the book comprises selected quotations from Mao's writings, presented according to subject or theme and reflecting the chairman's basic philosophy. The style of the book is deliberately simple and straightforward to encourage ease of understanding and

commitment to memory. In this feature, it is reminiscent of certain classical Chinese texts, especially the "Analects" of Confucius.

Following are selections, in some places edited, from the much longer text.

Document 7
THE "LITTLE RED BOOK": QUOTATIONS FROM CHAIRMAN MAO

I. THE COMMUNIST PARTY

The force at the core leading our cause forward is the Chinese Communist Party. The theoretical basis guiding our thinking is Marxism-Leninism.

[Opening address at the first session of the First National People's Congress of the People's Republic of China (1954)]

If there is to be a revolution, there must be a revolutionary party. Without a revolutionary party, without a party built on the Marxist-Leninism revolutionary theory and in the Marxist-Leninist revolutionary style, it is impossible to lead the working class and the broad masses of the people in defeating imperialism and its running dogs.

["Revolutionary Forces of the World Unite, Fight Against Imperialist Aggression!" (1948)]

A well-disciplined Party armed with the theory of Marxism-Leninism, using the method of self-criticism, and linked with the masses of the people; an army under the leadership of such a Party; a united front of all revolutionary classes and all revolutionary groups under the leadership of such a Party—these are the three main weapons with which we have defeated the enemy.

["On the People's Democratic Dictatorship" (1949)]

II. CLASSES AND CLASS STRUGGLE

In class society everyone lives as a member of a particular class, and every kind of thinking, without exception, is stamped with the brand of a class.

["On Practice" (1937)]

In our country bourgeois and petty-bourgeois ideology, anti-Marxist ideology, will continue to exist for a long time. Basically, the socialist system has been established in our country. We have won the basic victory in transforming the ownership of the means of production, but we have not yet won complete victory on the political and ideological fronts. In the ideological field, the question of who will win in the struggle between the proletariat and the bourgeoisie has not been really settled yet. We still have to wage a protracted struggle against bourgeois and petty-bourgeois ideology. It is wrong not to understand this and to give up ideological struggle. All erroneous ideas, all poisonous weeds, all ghosts and monsters, must be subjected to criticism; in no circumstance would they be allowed to spread unchecked. . . .

["Speech at the Chinese Communist Party's
National Conference on Propaganda Work" (1957)]

VIII. PEOPLE'S WAR

The revolutionary war is a war of the masses; it can be waged only by mobilizing the masses and relying on them.

["Be Concerned with the Well-Being of the Masses,
Pay Attention to Methods of Work" (1934)]

Considering the revolutionary war as a whole, the operations of the people's guerrillas and those of the main forces of the Red Army complement each other like a man's right arm and left arm, and if we had only the main forces of the Red Army without the people's guerrillas, we would be like a warrior with only one arm. . . .

["Problems of Strategy in China's Revolutionary War" (1936)]

XI. THE MASS LINE

The masses have boundless creative power. They can organize themselves and concentrate on places and branches of work where they can give full play to their energy; they can concentrate on production in breadth and depth and create more and more welfare undertakings for themselves.

[Introductory note to "Surplus Labour
Has Found a Way Out" (1955)]

Commandism is wrong in any type of work, because in overstepping the level of political consciousness of the masses and violating the principle of voluntary mass action it reflects the disease of impetuosity. Our comrades must not assume that everything they themselves understand is understood by the masses. Whether the masses understand it and are ready to take action can be discovered only by going into their midst and making investigations. If we do so, we can avoid commandism. Tailism in any type of work is also wrong, because in falling below the level of political consciousness of the masses and violating the principle of leading the masses forward it reflects the disease of dilatoriness. Our comrades must not assume that the masses have no understanding of what they themselves do not yet understand. It often happens that the masses outstrip us and are eager to advance a step and that nevertheless our comrades fail to act as leaders of the masses and tail behind certain backward elements, reflecting their views and, moreover, mistaking them for those of the broad masses.

["On Coalition Government" (1945)]

XV. DEMOCRACY IN THE THREE MAIN FIELDS

Anyone should be allowed to speak out, whoever he may be, so long as he is not a hostile element and does not make malicious attacks, and it does not matter if he says something wrong. Leaders at all levels have the duty to listen to others. Two principles must be observed: (1) Say all you know and say it without reserve; (2) Don't blame the speaker but take his words as a warning. Unless the principle of "Don't blame the speaker" is observed genuinely and not falsely, the result will not be "Say all you know and say it without reserve."

["The Tasks for 1945" (1944)]

XXI. SELF-RELIANCE AND ARDUOUS STRUGGLE

We stand for self-reliance. We hope for foreign aid but cannot be dependent on it; we depend on our own efforts, on the creative power of the whole army and the entire people.

["We Must Learn to Do Economic Work" (1945)]

There is an ancient Chinese fable called "The Foolish Old Man Who Removed the Mountains." It tells of an old man who lived in northern China long, long ago and was known as the Foolish Old Man of North Mountain. His house faced south and beyond his doorway stood the two great peaks, Taihang and Wangwu, obstructing the way. With great determination, he led his sons in digging up these mountains hoe in hand. Another graybeard, known as the Wise Old Man, saw them and said derisively, "How silly of you to do this! It is quite impossible for you few to dig up these two huge mountains." The Foolish Old Man replied, "When I die, my sons will carry on; when they die, there will be my grandsons, and then their sons and grandsons, and so on to infinity. High as they are, the mountains cannot grow any higher and with every bit we dig, they will be that much lower. Why can't we clear them away?" Having refuted the Wise Old Man's wrong view, he went on digging every day, unshaken in his conviction. God was moved by this, and he sent down two angels, who carried the mountains away on their backs. Today, two big mountains lie like a dead weight on the Chinese people. One is imperialism, the other is feudalism. The Chinese Communist Party has long made up its mind to dig them up. We must persevere and work unceasingly, and we, too, will touch God's heart. Our God is none other than the masses of the Chinese people. If they stand up and dig together with us, why can't these two mountains be cleared away?

["The Foolish Old Man Who Removed the Mountains" (1945)]

Source: Quotations from Chairman Mao Tse-tung (Peking: Foreigh Languages Press, 1972), 1–3, 8, 19, 45, 52, 54, 86, 88, 90, 118–19, 124–25, 127–28, 161–62, 194–95, 201–2.

> At the conclusion of President Richard Nixon's historic trip to China in February 1972, the United States and China issued a joint communiqué in Shanghai. The document addressed the common goals and essential differences remaining between the two countries and affirmed their mutual desire to normalize diplomatic relations. The most sensitive issue raised in the communiqué was that of Taiwan. In the end, the issue was finessed. "[A]ll Chinese on either side of the Taiwan Strait," the document declared, "maintain there is but one China and that Taiwan is a part of China. The United States Government does not challenge that position." Although the United States did not "challenge" that position, it did not state that it agreed with it, largely because there were awkward legal and ethical considerations with which to deal. To break relations with Taiwan, its loyal ally, might call into question the sincerity of America's commitments to its other allies. There was also the question of the U.S.-Taiwan Mutual Security Treaty. Finally, a large number of Taiwanese did not consider the island to be part of Chinese territory and have long been opposed to unification with a country to which they felt no ideological or emotional ties.
>
> Another seven years would pass before full diplomatic relations were established. In the intervening period, each side set up a liaison office in the other's capital, trade increased markedly, and contacts and exchanges took place in a number of areas. The Taiwan issue was somewhat defused when the United States ended formal ties with the island and the defense treaty was abrogated. To provide for Taiwan's security, the U.S. Congress passed the Taiwan Relations Act in April 1979 declaring that the U.S. would continue to sell such defensive weapons as were "deemed necessary" to maintain the balance of power in the Taiwan Strait.
>
> The text has been edited for inclusion here. Punctuation and spelling are as in the original.

Document 8
1972 SHANGHAI COMMUNIQUÉ

President Richard Nixon of the United States of America visited the People's Republic of China at the invitation of Premier Chou [Zhou] Enlai of the People's Republic of China from February 21 to February 28, 1972....

President Nixon met with Chairman Mao [Zedong] of the Communist Party of China on February 21. The two leaders had a serious and frank exchange of views on Sino-U.S. relations and world affairs.

During the visit, extensive, earnest and frank discussions were held between President Nixon and Premier Chou Enlai on the normalization of relations between the United States of America and the People's Republic of China, as well as on other matters of interest to both sides. In addition, Secretary of State William Rogers and Foreign Minister Chi Peng-fei [Ji Pengfei] held talks in the same spirit. . . .

The U.S. side stated: Peace in Asia and peace in the world requires efforts both to reduce immediate tensions and to eliminate the basic causes of conflict. The United States will work for a just and secure peace; just, because it fulfills the aspirations of peoples and nations for freedom and progress; secure, because it removes the danger of foreign aggression. The United States supports individual freedom and social progress for all the peoples of the world, free of outside pressure or intervention. The United States believes that the effort to reduce tensions is served by improving communication between countries that have different ideologies so as to lessen the risks of confrontation through accident, miscalculation or misunderstanding. Countries should treat each other with mutual respect and be willing to compete peacefully, letting performance be the ultimate judge. No country should claim infallibility and each country should be prepared to reexamine its own attitudes for the common good. The United States stressed that the peoples of Indochina should be allowed to determine their destiny without outside intervention; its constant primary objective has been a negotiated solution; the eight-point proposal put forward by the Republic of Vietnam and the United States on January 27, 1972, represents a basis for the attainment of that objective; in the absence of a negotiated settlement the United States envisages the ultimate withdrawal of all U.S. forces from the region consistent with the aim of self determination for each country of Indochina. The United States will maintain its close ties with and support for the Republic of Korea; the United States will support efforts of the Republic of Korea to seek a relaxation of tension and increased communication in the Korean peninsula. The United States places the highest value on its friendly relations with Japan; it will continue to develop the existing close bonds. Consistent with the United Nations Security Council Resolution of December 21, 1971, the United States favors the continuation of the ceasefire between India and Pakistan and the withdrawal of all military forces to within their own territories and to their own sides of the ceasefire line in Jammu and Kashmir; the United States supports the right of the peoples of South

Asia to shape their own future in peace; free of military threat, and without having the area become the subject of great power rivalry.

The Chinese side stated: Wherever there is oppression, there is resistance. Countries want independence, nations want liberation and the people want revolution—this has become the irresistible trend of history. All nations, big or small, should be equal; big nations should not bully the small and strong nations should not bully the weak. China will never be a superpower and it opposes hegemony and power politics of any kind. The Chinese side stated that it firmly supports the struggles of all the oppressed people and nations for freedom and liberation and that the people of all countries have the right to choose their social systems according to their own wishes and the right to safeguard the independence, sovereignty and territorial integrity of their own countries and oppose foreign aggression, interference, control and subversion. All foreign troops should be withdrawn to their own countries.

The Chinese side expressed its firm support to the peoples of Vietnam, Laos and Cambodia in their efforts for the attainment of their goal and its firm support to the seven-point proposal of the Provisional Revolutionary Government of the Republic of South Vietnam and the elaboration of February this year on the two key problems in the proposal, and to the Joint Declaration of the Summit Conference of the Indochinese Peoples. It firmly supports the eight-point program for the peaceful unification of Korea put forward by the Government of the Democratic People's Republic of Korea on April 12, 1971, and the stand for the abolition of the "U.N. Commission for the Unification and Rehabilitation of Korea." It firmly opposes the revival and outward expansion of Japanese militarism and firmly supports the Japanese people's desire to build an independent, democratic, peaceful and neutral Japan. It firmly maintains that India and Pakistan should, in accordance with the United Nations resolutions on the India-Pakistan question, immediately withdraw all their forces to their respective territories and to their own sides of the ceasefire line in Jammu and Kashmir and firmly supports the Pakistan Government and people in their struggle to preserve their independence and sovereignty and the people of Jammu and Kashmir in their struggle for the right of self-determination.

There are essential differences between China and the United States in their social systems and foreign policies. However, the two sides agreed that countries, regardless of their social systems, should conduct their relations on the principles of respect for the sovereignty and territorial integrity of all states, nonaggression against other states, noninterference in the internal affairs of other states, equality and mutual benefit, and peaceful coexistence. International disputes should be settled on this basis, without resorting to the use or threat of force. The United States and the People's Republic of China are prepared to apply these principles to their mutual relations.

With these principles of international relations in mind the two sides stated that:

- progress toward the normalization of relations between China and the United States is in the interests of all countries;
- both wish to reduce the danger of international military conflict;
- neither should seek hegemony in the Asia-Pacific region and each is opposed to efforts by any other country or group of countries to establish such hegemony; and
- neither is prepared to negotiate on behalf of any third party or to enter into agreements or understandings with the other directed at other states.

Both sides are of the view that it would be against the interests of the peoples of the world for any major country to collude with another against other countries, or for major countries to divide up the world into spheres of interest.

The two sides reviewed the longstanding serious disputes between China and the United States. The Chinese reaffirmed their position: The Taiwan question is the crucial question obstructing the normalization of relations between China and the United States; the Government of the People's Republic of China is the sole legal government of China; Taiwan is a province of China which has long been returned to the motherland; the liberation of Taiwan is China's internal affair in which no other country has the right to interfere; and all U.S. forces and military installations must be withdrawn from Taiwan. The Chinese Government firmly opposes any activities which aim at the creation of "one China, one Taiwan," "one China, two governments," "two Chinas," an "independent Taiwan" or advocate that "the status of Taiwan remains to be determined."

The U.S. side declared: The United States acknowledges that all Chinese on either side of the Taiwan Strait maintain there is but one China and that Taiwan is a part of China. The United States Government does not challenge that position. It reaffirms its interest in a peaceful settlement of the Taiwan question by the Chinese themselves. With this prospect in mind, it affirms the ultimate objective of the withdrawal of all U.S. forces and military installations from Taiwan. In the meantime, it will progressively reduce its forces and military installations on Taiwan as the tension in the area diminishes.

The two sides agreed that it is desirable to broaden the understanding between the two peoples. To this end, they discussed specific areas in such fields as science, technology, culture, sports and journalism, in which people-to-people contacts and exchanges would be mutually beneficial. Each side undertakes to facilitate the further development of such contacts and exchanges.

Both sides view bilateral trade as another area from which mutual benefit can be derived, and agreed that economic relations based on equality and mutual benefit are in the interest of the peoples of the two countries. They agree to facilitate the progressive development of trade between their two countries.

The two sides agreed that they will stay in contact through various channels, including the sending of a senior U.S. representative to Peking [Beijing] from time to time for concrete consultations to further the normalization of relations between the two countries and continue to exchange views on issues of common interest.

Source: New China News Agency, February 27, 1972.

Deng Xiaoping, emerging as the preeminent figure in the Chinese Communist Party by the late 1970s, for several years had been leading a wide-ranging assault on the legacies of the Cultural Revolution and Mao Zedong's radicalism. At the end of 1978, during the third plenum of the Eleventh Central Committee, Deng effectively silenced Hua Guofeng and other defenders of the Cultural Revolution and began emphasizing the principles of political stability, openness, and economic development. Intent on remaking China, Deng forged ahead without thinking through the details of the many reforms which he envisioned. By the spring of 1979, evidence was mounting quickly, however, that foreign debt was becoming unmanageable and inflation was climbing. In a phrase, the economy was "overheating." Moreover, political agitation from dissidents and students was reaching unacceptable levels.

In these circumstances, Deng responded on March 30, 1979, with a speech evoking the "four cardinal principles" that he hoped would dampen the excesses of reformism, cool inflationary fires, and provide the period of leadership "readjustment" to the changes already underway that moderate reformers, such as Chen Yun, were advocating. He also intended to impress on the public the unacceptability of questioning principles. In a speech he delivered at a party theoretical forum, Deng insisted that all future policies and public attitudes must be in conformity with (1) Marxism-Leninism and Mao Zedong Thought, (2) the socialist road, (3) continuation of the people's democratic dictatorship, and (4) absolute political domination by the Chinese Communist Party. Though the first three were subsequently subject to extensive debate and emendation, the fourth remained at the heart of Deng's basic viewpoint and amounted to a firm commitment on the party's part to suppress any challenge to its political hegemony. The significance of this would be revealed by the end of 1979 with the closure of Democracy Wall and again to the watching eye of the world in Tiananmen Square in 1989.

The text of the speech is presented here in substantially abbreviated form. Punctuation and spelling are as in the original.

Document 9
UPHOLD THE FOUR CARDINAL PRINCIPLES

Comrades,

This forum on the principles for the Party's theoretical work has been in session for some time. With the meeting drawing to an end, the Central Committee has asked me to set forth a few views on the subject.

I. THE PRESENT SITUATION AND OUR TASKS. . . .

We need to make an adequate assessment of all aspects of the situation since the toppling of the Gang of Four, and particularly since the Third Plenary Session. In the two and a half years since the overthrow of the Gang, we have destroyed most of its counter-revolutionary political forces and readjusted and strengthened our leading bodies at various levels. Leadership in the Party, the government and the army is now mainly in the hands of cadres worthy of the people's trust, and most of the work in these three spheres has returned to normal. This is a momentous, hard-won achievement. We have freed ourselves from the effects of the decade of turmoil created by Lin Biao and the Gang of Four and secured a political situation marked by stability and unity; this situation is both a prerequisite and a guarantee for our socialist modernization. . . .

But at the same time we are confronted with some rather serious difficulties, and failure to recognize that too will likewise lead to major errors. First of all, we must make a sober appraisal of our country's economy, which has long suffered damage from Lin Biao and the Gang of Four, and reach a common view of the subject. In the past decade we have failed to rid the economy of the serious imbalances which have made it impossible to achieve a steady and reliable high rate of growth. It appears that in the general process of advance, our economy—that is, our agriculture, industry, capital construction, transport services, domestic and foreign trade, and banking and finance—needs a period of readjustment in order to change from varying degrees of imbalance to relative balance. The present readjustment is different from that of the early 1960s. Being made at a time when the economy is growing, it aims to lay a solid foundation for the four modernizations. However, it is necessary to make a partial retreat. Some unrealistically high targets, which it would do more harm than good to aim at, must be resolutely lowered, and some ill-managed enterprises which run at a heavy loss must be consolidated within a certain time span or even temporarily shut down so that consolidation can be carried out. We must take one step back in order to take two steps forward. . . .

What is our main task at present and for a fairly long time to come? To put it briefly, it is to carry out the modernization program. The destiny of our country and people hinges on its success. Given our present conditions, it will be precisely by succeeding in the four modernizations that we will be adhering to Marxism and holding high the great banner of Mao Zedong Thought. And if we fail to proceed from this reality and to concentrate on the four modernizations, it will mean that we are departing from Marxism while indulging in empty talk about it. At the present time, socialist modernization is of supreme political importance for us, because it represents the most fundamental interest of our people. Today every member of the Communist Party and the Communist Youth League and every patriotic citizen must devote all his energies to the modernization drive and do all he can to overcome every difficulty under the unified leadership of the Party and government.

II. THE NECESSITY OF UPHOLDING THE FOUR CARDINAL PRINCIPLES IN THE DRIVE FOR THE FOUR MODERNIZATIONS

. . . At least two important features of our situation must be taken into account in order to carry out the four modernizations in China.

First, we are starting from a weak base. The damage inflicted over a long period by the forces of imperialism, feudalism and bureaucrat-capitalism reduced China to a state of poverty and backwardness. However, since the founding of the People's Republic we have achieved signal successes in economic construction, established a fairly comprehensive industrial system, and trained a body of technical personnel. From Liberation to last year, the average annual rate of growth in our industry and agriculture was fairly high by world standards. Nonetheless, because of our low starting point, China is still one of the world's poor countries. . . .

Second, we have a large population but not enough arable land. Of China's population of more than 900 million, 80 per cent are peasants. While there are advantages to having a large population, there are disadvantages as well. When production is insufficiently developed, it poses serious problems with regard to food, education, and employment. We must greatly increase our efforts in family planning; but even if the population does not grow for a number of years, we will still have a population problem for a certain period. . . .

What I want to talk about now is ideological and political questions. The Central Committee maintains that, to carry out China's four modernizations, we must uphold the four cardinal principles ideologically and politically. This is the basic prerequisite for achieving modernization. The four principles are:

1. We must keep to the socialist road.
2. We must uphold the dictatorship of the proletariat.
3. We must uphold the leadership of the Communist Party.
4. We must uphold Marxism-Leninism and Mao Zedong Thought. . . .

We have criticized, on both a theoretical and a practical level, the phoney, ultra-Left socialism pushed by the Gang of Four, which boils down to universal poverty. We have always followed the principles of socialist public ownership and distribution according to work. We have always followed the policy of developing socialist economic construction mainly through self-reliance—supplemented by foreign aid—and through the study and acquisition of advanced technology from abroad. We have tried to act in accordance with objective economic laws. In other words, we have adhered to scientific socialism. . . .

We have restored the three major features of the Party's style of work, which had been trampled upon, improved the system of democratic centralism in the Party, and reinforced unity throughout the Party and between the Party and the masses. All this has enormously enhanced the Party's prestige and strengthened its leadership of the state and society.

We have broken the mental shackles forged by Lin Biao and the Gang of Four and have insisted that leaders should be regarded as human beings, not demigods. We have always tried to understand Marxism-Leninism and Mao Zedong Thought correctly and as an integral, scientific system, and have always proceeded from reality and sought truth from facts. In other words, we have restored the original features of Mao Zedong Thought and defended the eminence of Comrade Mao Zedong as a great figure in the history of the Chinese revolution and of world revolution. Nevertheless, the Central Committee believes that today there is still a tremendous need to stress propaganda on the four cardinal principles. . . .

First, we must keep to the socialist road. Some people are now openly saying that socialism is inferior to capitalism. We must demolish this contention. In the first place, socialism and socialism alone can save China—this is the unshakable historical conclusion that the Chinese people have drawn from their own experience in the 60 years since the May 4th Movement [1919]. Deviate from socialism and China will inevitably retrogress to semi-feudalism and semicolonialism. . . . In the second place, although it is a fact that socialist China lags behind the developed capitalist countries in its economy, technology, and culture, this is not a result of the socialist system but basically of China's historical development before Liberation; it is the result of imperialism and feudalism. . . .

Second, we must uphold the dictatorship of the proletariat. We have conducted a lot of propaganda explaining that the dictatorship of the proletariat means socialist democracy for the people, democracy enjoyed by the workers, peasants, intellectuals, and other working people, the broadest democracy that has ever existed in history. In the past, we did not practice democracy enough and we made mistakes. Lin Biao and the Gang of Four, while boosting their so-called "all-around dictatorship," exercised a feudal fascist dictatorship over the people. We have smashed this dictatorship, which had nothing in common with the dictatorship of the proletariat but was its diametric opposite. . . .

Third, we must uphold the leadership of the Communist Party. Since the inception of the international communist movement, it has been demonstrated that its survival is impossible without the political parties of the proletariat. Moreover, since the October Revolution it has been clear that without the leadership of a Communist Party, the socialist revolution, the dictatorship of the proletariat, and socialist construction would all be impossible. Lenin said: "The dictatorship of the proletariat is a persistent struggle—bloody and bloodless, violent and peaceful, military and economic, educational and administrative—against the forces and traditions of the old society. . . . Without an iron party tempered in the struggle, without a party enjoying the confidence of all that is honest in the given class, without a party capable of watching and influencing the mood of the masses, it is impossible to conduct such a struggle successfully." This truth enunciated by Lenin remains valid today. . . . Without the Chinese Communist Party there would be no socialist new China. . . .

In the China of today we can never dispense with leadership by the Party and extol the spontaneity of the masses. Party leadership, of course, is not infallible, and the problem of how the Party can maintain close links with the masses and exercise correct and effective leadership is still one that we must seriously study and try to solve. But this can never be made a pretext for demanding the weakening or liquidation of the Party's leadership. Our Party has made many errors, but each time the errors were corrected by relying on the Party organization, not by discarding it. The present Central Committee is persistent in promoting democracy in the Party and among the people and is determined to correct past errors. Under these circumstances, it would be all the more intolerable to the masses of our people to demand the liquidation or even the weakening of leadership by the Party. In fact, bowing to this demand would only lead to anarchism and the disruption and ruin of the socialist cause. . . .

Fourth, we must uphold Marxism-Leninism and Mao Zedong Thought. One of the key points of our struggle against Lin Biao and the Gang of Four was opposition to their falsification, doctoring, and fragmenting of Marxism-Leninism and Mao Zedong Thought. Since the smashing of the Gang, we have restored the scientific character of Marxism-Leninism and Mao Zedong Thought and have guided ourselves by them. This is a resounding victory for the whole Party and people. But a few individuals think otherwise. Either they openly oppose the basic tenets of Marxism-Leninism, or else they uphold Marxism-Leninism in word only while in deed opposing Mao Zedong Thought, which represents the integration of the universal truth of Marxism-Leninism with the practice of the Chinese revolution. We must oppose these erroneous trends of thought. Some comrades say that we should uphold "correct Mao Zedong Thought," but not "erroneous Mao Zedong Thought." This kind of statement is also wrong. What we consistently take as our guide to action are the basic tenets of Marxism-Leninism and Mao Zedong Thought or, to put it another way, the scientific system formed by these tenets. When it comes to individual theses, neither Marx and Lenin nor Comrade Mao could be immune from misjudgments of one sort or another. But these do not belong to the scientific system formed by the basic tenets of Marxism-Leninism and Mao Zedong Thought. . . .

To sum up, in order to achieve the four modernizations we must keep to the socialist road, uphold the dictatorship of the proletariat, uphold the leadership of the Communist Party, and uphold Marxism-Leninism and Mao Zedong Thought. The Central Committee considers that we must now repeatedly emphasize the necessity of upholding these four cardinal principles, because certain people (even if only a handful) are attempting to undermine them. In no way can such attempts be tolerated. No Party member and, needless to say, no Party ideological or theoretical worker, must ever waver in the slightest on this basic stand. To undermine any of the four cardinal principles is to undermine the whole cause of socialism in China, the whole cause of modernization.

Source: Selected Works of Deng Xiaoping, 1975–1982 (Beijing: Foreign Languages Press, 1984), 166–91.

Following is a selection of documents relating to the situation of ethnic minorities in the PRC. In those reflecting "official" viewpoints, noteworthy are the arguments that ethnic dissension is inconsequential, foreign in origin or instigation, and limited to those who want one region or another to split from China. Likewise, China is regarded as the sole benefactor of the ethnic regions, without whose selfless support they would remain impoverished. The connection between economic development and remaining within the Chinese fold is a constant refrain, as is the implication that ethnic regions, such as Tibet, have always been parts of China.

The texts have been edited for inclusion here. Punctuation and spelling are as in the original.

THE NON-HAN CHINESE

Document 10
XINJIANG PARTY SECRETARY SAYS SITUATION "EXCELLENT"

Song Hanliang, secretary of the Xinjiang Uygur Autonomous Regional CCP Committee, denied yesterday that national separatist activities are going on in Xinjiang's border areas. Describing the current Xinjiang "situation as excellent," he held that so long as Xinjiang's economic construction is genuinely boosted, the "voice" of the Western forces of infiltration and national separatists will be stifled.

Song was interviewed by reporters here yesterday. Asked about the recent national separatist activities in Xinjiang in the wake of the Soviet disintegration, he said: Although there is one force abroad adopting unfriendly acts and uttering unfriendly remarks toward China's Xinjiang, this does not affect the situation as a whole; . . . Xinjiang will not split with China.

He said: There are various voices in any society. The dissenting voices are insignificant and, with the development of economic construction, will disappear spontaneously.

He stressed: The current situation in Xinjiang Region is excellent. The nationalities are united, the economy is developing, the living standard of the people is improving.

Source: Ming Pao (Hong Kong), March 29, 1992, p. 24; translated in *Foreign Broadcasting Information Services*, April 1, 1992.

Document 11
BOMB PART OF "ANTIGOVERNMENT ATTACK" IN XINJIANG

A bomb ripped a huge hole in a Kashgar city government building in the remote western Chinese Xinjiang Uygur Autonomous Region last week, in what was believed to be an antigovernment attack, sources said Thursday

[June 24]. The bomb, which exploded around 4 P.M. on June 17, killed and wounded up to ten people, the sources in the city of Kashgar said.

According to local Chinese sources, the four-story building belonged to the city municipal government and housed the offices of the agricultural machinery division. Public Security Bureau forces have already arrested one person allegedly involved in the bombing and are continuing their investigations, they said.

The sources said that the bombing could be related to antigovernment sentiments in the region, which is a predominantly Muslim-minority, non-Han, area of China. Minority peoples often take to the street to express their antigovernment feelings, the sources claimed, adding that peasants have recently been dissatisfied with the government's tax policy. . . .

The building, located in downtown Kashgar, is across the street from the Seman Guesthouse, a hotel popular with Western tourists.

Sources said that the bomb was placed on the third floor of the building, next to the offices of a private company involved in the purchase and sale of agricultural machinery. The company is owned by the city government. . . . Employees at the Seman Guesthouse estimated that between two and five people were killed in the blast.

Kashgar is close to the border of Pakistan and several former Soviet republics. . . .

In late May, citizens in Lhasa, the capital of Tibet, rioted over price rises, while other such incidents have reportedly occurred in Sichuan, Hunan, Henan, and Jinan provinces.

Source: Kyodo (Tokyo), June 24, 1993; translated in *Foreign Broadcasting Information Services*, June 24, 1993.

Document 12
TIBET'S DEPUTY PARTY SECRETARY RAIDI DISCUSSES "ANTISPLITTIST STRUGGLE"

Speaking at a recent work meeting held by the autonomous regional party committee and people's government, Raidi, deputy secretary of the autonomous regional party committee and chairman of the autonomous regional people's congress standing committee, pointed out: Tibetan people of various nationalities have waged resolute struggles against domestic and foreign splittist forces in recent years. They have achieved very considerable results in their antisplittist struggle and in their work to stabilize the situation. We must further strengthen our understanding of the protractedness, complexity, and arduousness of the antisplittist struggle; crack down, with a clear-cut stance, on splittist activities; and firmly maintain our initiative in the struggle.

Raidi pointed out: Party organizations at various levels should correctly and properly handle the relationship between economic construction and stabilizing the situation. They should understand that we must have a stable social environment if we are to take economic construction as our central task and if we wish to enhance economic progress. Without stability, we cannot possibly seize opportunities, develop social productive forces, or raise people's living standards. Therefore, issues concerning the situation's stability are major issues that concern the country's unification, the unity of nationalities, and Tibet's development and progress. . . . While properly enhancing economic construction, we should specifically, firmly, and realistically carry out antisplittist struggles and work to stabilize the situation.

Raidi stressed: The broad masses of party members and cadres should resolutely stand at the forefront of the antisplittist struggle; safeguard, with a clear-cut stance, the motherland's unification; strengthen the unity of nationalities; enhance social stability; self-consciously resist various infiltrations of hostile forces; and withstand the test of antisplittist struggles. We should persistently attach importance to teaching the history that Tibet has been an inalienable part of the motherland and to publicizing and promoting Tibet's future. We should enable the masses of various nationalities to profoundly understand that only by following the CCP's leadership and taking the socialist road can Tibet have a bright and splendid future. Only by living in the motherland's large family can Tibetan people have a rich and happy tomorrow. We should realize that no attempts can restore Tibet to its former state. The schemes of domestic and foreign splittist forces will never succeed. Their activities to split the motherland can only fail totally in the end.

Raidi said: Strengthening the administration of temples and religious activities has a special practical significance in comprehensively implementing the party's policy on religion, in better resisting the splittist forces that conduct splittist activities and sabotage under the pretext of religion, and in stabilizing Tibet's situation. Religious activities can only be conducted within the realm of the law. Normal religious activities should be protected by law; however, no one is allowed, under the pretext of religion, to oppose the party's leadership or the socialist system, or to carry out crimes that violate the law, including splitting the motherland's unification.

In conclusion, Raidi stressed: Strengthening antisplittist struggles and properly performing work to stabilize the situation are the current important tasks for party and government organizations at various levels in Tibet. All party and government organizations should uphold the party's basic line and persistently pursue the policy of grasping two links at the same time and of attaching importance to both. While upholding the central task of economic construction and properly carrying out reform and opening up, we should regard launching antisplittist struggles and work to stabilize the situation as important parts of our agenda.

Source: Tibet People's Radio Network (Lhasa), August 11, 1993; translated in *Foreign Broadcasting Information Services*, August 24, 1993.

> The author of this essay, Wang Ruoshui, served as deputy editor-in-chief of the *People's Daily* until his dismissal in 1983 during a campaign against "spiritual pollution," or unappreciated influences from abroad, particularly from Western cultures. The following article, dated January of that same year and appearing here in condensed form, captures the themes of socialist humanism and alienation that have figured prominently in Wang's writings.
>
> This essay is important for several reasons. It argues in favor of a theme—humanism—that Wang correctly identifies as having been misinterpreted frequently by supporters of China's revolution, with disastrous consequences. Rather than seeing humanism as merely an element within bourgeois ideology, he insists that it belongs to all ideologies and has always possessed revolutionary implications. Bourgeois advocacy of humanism ought not serve to deny its value in the larger process of mankind's liberation from exploitation. Shrewdly using words carefully chosen from Marx and Mao about the importance of people (the opening phrase about there being a ghost haunting China's intellectuals is a paraphrase of Marx's *Communist Manifesto*), Wang "proves" those revolutionaries' fundamental commitment to a humanist viewpoint that, while not supportive of crude individualism, holds nothing more important than each person. Appeals to the Renaissance and the long tradition of humanist thought in European culture are themselves pointed criticisms of the Maoist legacy as epitomized by the Cultural Revolution, as are positive use of phrases such as "human dignity," "human value," and "human freedom."
>
> The text is presented here in its entirety. Punctuation and spelling are as in the original.

Document 13
IN DEFENSE OF HUMANISM

There is a ghost haunting China's intellectuals: the ghost of humanism. Over the past three years, more than four hundred articles have been written discussing the problem of "humanity," and quite a few of them have explored Marxist humanism. That it has evoked such strong interest is not just a reaction to the ten years of turmoil (during the Cultural Revolution): it is also an expression in our new era of the need to build a socialist society with a high degree of culture and democracy. But some well-intentioned comrades reject any humanist slogan, on the grounds that humanism is unorthodox.

The main reasons they put forward are: humanism is an ideology of the bourgeoisie; humanism discusses humanity as something abstract; and humanism was early on denounced and abandoned by Marx. So they use Marxism to oppose humanism, instead of using Marxist humanism to oppose bourgeois humanism. They do not just disavow specific forms of humanism, but negate it as a fundamental principle. In this article, then, I shall defend humanism in general and Marxist humanism in particular.

"Humanism is an ideology of the bourgeoisie." If this means that humanism was the ideology of the bourgeoisie, then it is a statement of historical fact not open to dispute. But if it means that humanism can *only* be an ideology of the bourgeoisie, then I challenge it. We must never confound the two meanings; the second cannot be deduced from the first.

Materialism too was an ideology of the capitalist class (and even of the slaveholder class and the feudal class), but that did not stop materialism from becoming the worldview of the proletariat. Can we say the same of humanism? First we must look at its inner meaning. If humanism (like individualism) is essentially and inexorably linked with the bourgeoisie, then it can only be a bourgeois ideology; otherwise it will not be thus restricted. "Humanism" is a word of foreign origin, and many Chinese have only a vague and inaccurate idea of its meaning. There are many schools of humanism, each with a different interpretation, but there is one that is generally recognized.

The word "humanism" originally referred to the main ideological theme of the Renaissance (humanism in a narrow sense, also called "humanitarianism"), but it was later broadened to embrace concepts that have humans as their main purport, that is, human value, human dignity, human interests or happiness, and human development or freedom. Humanism is a long-standing and well-established trend of thought that in the Western world has existed for at least six hundred years. Since the Renaissance, we have seen the humanism of the Enlightenment, utopian socialist humanism, Feuerbach's humanism, and various shades of modern humanism. The concept "humanism" is derived from all these sources. Why do so many schools of thought call themselves "humanist"? Because they all acknowledge a common principle: the value of human beings.

Many comrades are perhaps not accustomed to the term "value of human beings," but everybody will be familiar with the words of Mao Zedong: "Of all things in the world, people are the most precious." Does that not put the highest value on human beings? True, Mao did not use the term "value of human beings," but that is only a difference of terminology. I shall now show that Marx had already used the term in a positive sense.

Many comrades mistrust the term "value of human beings" because they feel that affirming "human value" means affirming "the value of the individual," which makes them think of individualism. But it is not an affirmation of individualism, any more than affirming that "people are the most precious" is. During the development of humanism, some forms of it have borne the stamp of individualism, but others have carried connotations of universal love and altruism. Feuerbach propounded universal love between human beings; his humanism opposed selfishness. But Max Stirner, Feuerbach's contemporary and the founder of anarchist individualism, was firmly opposed to humanism. This shows that there is no cast-iron link between humanism and individualism, and that "the value of human beings" does not equal individualism. We are advocating collectivism; collectivism is the opposite of individualism, but it is not opposed to the value of human beings, correctly understood. A collective is made up of individuals. If one individual or a group of individuals in a collective is without value, in Marx' view that collective is illusory and alienated (capitalist countries are collectives of this sort). The value of the individual can only be realized within a collective.

Some comrades may admit the slogan "revolutionary humanism," but only in connection with such matters as healing the wounded, rescuing the dying, and treating prisoners of war leniently. They insist that we should not broaden its meaning and expand the sphere of its application. And here lies a problem. In the modern world healing the wounded, rescuing the dying, and treating prisoners of war leniently are international norms. Although these norms are repeatedly violated, international public opinion has always condemned such violations. If we restrict the practice of "revolutionary humanism" so narrowly, we will be unable to distinguish it from bourgeois humanism. What makes humanism revolutionary is not the humane treatment of the wounded or of prisoners of war, but its use of revolutionary means to realize human value. We cultivate the fields for the revolution, we work for the revolution, we do everything for the revolution. But for what is the revolution? Revolution is a means, not an end. We work for socialism and communism, for the interests and happiness of the people, for the liberation of all humanity. That is the meaning of revolutionary humanism.

It is a pity that during the "great cultural revolution" we counterposed "revolution" and "humanism." People thought then that since humanism was not revolutionary, the revolution must not concern itself with humanism. So the "capitalist-roaders," "revisionist elements," and "monsters and demons" of those days were treated even less humanely than prisoners of war.

The reason people view humanism as part of bourgeois ideology is because they believe that it merely opposed feudalism. Yet historically it has played a role against capitalism too. The originator of utopian socialism, Henry [*sic*, Sir Thomas] More, was a believer in humanism. In the eighteenth century, champions of the French bourgeois enlightenment raised the slogan of "freedom and equality" on the basis of humanism and in opposition to feudalism. In the nineteenth century, British and French utopian socialists seized this weapon, turned it around, and used it against capitalism. They exposed the hypocrisy of bourgeois "freedom" and "equality" and propagated true freedom and equality. A society that conforms to humanist norms is socialist. Speaking of the relation between French materialists and utopian socialists in the eighteenth century, Marx said that Fourier, Owen, Dezamy, and Gay treated the materialist doctrine as real humanism and as the logical foundation of communism and developed it further.

Marx criticized Feuerbach's humanism, but he never radically negated it. Rather, he advanced it to a new stage. Likewise, he criticized Feuerbach's materialism, but he never radically negated materialism: instead he developed Feuerbach's intuitive materialism into practical materialism. Feuerbach said that "humans are humanity's highest essence." He criticized the theological view that "God is humanity's highest essence" and instead showed that "God is nothing but the essence of humanity." Feuerbach believed that it was not God who created humans, but humans who created God, by projecting their own nature onto him, that is, by alienating their own nature. The problem is that Feuerbach regarded humans only in the abstract and saw their essential nature as reason, will, and affection.

Religion depreciates human value, but does only religion do that? Humans need the opiate of religion because the real world is full of misery and alienation. After exposing religious alienation, we must expose the alienation of real life. We must criticize all social relations that humiliate, enslave, forsake, and despise humans. Since these forms of alienation are not just figments of the imagination but lived reality, they cannot be overcome by relying only on "weapons of criticism"; we still need the "criticism of weapons," that is, revolution. We must rely on that class for which inhuman conditions have reached the limit: the class that must liberate all humanity to liberate itself, that is, the proletariat.

Marx proceeds from the idea that "humans are humanity's highest essence" to the necessity of revolution. He establishes a link between humanism and violent revolution. This is revolutionary humanism or proletarian humanism. Both Marx and Feuerbach place humans highest, and recognize no essence above them. But Feuerbach opposes illusory superhuman forces only in the ideological field, while Marx opposes the social relations that degrade humans to an inhuman level. Marx arrives at this revolutionary conclusion because of his firm grasp of real humanity, social humanity.

In 1844 Marx pointed out that productive life is the life of the species, and that the activities of the human species are characteristically free and conscious; which is where humans differ from beasts. But alienated labor under private ownership is forced labor, done merely to subsist. In 1844 Marx was still a young man. Did he later discard his humanism? The mature Marx's *Communist Manifesto* criticizes "transforming the dignity of human beings into exchange value" and "leaving no bond between human beings other than naked interest and unfeeling 'cash transactions'." "In bourgeois society, capital possesses independence and individuality, but the individual operator has neither independence nor individuality." Marx and Engels pointed out that under communism the free development of each individual will be the condition for the free development of all.

Capital, a representative work of the older Marx, indignantly and at great length exposed capitalist exploitation, both physical and mental, of the workers and showed how large-scale industry turns the worker into an appendage of machines; it also exposed the pitiful fate of women and child workers. Marx further developed his idea of "alienation of labor" and expounded the doctrine of surplus value. Of human nature, he said: "We must first study general human nature, and then the changes in human nature that have typified each era." He believed that in communist society workers would live their material lives "under conditions most adequate to their human nature and most worthy of it," and "will begin that development of human power that is its own end, the true realm of freedom." This shows that Marx all along connected proletarian revolution and communism with questions of human value, dignity, emancipation, and freedom. This is the most thoroughgoing humanism.

"Humanism" is simply a word for various systems and trends of thought that emphasize human value. We must not confuse general humanism with the forms that humanism has taken in specific historical phases. Marxism is not identical with humanism, but it does include humanism. We propound Marxist humanism (socialist humanism, revolutionary humanism), just as we propound Marxist materialism.

Today, in the age of socialist modernization, we need socialist humanism. Humanism implies resolute rejection of the "all-round dictatorship" and cruel struggle of the Cultural Revolution. It rejects cults of personality that degrade the people. It firmly upholds the principle of universal equality before truth and the law, personal freedom, and personal dignity. It opposes the feudal concept of ranks and privileges, capitalist money worship, and the treatment of people as commodities or tools, and it demands that people be truly regarded as human beings. It sees people rather than socialist production as the goal, and aims to build up and develop a new type of relationship grounded in mutual respect, mutual concern, mutual assistance, and friendly cooperation as an embodiment of socialist civilization. It opposes bureaucratism, which ignores people, and extreme individualism, which strives for personal gain at others' expense. It promotes the human element in socialist construction and sees the workers as masters of their own affairs and creativity. It stresses education, the nurturing of talents, and the full development of humanity.

Is socialist humanism not already present in our practice? Is it not continuously developing? Why treat it as strange and alien?

There is a ghost haunting the vast expanse of China.

"Who are you?"

"I am humanity."

Source: Initially published in Beijing in 1986; a full English translation is in *Joint Publications Research Service* (Translations on People's Republic of China), October 3, 1988.

Glossary of Selected Terms

Anti-Lin Biao, Anti-Confucius Campaign: Campaign launched in late 1973 calling for criticism of the reactionary (feudal) features of Chinese society that Lin Biao, now disgraced and dead, and Confucius allegedly symbolized. The campaign was the third of Mao's efforts, following the Great Leap Forward and the Cultural Revolution, to ensure permanent revolution in China.

Anti-Rightist Campaign: A widespread attack upon intellectuals principally, under the banner of rooting out counterrevolutionaries. The campaign was launched by Mao Zedong in 1957 following bold public criticism of the CCP and its leaders during the Hundred Flowers Campaign of 1956.

Anti-Spiritual Pollution Campaign: Launched in 1982 by the CCP against Western influence in Chinese writing and the other arts. It lasted until October 1984 and focused on crime, corruption, pornography, and other social ills seen as consequences of the "open policy."

Basic Law: A document adopted by China's National People's Congress in April 1990 that was to serve as the constitution for Hong Kong after it reverted to Chinese sovereignty on July 1, 1997. The Basic Law is particularly important for its description of the relationship between the Hong Kong Special Administrative Region (SAR) and the central government in Beijing, the rights and duties of SAR residents, and the structure of the SAR government.

Central Committee: The central coordinating organ of the Chinese Communist Party, from which the even more powerful Politburo and its Standing Committee draw their members.

Democracy Wall: Situated along the edge of the Forbidden City, a stretch of wall where "big character" posters advocating democratic freedom were displayed in 1978–1979.

Fifth Modernization: Phrase taken from the title of a "big character" poster written by Wei Jingsheng and posted on Democracy Wall. Wei called for the addition of democracy as the "fifth modernization" to accompany and ensure the success of the "four modernizations" promoted by the CCP.

Five Anti Campaign: CCP-led "struggle" against Chinese entrepreneurs (industrialists and businessmen) who had remained in China after the communist victory in 1949. Carried out in 1951–1952, the campaign helped consolidate CCP authority over the economy by removing the last vestiges of independent capitalist activity.

Four Basic Principles: Outlined in China's state constitution, these principles have been used to distinguish between permissible and impermissible dissent. They include adherence to socialism, the dictatorship of the proletariat, rule by the CCP, and Marxism-Leninism-Mao Zedong Thought.

Four Modernizations: A policy first enunciated by Zhou Enlai in 1974 but fully implemented only under Deng Xiaoping in 1978. Its goals were the development of agriculture, industry, national defense, and science and technology. To accompany the four modernizations, Deng also inaugurated an open-door policy to the outside world, particularly the West, that included sending Chinese students abroad, encouraging foreign investment in Chinese enterprises, and developing special economic zones.

Gang of Four: Group led by Mao Zedong's wife Jiang Qing that also included Yao Wenyuan, Zhang Chunqiao, and Wang Hongwen. All rose to prominence during the Cultural Revolution and were later blamed officially for its excesses. On order of Hua Guofeng, they were arrested in October 1976, shortly after Mao's death, and were subsequently convicted in a national show trial.

Great Leap Forward (GLF): Campaign launched under Mao Zedong's auspices late in 1958 to raise China's economic production rapidly while avoiding the dangers (contradictions, in Mao's phrase) that typically accompany such development. The mechanism was a combination of mass organization and revolutionary fervor, highlighted by the notion that a properly harnessed popular will could overcome the obstacles to genuine revolutionary achievement. An economic and social disaster, the GLF was officially ended in 1961.

Great Proletarian Cultural Revolution (GPCR): Campaign by Mao Zedong against the moderate policies of Communist party pragmatists and the values and attitudes of traditional China. Like the Great Leap Forward, the GPCR was aimed at correcting China's drift away from socialism and toward capitalism. It lasted from 1966 to 1969.

Guomindang (GMD) (Kuomintang, Nationalist Party, KMT): Organized in 1912 by Sun Yat-sen, the party became a major political force in China. In 1949 the Guomindang government on the mainland collapsed, and Chiang Kai-shek, its leader since 1928, retreated with his supporters to Taiwan.

Household Responsibility System: Since the early 1980s, the system of agricultural organization whereby decisions concerning farm production are made by individual households, contracting land from their village, rather than by a collective or the government. Most of the annual production is left to the households, and losses are not protected by state subsidy.

Hundred Flowers Movement: Short-lived campaign launched by Mao in May 1957, ostensibly to encourage frank and public discussion of the CCP and its policies. Mao's call for "the blooming of a hundred flowers and the contending of a hundred schools of thought" led to an unprecedented outpouring of opinion, especially from intellectuals, that proved unwelcome politically and led to suppression by the end of June.

Iron Rice Bowl: A term referring to lifetime guaranteed employment at a fixed wage. A hallmark of CCP social policy until Mao's death in 1976, it was one of the casualties of Deng Xiaoping's reforms.

Long March: The trek of about 80,000 CCP supporters to escape the forces of Chiang Kai-shek in 1934–1935. Covered 6,000 miles from southeastern to northern China in about one year. Barely 10 percent of those who began the march survived. The event confirmed Mao Zedong's leadership.

Marshall Mission: Unsuccessful attempt by the American general George C. Marshall to mediate a peace between the Chinese communists and the Nationalists from 1945 to 1947.

Mass Line: Technique developed by the CCP during the Yan'an Period (1935–1947) to facilitate mass mobilization by providing a link between the party and the masses.

May Fourth Movement: Describes the intellectual and social movement growing out of the demonstrations by Chinese students in Tiananmen Square on May 4, 1919. It was precipitated by resentment against the weak warlord government in Beijing as well as the unfair terms of the Versailles Treaty that granted territorial concessions to Japan.

New Life Movement: Promoted by Chiang Kai-shek's government during the 1930s to foster moral development in the Chinese people and make them more amenable to mobilization. It comprised an ideology containing a mix of Confucian, Christian, and fascist beliefs.

Northern Expedition: Military campaign, beginning in 1926, under the leadership of Chiang Kai-shek. Troops set out from Canton to attack the warlords who had fragmented the country. By 1928 most of China was reunited under GMD control.

One Country, Two Systems: Policy enunciated by Deng Xiaoping for reuniting Hong Kong and Taiwan with the mainland. As special administrative regions, each would be able to maintain its current system under the administration of the Beijing government. The return of Hong Kong on July 1, 1997, represents partial fulfillment of this policy.

People's Communes: Large-scale collectives established beginning in 1958 to mobilize rural labor and prepare for the transition to communism. They were expanded to the cities during the Cultural Revolution and associated with Maoist economic theories. They were eliminated under Deng Xiaoping's reforms.

Rectification Campaign: Launched in Yan'an in 1942 by Mao Zedong as a political struggle to bolster the dominance of his ideology in the CCP. Wang Ming, a party rival, was a prime target of the campaign, as was Ding Ling, a feminist writer.

Red Guards: During the Cultural Revolution groups of university and middle-school students, who rose to Mao Zedong's challenge to follow his path and rekindle the revolutionary spirit in China. Red Guards swept the country, increasingly engaging in violent behavior against authority of all kinds, eventually struggling among themselves and their PLA allies in the late 1960s.

Sino-Soviet Split: Dispute between the Soviet Union and the PRC, emerging in the aftermath of Premier Nikita Khrushchev's denunciation of Stalin's "cult of personality" in 1956. The quarrel raged over historical, doctrinal, territorial, and strategic issues.

Socialist Education Campaign: Mass movement promoted by Mao Zedong beginning in 1963 to promote socialist values in Chinese society. To help break down the contradiction between urban and rural labor, as Mao saw it, urban cadres were sent to the countryside to work among peasants.

Special Economic Zones (SEZ): As part of the "four modernizations" program implemented under Deng Xiaoping, certain cities have been identified as sites for direct foreign investment and adoption of foreign technology. The special economic zones are to contribute to an increase of Chinese exports, thereby generating much needed capital and serving as models for the rest of the country. Four cities were originally designed SEZs in 1979, with fourteen others added in 1986, along with the island of Hainan.

Three Anti Campaign: CCP-sponsored mass movement launched in 1951 seeking to eliminate the vices of "corruption, waste, and obstructionist bureaucracy" among party, government, and economic elites.

Three Noes Policy: Official policy of the Republic of China on Taiwan against the PRC's requests for discussion of reunification. Included no contact, no negotiation, and no compromises.

Tiananmen Incident: Popular demonstrations occurring in Tiananmen Square on April 5, 1976. Spontaneous expressions of grief over the death of Zhou Enlai, the event was interpreted as a criticism of Mao Zedong and the Cultural Revolution.

Ti/yong ("Substance/Function"): From the slogan "Chinese learning for substance, Western learning for function." The approach to reform characteristic of the so-called self-strengtheners of the late nineteenth century.

United Front: A term describing the tenuous alliance between the usually hostile CCP and GMD, agreed to on two occasions—1923–1927 and 1937–1945— for purposes of achieving national goals. The first sought to wrest China from the warlords and restore national unity; the second aimed at resisting Japanese military intervention.

Yan'an Era: Refers to the period from 1937 to 1947 when Yan'an, a city in northern Shaanxi province, was the headquarters of the CCP. In Yan'an, the party was transformed into a serious threat to the Guomindang, and Mao Zedong became its principal ideologist.

Annotated Bibliography

BOOKS

General

Anderson, E. N. *The Food of China*. New Haven: Yale University Press, 1988. A rich and engrossing treatment of how the Chinese have managed to sustain themselves for centuries.

DeBary, William Theodore, Wing-tsit Chan, and Burton Watson, comps. *Sources of Chinese Tradition*. Two vols. New York: Columbia University Press, 1964. A rich introduction to the background of contemporary civilization in China. Offers translations from Chinese sources that illustrate Chinese thought since earliest times, from Confucius to Mao Zedong.

Ebrey, Patricia. *Chinese Civilization and Society: A Sourcebook*. 2nd ed. New York: Free Press, 1995. Primarily focused on social rather than intellectual history (see the previous work by DeBary et al.), this volume offers a chronological approach to revealing how institutions and historical developments affected ordinary Chinese.

Lindqvist, Cecilia. *China: Empire of Living Symbols*. Reading, MA: Addison-Wesley, 1989. Using language and the Chinese written script, the author offers a wealth of information on a large number of topics from Chinese cultural history.

Mote, Frederick W. *Intellectual Foundations of China*. 2nd ed. New York: McGraw-Hill, 1989. A brief but insightful introduction to the major schools of thought that had the most impact on the development of Chinese culture.

Ramsey, Robert S. *The Languages of China*. Princeton: Princeton University Press, 1987. Places China's linguistic diversity in historical, geographical, and social context.

Spence, Jonathan D. *The Search for Modern China*. New York: W. W. Norton & Co., 1990. Covers the period of China's history from the mid-seventeenth century to 1989. A comprehensive but highly readable and fascinating account.

Van Slyke, Lyman P. *Yangtze: Nature, History, and the River*. Reading, MA: Addison-Wesley, 1988. An effort to examine Chinese history from the perspective of one of its greatest rivers, showing how it has been a catalyst for major events and movements for millennia.

Late Imperial China (to 1911)

Pomeranz, Kenneth. *The Making of a Hinterland: State, Society, and Economy in Inland North China, 1853–1937*. Berkeley: University of California Press, 1993. An award-winning monograph that looks closely at a section of North China during the late imperial and early republican periods. The author uses a microanalytical approach to reveal the distinctiveness of the region and a much more complex interaction among divergent interests and forces than one tends to see by focusing on the state and China as a whole.

Scalapino, Robert A., and George T. Yu. *Modern China and its Revolutionary Process: Recurrent Challenges to the Traditional Order, 1850–1920*. Berkeley: University of California Press, 1985. A highly detailed, wonderfully informative, and intelligent examination of the decades that witnessed the death of the old regime and confused but determined efforts to create something better in its wake.

Teng, W. Y., and J. K. Fairbank, eds. *China's Response to the West: A Documentary Survey, 1839–1923*. 2nd ed. Cambridge, MA: Harvard University Press, 1979. A classic anthology of primary sources revealing the evolution of Chinese perceptions of European culture and capabilities.

Wakeman, Frederic, Jr. *The Fall of Imperial China*. New York: The Free Press, 1975. A good survey of the last century and one-half of the imperial order.

Wright, May C., ed. *China in Revolution: The First Phase, 1900–1913*. New Haven: Yale University Press, 1968. An important and still valuable early collection of essays treating the first years of revolutionary thought and activities.

Republican China (1911–1949)

Bianco, Lucien. *Origins of the Chinese Revolution, 1915–1940*. Stanford: Stanford University Press, 1967. An extended essay that is one of the best short accounts of the period, focusing especially upon social realities that affected ordinary Chinese.

Chang, Jung. *Wild Swans: Three Daughters of China*. New York: Simon and Schuster, 1992. A wonderful biographical account of three women in the same family over three generations, and their experiences during a century of dramatic change in China.

Gilmartin, Christina Kelley. *Engendering the Chinese Revolution: Radical Women, Communist Politics, and Mass Movements in the 1920s*. Berkeley: University of California Press, 1995. The author explores the experiences of radical Chinese women in revolutionary movements in Shanghai in the 1920s, as well as the role of gender in revolutionary politics.

Grieder, Jerome. *Intellectuals and the State in Modern China: A Narrative History*. New York: The Free Press, 1981. Covers the period from the early nineteenth century into the middle of the twentieth century, with a focus on Chinese liberalism and radicalism.

Hinton, William. *Fanshen: A Documentary of Revolution in a Chinese Village*. New York: Random House, 1966. A gripping account, based on the author's eyewitness experiences, of land reform carried out by the CCP in the North China village of Long Bow between 1947 and 1949. Hinton wrote a sequel that continues the story of the village to 1971 (*Shenfan: The Continuing Revolution in a Chinese Village* [New York: Random House, 1983]).

McCord, Edward A. *The Power of the Gun: The Emergence of Modern Chinese Warlordism*. Berkeley: University of California Press, 1993. A detailed analysis of military politics in Hubei and Hunan, neighboring provinces that played key political roles during the early Republic. The book's thesis is that warlordism emerged not from the general collapse of political authority at the end of the Qing dynasty but rather from the specific circumstances surrounding Yuan Shikai's effort to establish his centralized personal dictatorship.

Saich, Tony, ed. *The Rise to Power of the Chinese Communist Party: Documents and Analysis*. Armonk, NY: M. E. Sharpe, 1996. An imposing work containing 212 major Communist party documents along with lengthy analysis that together provide a very useful short history of the rise of the CCP.

Schiffrin, Harold Z. *Sun Yat-sen and the Origins of the Chinese Revolution*. Berkeley: University of California Press, 1968. A full and still valuable biography of China's most famous and important early revolutionary.

Schwarcz, Vera. *The Chinese Enlightenment: Intellectuals and the Legacy of the May Fourth Movement of 1919*. Berkeley: University of California Press, 1986. An important study that focuses on the May Fourth Movement and its lasting impact on twentieth-century Chinese thought and aspirations.

Sheridan, James E. *China in Disintegration: The Republican Era in Chinese History, 1912–1949*. New York: The Free Press, 1975. A solid treatment of the republican era that emerged out of one revolution in 1912 and was destroyed by a second in 1949.

Snow, Edgar. *Red Star over China*. Revised and enlarged ed. New York: Grove Press, 1968. An influential work first published in 1938 and containing unique autobiographical information from Mao Zedong. Snow spent months with the CCP Red Army in Yan'an in 1936.

Maoist China (1949–1978)

Becker, Jasper. *Hungry Ghosts: Mao's Secret Famine*. New York: The Free Press, 1997. The author reconstructs in agonizing detail the famine during the early 1960s in which 20–30 million people perished—a famine that the world did not hear about until recently. The revolution at its most self-destructive.

Cheng, Nien. *Life and Death in Shanghai*. New York: Grove Press, 1987. The autobiographical account of a woman persecuted during the Cultural Revolution. Her "crimes" included fraternizing with Westerners, elitism, and a love of the good life.

Goldman, Merle. *China's Intellectuals: Advise and Dissent*. Cambridge, MA: Harvard University Press, 1981. An informative work that unravels the relationship between China's intellectuals and the regime during the Cultural Revolution.

Hinton, Harold C., ed. *The People's Republic of China, 1949–1979: A Documentary Survey*. 5 vols. Wilmington, DE: Scholarly Resources, 1980. A full collection of material translated into English, covering many aspects of both domestic and foreign policy.

———. *The People's Republic of China, 1979–1984: A Documentary Survey*. 2 vols. Wilmington, DE: Scholarly Resources, 1986. A continuation of the previous collection.

Li, Zhisui. *The Private Life of Chairman Mao*. New York: Random House, 1994. A deeply personal narrative based almost exclusively on the author's memory of his own encounters with Mao and conversations with members of the Chairman's inner circle. Unflattering in its conclusion that once we strip away all of the mythical images that have surrounded Mao, the man we are left with is nothing more than a tyrant.

MacFarquhar, Roderick. *The Origins of the Cultural Revolution*, Vol. 1: *Contradictions among the People 1956–1957*. Oxford, England: Oxford University Press, 1974. This and the following volumes provide an extremely detailed and scholarly examination of Chinese politics in the years leading up to the Cultural Revolution.

———. *The Origins of the Cultural Revolution*, Vol. 2: *The Great Leap Forward 1958–1960*. New York: Columbia University Press, 1983.

———. *The Origins of the Cultural Revolution*, Vol. 3: *The Coming of the Cataclysm*. New York: Columbia University Press, 1997.

MacFarquhar, Roderick, and John K. Fairbank, eds. *The Cambridge History of China*, Vol. 14, *The People's Republic*, Part 1: The Emergence of Revolutionary China 1949–1965. Cambridge, England: Cambridge University Press, 1987. Part of the multi-volume, and as yet incomplete, *Cambridge History of China*, this volume covers the first sixteen years of the People's Republic and its development. The work is a collection of essays by eminent scholars covering politics, economics, culture, education, and foreign relations.

———. *The Cambridge History of China*, Vol. 15, *The People's Republic*, Part 2: Revolutions within the Chinese Revolution 1966–1982. Cambridge, England: Cambridge University Press, 1991. A continuation of the previous volume, covering developments through the early phase of Deng Xiaoping's redirection of Chinese life following the death of Mao Zedong in 1976.

Meisner, Maurice. *Mao's China and After: A History of the People's Republic.* Rev. ed. New York: The Free Press, 1986. A general history of the PRC from the standpoint of a political scientist who approaches his subject in the light of the Chinese leaders' own Marxist goals and standards. The assessment of Deng Xiaoping and his policies is generally negative.

Perry, Elizabeth I., and Li Xun. *Proletarian Power: Shanghai in the Cultural Revolution.* Boulder, CO: Westview Press, 1997. Helps unravel some of the complexity of the Cultural Revolution and clarify what drove ordinary people to political activism.

Smil, Vaclav. *The Bad Earth: Environmental Degradation in China.* Armonk, NY: M. E. Sharpe, 1984. Another grim evaluation of China's deteriorating environment as a result of modernization.

China under Deng Xiaoping (1979–1997)

Gladney, Dru C. *Muslim Chinese: Ethnic Nationalism in the People's Republic.* Cambridge, MA: Harvard University Press, 1991. Focuses on the resurgence of nationalism in the People's Republic among Chinese Muslims (known as the Hui people). An important anthropological study.

Han, Minzhu, ed. *Cries for Democracy: Writings and Speeches from the 1989 Chinese Democracy Movement.* Princeton: Princeton University Press, 1990. The words of various participants in the protest movement.

Lieberthal, Kenneth. *Governing China: From Revolution through Reform.* New York: W. W. Norton, 1995. The basic thesis of this book is that the way China is governed today is the product of several legacies—the imperial tradition, the Republican period, and the Chinese Communist Revolution. A comprehensive analysis that sees governance as reflecting a two-thousand-year continuum.

Meisner, Maurice. *The Deng Xiaoping Era: An Inquiry into the Fate of Chinese Socialism 1978–1994.* New York: Hill and Wang, 1996. Pursues the story of how the promise of socialist democracy, proclaimed by Deng

Xiaoping when he came to power in 1978, has degenerated into bureaucratic capitalism.

Nolan, Peter. *China's Rise, Russia's Fall: Politics, Economics and Planning in the Transition from Stalinism.* New York: St. Martin's Press, 1995. Focuses on the differences between the incremental approach to reform taken by the Chinese and the "shock therapy" approach tried in the former Soviet Union and communist eastern Europe.

Saich, Tony, ed. *The Chinese People's Movement: Perspectives on Spring 1989.* Armonk, NY: M. E. Sharpe, 1991. A fine collection that includes essays on the background and context of the Tiananmen events.

Unger, Jonathan, ed. *The Pro-Democracy Protests in China: Reports from the Provinces.* Armonk, NY: M. E. Sharpe, 1991. An anthology of reports from outside the capital that reveals the range and intensity of protest during the events of 1989.

Wei Jingsheng. *The Courage to Stand Alone: Letters from Prison and Other Writings.* Edited and translated by Kristina M. Torgeson. New York: Viking, 1997. A collection of writings, mostly from his fifteen years in prison, by China's most famous and persistent dissident. The "letters," written to China's leaders (especially Deng Xiaoping), are an extraordinary and moving record of a courageous, compassionate, and obstinate mind dedicated to democratic principles and the amelioration of the Chinese people's political fate.

Zha Jianying. *China Pop: How Soap Operas, Tabloids, and Bestsellers Are Transforming a Culture.* New York: The New Press, 1995. An attempt to reveal the extent to which Deng Xiaoping's open-door economic reforms have eroded Mao Zedong's revolutionary culture.

Zhang Xinxin, and Sang Ye. *Chinese Lives: An Oral History of Contemporary China.* New York: Pantheon Books, 1987. A rare look at recent China through the eyes of more than sixty ordinary people from all walks of life.

Hong Kong and Taiwan

Chan, Ming K., ed. *Precarious Balance: Hong Kong between China and Britain, 1842–1992.* Armonk, NY: M. E. Sharpe, 1994. A good introduction to various aspects of Hong Kong's efforts to balance its relations with these two countries.

Harrell, Stevan, and Chun-chieh Huang, eds. *Cultural Change in Postwar Taiwan.* Boulder, CO: Westview Press, 1994. A collection of essays examining the ways in which modernization has undermined many Chinese values and traditions on Taiwan. Covers trends in governmental cultural policy, literature, the arts, religion, and recreation, among others.

Hickey, Dennis. *United States-Taiwan Security Ties: From Cold War to Beyond Containment.* Westport, CT: Praeger, 1994. Besides discussing U.S.-Taiwan relations, Hickey focuses on Taiwan's own efforts to ensure military preparedness in the face of the PRC's threat.

Kemenade, Willem van. *China, Hong Kong, Taiwan, Inc.* Translated by Diane Webb. New York: Alfred A. Knopf, 1997. Focuses on "Greater China." The author marshals statistics, history, and other information about the complexities of China and how it is merging with the Chinese diaspora to create the newest economic powerhouse.

Klintworth, Gary. *New Taiwan, New China: Taiwan's Changing Role in the Asia-Pacific Region.* New York: St. Martin's Press, 1995. Argues that Taiwan's strategic position among the Pacific powers of Japan, China, and the United States has made Taiwan a particularly resilient and increasingly consequential factor in the development and future of the region.

Shambaugh, David, ed. *Greater China: The Next Superpower?* Oxford, England: Clarendon Press, 1995. This book is the product of a 1993 conference that focused on the potential for China, Taiwan, and Hong Kong together to become a major player in world economic, political, and strategic relations.

Sutter, Robert G., and William R. Johnson, eds. *Taiwan in World Affairs.* Boulder, CO: Westview Press, 1994. A collection of essays that attempts to assess the impact of political and economic changes since the 1980s upon Taiwan's place in world affairs, U.S. foreign policy generally, and U.S.-PRC relations in particular.

Welsh, Frank. *A Borrowed Place: The History of Hong Kong.* New York: Kodansha International, 1993. A full narrative of Hong Kong's history since the early nineteenth century.

FILMS AND VIDEOS

Documentaries

Art in the Cultural Revolution (33 minutes, 1997). Examines the Communist party's rigorously enforced art policies during the Cultural Revolution, when pictorial artists were given strict aesthetic guidelines for the production of works designed to promote the ideology and imagery of Mao Zedong's new society.

Born under the Red Flag, 1976–1997 (180 minutes, 1997). Examines China's journey from Mao's vision of the country's future to Deng Xiaoping's on the eve of the twenty-first century. Part Three of a three-part PBS series (Part One: *China in Revolution, 1911–1949*; Part Two: *The Mao Years, 1949–1976*).

The Cat and the Mouse: China and Tibet (50 minutes, 1996). An intimate portrayal of Tibetan resistance to Chinese occupation of their country. It contrasts the moderate approach of the Dalai Lama with that of the young rebels who employ more-direct forms of protest.

China: The Great Leap Forward (40 minutes, 1997). Focuses on one earnest young man who leaves his struggling rural family to seek his fortune in a big city. His long hours at work and low pay leave him little time or disposable income to participate in the new China that is being created.

China: Trading in Death (30 minutes, 1997). Examines the coercive side of the Chinese government through its Public Security Bureau, system of labor camps, and use of torture.

China in Revolution, 1911–1949 (120 minutes, 1997). A two-hour video replete with rare news footage. Describes the epic upheaval that began with the fall of the last emperor in 1911 and culminated with the communist victory in 1949. Part One of a three-part PBS series (Part Two: *The Mao Years, 1949–1976*; Part Three: *Born under the Red Flag, 1976–1997*).

China Rising: The Epic History of 20th-Century China (three tapes, 50 minutes each, 1996). A video set that explores major events in twentieth-century Chinese history. Uses archival footage and interviews with participants and ordinary citizens.

The Chinese (twenty-six programs, approximately 30 minutes each, 1986). A fine set of videotapes that documents Chinese life in all its aspects as set against the country's historical experiences.

Chinese Cultural Values: The Other Pole of the Human Mind (60 minutes, 1996). A young Chinese woman talks about her childhood, her relationship with her family, and her work. Focuses the viewers' attention on the endurance of traditional Chinese cultural values.

Half the Sky (27 minutes, 1997). Draws negative conclusions to the question of women's status in contemporary China, compared with the promise of the revolution. The film visits remote villages and urban factories to present sometimes candid remarks from women of diverse backgrounds.

Imprisoned Dragon: The Last Chinese Emperor (50 minutes, 1997). The story of Puyi, the last Chinese emperor, his use by the Japanese during World War II as titular head of their puppet government in Manchuria, his subsequent trial by an International Military Tribunal, and his imprisonment by Soviet and then Chinese authorities.

Inner Visions: Avant Garde Art in China (28 minutes, 1995). Gives a rare opportunity to meet young artists and intellectuals in Beijing and hear how they steer a course between survival and artistic expression.

The Mao Years, 1949–1976 (180 minutes, 1997). Tells the story of how Mao Zedong and his colleagues tried to build a "new China," and in the process drew the Chinese people into the largest political experiment in history. Part Two of a three-part PBS series (Part One: *China in Revolution, 1911–1949*; Part Three: *Born under the Red Flag, 1976–1997*).

Salisbury's Report on China: The Chinese Revolution and Beyond. Hosted by Harrison Salisbury, the noted *New York Times* correspondent who followed events in China for decades, this series is in three parts. Part One (*The Leaders of the Revolution*, 45 minutes, color) examines the roles of

Zhou Enlai and Mao Zedong, intraparty struggles and confrontations, Lin Biao's plotting, the activities of the Gang of Four, and the rise of Deng Xiaoping since 1949. Part Two (*Slogans and Policies*, 45 minutes, color) focuses on China's economic transformation as guided by slogans like "land reform," the "Great Leap Forward," "Learn from Dazhai," and the "Four Modernizations." Part Three (*From Liberalization to Crackdown*, 59 minutes, color) follows the opening to the West launched in 1972 by the rapprochement between China and the United States, the subsequent emphases on modernization that necessitated liberalization, and the pressure for democratization.

The Silk Road (six tapes, approximately 55 minutes each, 1990). Produced by the Japanese National Television Network, this documentary offers a panoramic tour of the most historic and inaccessible locations along the Silk Road.

Wild Swans—Jung Chang (59 minutes, 1995). The autobiographical account of three generations of Chinese women, capturing all the turbulence of China in the twentieth century.

Women in China (two parts, 50 minutes each, 1997). Documents the condition of women in today's market-oriented China. By visiting four different parts of China, the film proves to be a representative view of the opportunities and living conditions of Chinese women today.

Women of the Yellow Earth (50 minutes, 1996). This film takes the viewer to the heart of rural China, introducing two village women. A major theme is state intervention into family life.

Feature Films

The Blue Kite (1993). Directed by Tian Zhuanghuang, this film focuses on a boy's experiences growing up in China in the 1950s and 1960s. Banned in the People's Republic of China.

Farewell, My Concubine (1993). Directed by Chen Kaige, the story begins with the induction into the Beijing Opera's training academy of two boys whose lives and relationship then span the political turmoil of World War II, the Communist Revolution, and the Cultural Revolution. The film intertwines a turbulent personal relationship with the political context.

Ju Dou (1990). Directed by Zhang Yimou. An aging factory owner, hoping for an heir, takes a third wife. Mistreated by her new husband, the wife (Ju Dou) finds comfort in an adulterous relationship. The theme of the film is that of the protagonist's individual struggle against her social placement as a woman in China. The narrative of liberation also serves as an allegory in which the "Chinese people" struggle against the Communist party.

The Last Emperor (1987). Directed by Bernardo Bertolucci. The story of the child-emperor Puyi, who abdicated in 1912. The film elegantly portrays his rather passive life in the Forbidden City until 1924, as an admirer of the West in Shanghai, as a puppet of the Japanese occupation in Manchuria, and in the process of re-education in Communist China, where he becomes a gardener.

Raise the Red Lantern (1991). Directed by Zhang Yimou. Set in the 1920s, this film is about four consorts in a rich prerevolutionary household. The poetic title describes the daily event that determines their lives: which of the wives will be visited by the husband that night. The story is about the struggles among the wives for this honor, which crucially affects their standing in the larger household, their chance of giving birth to a male heir, and to some extent their diet and material comforts.

Red Sorghum (1988). Directed by Zhang Yimou. Set in Shandong province during the Sino-Japanese War of 1937–1945. The story surrounds the struggle of villagers against Japanese occupation, but also that of a woman against the demands of an arranged marriage.

To Live (1994). Directed by Zhang Yimou, this film follows the lives of a family from the 1940s through the Cultural Revolution of the 1960s. The film depicts the intersection between personal lives and momentous political upheaval. Each family member is provided with great character depth. It is quite critical, particularly of the Cultural Revolution.

Yellow Earth (1984). Directed by Chen Kaige. The first post-Cultural Revolution film to win a reputation both in China and abroad. A soldier, arriving in a village to research folk songs in 1939, becomes involved in the lives of a peasant family. A main focus is the attempt of a daughter (Cuiqiao) to escape an arranged marriage.

TEACHING MATERIALS

Berkman, P. "The Three Gorges Dam: Energy, the Environment, and the New Emperors," *Education about Asia*, 3, no. 1 (Spring 1998): 27–35.

Concept of Order in Ancient China. Stanford: Stanford University Program on International and Cross-Cultural Education. Though focused on the Han dynasty (202 B.C.E.–A.D.220) this unit explores a concept—unity—that figures prominently across the length of Chinese historical experience.

Demystifying the Chinese Language. Stanford: Stanford University Program on International and Cross-Cultural Education. Examines the evolution of Chinese characters to their present forms and addresses the issues of oral and written-language reform in the PRC.

Feeding a Hungry World: Focus on Rice in Asia and the Pacific. Stanford: Stanford University Program on International and Cross-Cultural Education. A classroom unit that introduces students to the diversity of rice cultures and rice-based farming systems of the region through a study of six rice-producing countries—China, Bangladesh, Indonesia, Japan, Philippines, and Thailand.

Journey to the Source: An Expedition along the Yangzi River. Hong Kong: Grid Media, Ltd. CD-ROM. An expedition up the Yangzi River, one of China's most important, illustrated with over 400 photographs and 70 QuickTime movies. Requires Apple Macintosh computer, system 6.0.7 or higher, with a minimum of 4MB RAM.

The Silk Road: Digital Journey. Vancouver, BC: DNA Multimedia Corp. CD-ROM. Interactive multimedia journey along the historic Silk Road that connected Asia with Europe from ancient times, introducing peoples, history, languages, and religions. Requires Apple Macintosh computer, system 7 or higher, with a minimum of 2.5MB RAM; 486SX-25 MHz PC running Windows 3.1 or 95, with a minimum of 4MB RAM.

Understanding China in the 21st Century: Political, Economic, and Security Issues in the Asia/Pacific Region. Stanford: Stanford University Program on International and Cross-Cultural Education. A classroom unit that describes China's political situation and economy in transition and explores issues relating to human rights and security.

INTERNET SOURCES

It is something of a futile exercise to identify sites on the World Wide Web in the hope that they will remain active, but Cyberspace is becoming such an important source of information that it is worth pointing to those that exist in the fall of 1998, are likely to exist for the foreseeable future, and will provide extensive information or lead to other China-related Internet resources.

Asian Studies WWW Virtual Library. The Asian Studies WWW Virtual Library was established in March 1994 by Dr. T. M. Ciolek, Research School of Pacific and Asian Studies, The Australian National University. The Virtual Library provides an authoritative, continuously updated hypertext guide and access tool to scholarly information resources on the Internet. It deals with the Asian continent as a whole, as well as with individual Asian regions, countries, and territories, China among them.
     http://coombs.anu.edu.au/WWWVL-AsianStudies.html

China Education and Research Network. The China Education and Research Network (CERNET) is funded by the Chinese government and directly managed by the Chinese State Education Commission. CERNET is scheduled to connect all education and research institutions by the end of this century.
     http://www.cernet.edu.cn

China News Digest. China News Digest International, Inc. (CND) is operated by volunteers with a mandate to provide timely and balanced news coverage on China and China-related affairs. CND also provides other information services to Chinese communities around the world. Its services are free of charge. CND is independent of any other organizations and strives to be impartial on the issues and news it reports.

http://www.cnd.org

Chinascape Chinese Web Index. This site is to provide information related to China, Taiwan, and Hong Kong and Macao, to people who are interested in Chinese culture.

http://www.chinascape.org

Complete Reference to China-Related Web Sites. A major reference to China/Chinese-related Web sites.

http://www.chinasite.com

Index

About the Author

EDWARD J. LAZZERINI is Professor of History at the University of New Orleans.